EISENHOWER
Declassified

EISENHOWER
Declassified

VIRGIL PINKLEY

with

JAMES F. SCHEER

FLEMING H. REVELL COMPANY
OLD TAPPAN, NEW JERSEY

Scripture quotations in this volume are from the King James Version of the Bible.
Excerpts from AT EASE by Dwight D. Eisenhower. Copyright © 1967 by Dwight D. Eisenhower. Reprinted by permission of Doubleday & Company, Inc.
Excerpts from WHEN EVEN ANGELS WEPT by Lately Thomas. Copyright © 1973 by William Morrow and Company, Inc. Used by permission of the publishers.
Excerpts from CRUSADE IN EUROPE by Dwight D. Eisenhower. Copyright © 1948 by Doubleday and Company, Inc. Reprinted by permission of the publisher.
Excerpts from MANDATE FOR CHANGE, 1953–1956 by Dwight D. Eisenhower. Copyright © 1963 by Dwight D. Eisenhower. Reprinted by permission of Doubleday and Company, Inc.

Library of Congress Cataloging in Publication Data

Pinkley, Virgil.
  Eisenhower declassified.

  Includes bibliographical references.
  1. Eisenhower, Dwight David, Pres., U.S.,
1890–1969.   2. Presidents—United States—Biography.
3. Generals—United States—Biography.   4. United
States.   Army—Biography.   I. Scheer, James F.,
joint author.   II. Title.
E836.P56   973.921′092′4 [B]   79-20763
ISBN 0-8007-1063-0

TO *my parents, Dr. Virgil Milo Pinkley and Gussie Virginia Pinkley, who, like millions throughout the world, loved Ike*

Contents

Preface

Two significant events occurred to Dwight David Eisenhower and me under the desert sun of two continents—events separated by 8,000 miles and 27 years which had an important bearing on his career, world history, our relationship and the writing of this book. In late 1942, General Eisenhower was headquartered in Algiers and in command of Allied forces that had invaded North Africa and were trying to drive Axis troops off the continent. I was a war correspondent in charge of the United Press service in Europe, Africa, the Near East and Middle East, and had observed Eisenhower closely under many trying circumstances.

One afternoon in his offices in the Saint George Hotel, overlooking the harbor, we were talking about the successful progress of the war. He was wearing his self-designed Eisenhower jacket, with no medals or ribbons—only two stars on his shoulders—and pacing. I remarked that he was a strong possibility for the presidency of the United States. He looked shocked. (It was the first time anyone had suggested such an idea to him, as he later wrote on pages four and five of his book *The White House Years: Mandate for Change.*)

Disdain showed in his blue eyes. "Virgil, that's crazy. If the two parties are so bad off that they have to come to Africa to get an old, broken-down general to become head of the party, the country must be in a mess."

But my conviction persisted, and, on other occasions, I predicted to him that he would become president, pointing out many generals who had commanded major military campaigns and had made the presidency: George Washington, Andrew Jackson, William Henry Harrison, Zachary Taylor and Ulysses S. Grant.

From his strange expression, I knew he felt it absurd to mention him and the presidency in the same breath. "Virgil, almost every time we talk, you say I'm going to be president. That's ridiculous. I have already received more honors than any human being could hope for. If I were to become involved in politics, I could go only one way—down.

"The trouble with you, Virgil, is that you've been standing out in the Algerian sun too long, and you've gone soft in the head."

So the friendship between the "old, broken-down general" and the "soft in the head" newspaperman grew during the war years and after. I was with General Ike in London, North Africa, Sicily, Malta, Italy, France, the American Occupied Zone in Germany. I was in Washington when he was Army Chief of Staff; in New York City when he was president of Columbia University; in Paris while he was supreme commander of NATO; in Washington during the White House years and in California after his retirement.

Henry Cabot Lodge, General Lucius Clay, Paul Hoffman and I flew to Paris on several occasions to persuade him to run for the presidency. They all made many trips, especially Clay and Lodge.

I saw him in Chicago before, during and after the 1952 Republican convention, where he was nominated for the presidency. I went to Denver with Paul Hoffman, to see him and vice-presidential-nominee Richard M. Nixon, and I also attended the 1956 GOP convention in San Francisco.

Sadly, I attended Ike's funeral in Washington, D.C., when invited to do so by Mamie and his son, General John Eisenhower.

While he was in the White House, I was invited to stag dinners. He frequently enjoyed the sun and golf of Palm Desert, California, where I was living. During retirement, he came there in late fall. Often I visited him in his office at the Cochran-Odlum Ranch in nearby Indio.

Through twenty-seven years, wherever we happened to be, I enjoyed plying him with questions to satisfy my curiosity about his life, career and crises. It was not my intention to use this information for news stories or any other public purpose, unless he authorized me to do so. His friendship and confidences were more valuable to me than any story could possibly be.

When he retired from the presidency, and he and Mamie occupied their home on the eleventh fairway at Eldorado Country Club in Palm Desert, I would play golf with him and then enjoy lunch or dinner in his company.

One day when we were golfing, he hit a very good drive some 210 yards right down the fourth fairway and turned to me. "You've never written a book about the war, have you?"

"No, unfortunately, I haven't."

"Why haven't you?"

"There have been so many bad ones that I didn't want to add to the list," I replied.

"That's ridiculous, Virgil. I want you to do me a favor. I would like you to write a book about major decisions I have made . . . ."

I must have looked stunned, because that is exactly how I felt. Although I had written millions of words as a newspaper editor, foreign correspondent and syndicated columnist—and edited millions more—I had never written a book and hadn't the slightest desire to do so.

The proposal seemed preposterous—perhaps as preposterous as my 1942 suggestion to the general that he would one day become president of the United States—and I smiled to myself, wondering whether my golfing companion had been exposed to excessive Palm Desert sun.

General Ike continued forcefully: "These would be major decisions I made before, during and after World War Two—and why I made them. I'm so sick and tired of hearing people say that I was the recipient of lucky breaks—that I just happened to be in the right place at the right time, and never made a major decision in my life.

"Why don't you write a book about these decisions and let the chips fall where they may? It might take three or four years to do the necessary research. You should go to England, the continent, the Philippines, the Panama Canal Zone, around the United States and Canada; and talk to my associates and friends. I'd certainly appreciate it."

How does one say no to an individual who has prevailed over a distinguished and formidable group of supermen: General George S. Patton, General Douglas MacArthur, Field Marshal Sir Bernard Montgomery and even Sir Winston Churchill? How does one turn down someone who has been president of the United States for eight years and commander in chief of the armed forces?

"That's very kind of you, General," I replied. "I'm flattered, but I need a little time to think."

About two weeks later, I was walking through Eldorado Country Club, where General Ike was lunching with Freeman Gosden (Andy of the "Amos and Andy" program), Charlie Jones of Richfield and George Allen. He gestured for me to come over.

"Why don't you join us for lunch?" And then, with no transition, "You know I made a hole in one yesterday at Seven Lakes."

"I read about it this morning. Congratulations!"

He took twenty minutes to tell me about every blade of grass from the tee to the green and how he approached and hit the ball, then asked, "Why don't you play golf with me next Thursday?"

"Fine, General. What time should I pick you up?"

"Oh, about a quarter of ten. I need to practice my putting and chip shots. My short game has become lousy."

Several days later, I heard the devastating news: He had had another heart attack—this one while practicing at the club. I sent him a couple of telegrams and two or three airmail letters at Walter Reed Hospital.

Shortly after that, his military aide, Brigadier General Bob Schulz, phoned me. "I've just been talking with the Boss, and he said, 'I want you to call Virgil Pinkley and ask how he's getting along with that book he's writing.'"

"Well," I said, "tell the general I haven't done much so far, but if he wants a book written so badly, I'll write it."

I never saw Ike alive again.

For ten years, I have worked to keep that promise, doing research, talking in depth to more than 600 individuals who knew or were associated with Eisenhower—the boy, the youth, the cadet, the general, the president, and the ex-president.

Sherman Adams, former governor of New Hampshire and top presidential assistant during the Eisenhower years, repeatedly urged me not to do a rehash of rehashes, but to probe for new information and to show the warm and human side that Ike's associates and friends knew.

Wherever in the world Eisenhower lived or was stationed, I visited to absorb the flavor and color of the places: the Panama Canal Zone, the Philippine Islands (where he served as General Douglas MacArthur's chief of staff) and England and Europe. I have also stayed in his hometown of Abilene, Kansas, for substantial periods.

Most historians encounter their subjects on a secondhand basis, through libraries. My approach has been tridimensional: interviews with the subject, interviews and correspondence with persons who knew him intimately, and library research.

In addition, I have read 800 books based totally or substantially on Eisenhower and have done extensive research work in libraries containing an aggregate of 80 million units of material on him: Columbia University, Dartmouth, Harvard, Princeton and—many times—the Dwight D. Eisenhower Library in Abilene, Kansas.

Through years of assembling pertinent data—interviewing, probing, reading, recording, jogging my memory, categorizing and analyzing—one fact emerged with the clarity of a lightning flash. No book on the major decisions of Eisenhower could possibly be written without considering Eisenhower the boy, the youth, and the man, his times, home life, education, military training, experience, associates, friends and philosophical stances.

Time has its own casual way of distilling the relevant from the irrelevant. Its distillation tells me that perhaps no other man in recorded history was called upon to pit his mind, reputation and career against so many incredibly complex problems (with such high risk factors) and before so many eyes.

Nothing reveals an individual more starkly and more humanly than his currents and crosscurrents of thought processes in problem solving and, of course, his actual decisions under the severe stress of crises. This is especially true when those decisions involve the lives of millions and the very survival of his nation and the rest of the world in a hostile climate.

So, in a sense, this is a book of revelation—a book about inseparables: a man to remember and his decisions.

Washington Runaround

Outside of Hollywood's make-believe, a newspaper editor has no business getting involved in United States State Department affairs—no matter how innocently. Yet that is exactly what I did in 1953, while a guest of President Ramón Magsaysay in the Malacanang (Philippine White House).

This complication, which I neither sought nor evaded, transported me smack into the middle of Washington, D.C.'s bureaucratic buck-passing, until my problem and I ended up with the man at the top, my friend of long-standing: President Dwight D. Eisenhower.

But I'm getting ahead of my story.

As editor and publisher of the Los Angeles *Mirror-News*, I had visited the Philippine Islands to gather material for a series of articles and, suddenly, found myself trying to help President Magsaysay secure United States supplies to prevent Communist infiltration. I had made previous trips to the Philippines and accompanied him as he campaigned, first for national defense minister and then for the presidency.

During breakfast of eggs over easy, brown-fried pork sausages, papaya and tea, on my final day, the president leaned toward me, touched my arm and confided: "Only last week, a Communist agent came in from Malaysia and, when apprehended, had more than seven hundred thousand dollars in greenbacks with which to carry on subversion. Another agent whom we managed to pick up had more than five hundred thousand dollars. That's the kind of thing we're fighting.

"These agents come in boats with powerful engines, race up our rivers and then into swampy areas so that we lose them. Landing craft which the United States gave us may attain speeds of eight or twelve miles per hour, but the Communists can reach speeds of thirty-to-thirty-five miles per hour, and quickly outdistance us. Our craft do not have a sufficiently shallow draft.

"We desperately need fast outboard motors and shortwave radio equipment. I know your government is interested in helping, but, somehow, my requests have not been fulfilled."

"Mr. President, through whom have you worked?"

"Through Carlos Romulo, president of the UN General Assembly and our ambassador to the United States, and American agencies here. Several Washington bureaus have turned down Romulo's requests. Virgil, we need these supplies to fight a common cause."

Ingenuously, I replied, "Mr. President, write out a list of required equipment and amounts. I will try to help."

Hastily, he scribbled on notepaper. "What we need will cost sixty to seventy thousand dollars. You have it in mothballs and stacked to the skies in San Diego, San Pedro, San Francisco and Seattle." He signed his name at the bottom of the list.

Right after landing in Los Angeles, I telephoned Senate Majority Leader Bill Knowland and told him the Magsaysay story. "Virgil, jump on a plane as quickly as you can and come to my office!"

Tired and groggy after eighteen consecutive flying hours, I managed to get a plane, an hour later, for Washington. In the senator's office, I reviewed the situation in detail. A perplexed look came over Bill's face.

"There's nothing I would like more to do than help President

Magsaysay and you, but this is a State Department matter. Why don't you go down there and see Walt Robertson, undersecretary in charge of Asian and Far Eastern Affairs?"

I arranged an immediate appointment. Robertson and I chatted for a while and, finally, he said, "Unfortunately, all matters like this must be handled by our military mission and embassy in Manila and be approved there before we can take action."

"Well, I'm here now," I replied. "Can't we dispense with procedure? Surely there's someone else I might see in Washington."

"Do you know Charles Thomas, secretary of the navy?"

"I've known him on a personal basis for years."

Thomas could not have been more amiable, but in the end, he gave me chapter and verse on specific procedures that had to be followed. "The recommendation for these supplies has to come from the mission and embassy in Manila," he informed me, "and this has not been the case."

My long and fatiguing flight, lack of sleep, a dull headache and Washington inflexibility began to wear on my limited patience. Couldn't anybody understand the desperate situation? Couldn't anybody tell me how to get the job done, rather than explain why it couldn't be done?

I would see Vice-President Richard Nixon. Surely he would know how to snip the red tape. I had known him intimately for years. That should help.

Nixon, too, was most cordial. "Virgil, I have complete sympathy with President Magsaysay. His request is reasonable, but I suggest you follow the method prescribed by Thomas."

Now I was angry, and didn't care if it showed, but how do you motivate a vice-president who doesn't want to be motivated?

As a last resort, I charged into the Department of Justice to see my old friend, J. Edgar Hoover. When I had been a green cub reporter in Washington, he had just taken over the FBI, and I used to cover his department daily on my news-beat. I told him my story.

He stormed to his feet. Sizzling unprintables erupted from

his mouth. "Here's a man in the Philippines who's more American than we are. All he wants is a measly sixty thousand dollars worth of equipment. It's no good to us, and we won't give it to him."

Finally he stopped pacing, impatiently phoned Sherman Adams in the White House, and told the story of my Washington runaround.

"Why doesn't Virgil come down here immediately?" Adams asked.

"Fine," replied Hoover. "I'll send him right over in my car."

Adams, in his gruff voice and clipped New England speech, asked me for a full briefing and list of needed supplies. I filled him in.

"Wait just a minute, Virgil, while I see the Boss."

Five minutes later, he came back to me. "The Boss wants to see *you.*"

When I entered the Oval Office, President Eisenhower hurried across the room, a welcoming grin clear across his pink face, and embraced me in warm bear hug. After a few minutes of reminiscences, he asked, "What's this about our friend, Magsaysay?"

I told him, handing over the list, which he studied. Abruptly, he turned to his private secretary, Ann Whitman. "Ann, get Foster on the phone!"

As soon as Secretary of State John Foster Dulles came on, Eisenhower shouted, "Foster, this is the president. We've got a silly, stupid situation out in Manila that makes me angry."

His face flushed, and the blood vessel over his right eye expanded visibly as he related the situation. "I want all of that material enroute to Manila Bay by 0600 hours tomorrow. I don't care where or how we get it there, but I want it on the water and headed toward Manila not later than that time. Please report when the job is done!"

Suddenly it was as if the weight of the world was off my shoulders. I exhaled in deep relief. A newspaperman, J. Edgar Hoover, Sherman Adams and the president had won a victory over bureaucracy.

Somehow the president's voice penetrated my triumphant reverie. "Virgil, we haven't talked in private for some time. There's a matter I've wanted to ask you about that happened in 1942."

"Sure, Mr. President."

"Aside from being aware that a number of the United States Army generals in command of major military operations had become president, how did you know then that I would be a presidential candidate and win the office?"

"Mr. President, so far as I can determine, my bloodlines do not go back to Nostradamus, but my prediction was more than a wild guess. I knew that your training and preparation were broad and deep. I watched how you dealt with difficult diplomatic situations in England—the wholesale influx of American troops, which caused many complications—then how effectively you directed the North African invasion and handled Prime Minister Churchill, FDR and the British chiefs of staff.

"Later, I knew for sure, when I saw your concern for the people of North Africa. You repaired war damage rapidly—reopening public utilities, schools, fresh-water supplies, transportation and communication systems, medical centers and hospitals. You had food, clothing and currency ready for use.

"You showed me a dimension that most military men did not have. You acted more like a civilian—a president—than a military man. There was no doubt in my mind that Allied troops under your command would eventually defeat the Germans and Italians. After victory in Europe, I felt it inevitable that you would become president."

He listened thoughtfully, his alert blue eyes never leaving mine.

"And, then, at that time, a great deal of publicity began coming out about you, your boyhood in Abilene, Kansas, your parents, your brothers and your upbringing. In a home such as yours, you had to develop the qualities of self-reliance, leadership, tolerance, consideration and humanity so important to a

president. In other words, your unusual past showed in your
present and pointed toward the future."

President Eisenhower nodded. "Virgil, thank you." Suddenly
amusement danced in his eyes, and the corners of his broad
mouth lifted upwards. "You know, when you first made your
prediction to me, I recall having said something a little unkind
to you about standing too long in the Algerian sun. . . ."

The backhanded apology made us both laugh. He thanked
me for alerting him to the Magsaysay matter.

I went back to the office of Sherman Adams, who invited me
to breakfast the next morning at 7:00 in the navy-run mess in
the White House basement.

When I entered the room, I saw Adams with senators Mundt,
of South Dakota, and Carlson, of Kansas. We had been breakfasting for several minutes, when an orderly rushed over to
Governor Adams. "The president wants to speak to you on the
phone."

Five minutes later, Adams returned, grinning broadly. "Vir-
gil, the Boss is at his desk, where he has been for thirty minutes.
He has asked me to tell you that all of the material left San
Pedro at 0600 hours."

What thrilling news!

Soon Magsaysay would have his supplies, thanks to President
Eisenhower's decisive action through the state department.

On my return flight to Los Angeles, I recalled other factors
about Ike Eisenhower's past—his knowledge, training and
character traits—that had led me to believe that, one day, he
would become president.

His depth of specific information on a multitude of subjects
was awesome to me and surprising to many; particularly his
knowledge of history, a subject to which he became addicted in
grade school. He had a phenomenal understanding of
government—theory and practice—of transportation, communication and industrial production. Although unmistakably
a military man, he preferred to request, rather than order, and
still got desired results. He had an uncanny knack for choosing
high-quality associates and then delegating powers. I also remembered a negative quality, a major flaw that could have

blasted his entire career before it ever got started: a volcanic temper.

Once he told me how, in his early years, he learned to control it through an unforgettable, life-shaking experience that he called the "Halloween Incident."

Halloween Incident

Although many trees of Abilene, Kansas, were still clothed for Indian summer with breathtaking yellows, scandalous scarlets and conservative russets, occasional chilly gusts of wind began undressing them for autumn and winter.

It was twilight, on Halloween of the year 1900.

In the kitchen of the two-story, boxlike white house of David Jacob Eisenhower, set like a postage stamp on the corner of three acres just south of the Union Pacific tracks, Ida Eisenhower turned up the glowing wick of the coal-oil lamp. Now her husband would have more light for reading the Bible.

Down the dark hallway at the front door, ten-year old, blond-haired Dwight peered eagerly toward the street. Not far away, he heard laughter and shouts of children about his age. Hurrying feet drummed on the wooden sidewalk and, when the sidewalk ended, slapped on the hard-packed earth. He tingled with excitement.

The kids were really having a good time. Oh, how he wanted to go out with them!

Arthur and Edgar, his older brothers, were already in on the Halloween fun. He would ask his mother again. Dwight rushed down the hallway, into the bright kitchen. "Please, Mom, let me go out!"

As she turned from the sink, the lamplight accented her lustrous, light-brown hair, parted in the middle and gathered in a bun. The good-humored uptilt at the corners of her ample mouth settled back. "Dwight, for the last time, you are too young."

"Lots of kids younger than I am are out there!"

"That may be, but they aren't members of the Eisenhower family."

"Yes, but. . . . "

"*Dwight.*" She raised her voice ever so slightly. "That's final."

Now Dwight was mad. The blood rushed upward. His face became red. It felt as if his head would explode. He wanted to smash something—*anything*. He rushed out the door. Suddenly an old apple-tree trunk loomed up in Dwight's path. He began pounding it with his fists. Almost blind with anger, he remembered nothing more until his father's strong workman's hands gripped his shoulders and pulled him away.

It was almost as if Dwight came back to consciousness. Oh, how his knuckles hurt! He could feel warm blood oozing from them. Only then did he realize what he had done.

The next thing he knew, he was across his father's knees in the kitchen. He felt the sting of the hickory switch. David Eisenhower's dark handlebar mustache trembled as he commanded, "To bed! Right *now!*"

Tears streamed down Dwight's cheeks. All he could think of, as he lay facedown on his feather-stuffed pillow, was how much his fists hurt and how mad he was about the whipping and not being able to go out with the kids.

After about an hour, the bedroom door opened and a shaft of light cut through the darkness. He listened. Someone came in quietly and sat down in a creaky old rocking chair near the bed.

It was his mother. He knew that. She creaked back and forth for a while and said nothing.

"Dwight," she finally whispered.

He stopped sobbing for a second.

"Dwight, let me see your hands."

He turned slowly and put them out for her.

Ida Eisenhower sucked in her breath. With her six boys, she had seen every kind of injury and ailment, but this was the ugliest. These unusually large hands for a small boy looked like raw meat.

She cleaned the wounds and gently applied a soothing salve and bandages to the worst areas.

"Dwight, you've read enough in the Bible to know how important obedience is. Without obedience, there could be no order in the world. It is important always to obey the word of God and to obey your parents, your teachers, your boss (someday when you go to work) or the coach or captain of a football or baseball team."

At the words *football* and *baseball*, Dwight's attention perked up; a fact that did not escape Ida. She knew that nothing interested him more than these two sports.

"If everybody did whatever he wanted, whenever he wanted there would be no civilization as we know it. There could be no peace. Everybody would fear for his life and property. Nothing good could be accomplished. All you would have is rebellion, quarreling and confusion."

Dwight looked up at her and listened with more interest.

"Hatred can only get you into trouble. Look what you have to show for hatred and disobedience: two sore hands. They will hurt for many days and remind you over and over again how much it costs to hate. Do you realize that you won't be able to throw or catch the football for a long while?"

Now he really began to pay attention.

"Of all my boys, you have the most to learn. Think about this. The person who caused you to hate may not even know that he has done so—or, maybe, doesn't care. So when you hate, it comes back to you. You only hurt yourself."

She finished her first aid.

"Dwight, if there's nothing else you remember, remember that the Bible is the most wise adviser anybody can find—for any problem. In Proverbs 16:32, it talks right to you about what happened tonight."

How's that? he asked himself.

She noted his puzzled expression. "It says: 'He that is slow to anger is better than the mighty; and he that ruleth his spirit than he that taketh a city.' "

Dwight didn't know how long she talked, but it seemed as if her words were taking away the hurt of his feelings like the salve on his bruised hands.

"Now, what do you think, Dwight? Is the Bible wrong on that point?"

"No, I guess not."

"Then was Dwight Eisenhower wrong?"

Dwight knew the answer. "Yes."

It was a simple answer, but it did something important to Dwight. The last bit of hurt and anger went out of him. He began feeling warm and comfortable. How nice it was to have his mother near. In a few minutes, he drifted off into sleep.

Never again did his mother mention the incident, but Dwight Eisenhower remembered every small detail of that Halloween, as if it had been tattooed on his brain.

His mother's words guided him in learning how to control his temper and making certain he never again hated anyone. He found a way of letting off steam. If someone did a hateful thing to him, he would write that person's name on a sheet of paper, crumple the paper hard and throw it into a bottom desk drawer. Then he would say, and mean, "That's the end of that."

An offshoot of his mother's advice was the strict lifetime practice of not naming or reacting in public to a person who had offended him or whose conduct or words ran against his own code of ethics or morals.

Early in my friendship with Ike Eisenhower, I knew many

general details about him, but often wondered about the specific details of his family tree, education and life experiences that destined him to become the greatest military man of all times.

One thing, especially, mystified me: How could he have come from parents—and relatives before them—who, by deep spiritual conviction, were pacifists?

Answers could come only from examining his roots and the most-important events of his life.

In the Beginning

Frustration. That is what genealogists feel when they try to get to the bottom of the Eisenhower family roots. Somewhere between the present generation and Adam and Eve, they lose track and zest.

One thing is clear. Many centuries ago in Germany, some member of the family got his name from his trade. *Eisen* (iron) and *hauer* (hewer or cutter) add up to "iron hewer."

A blacksmith?

No. That is *Eisenschmidt* in German.

An *eisenhauer* hews iron into ornamental or functional shapes, such as interior design accessories, armor, shields or weapons. The spelling *eisenhower* is an Americanization of *eisenhauer*.

Weapon making wasn't out of character for the Eisenhowers of antiquity, because, as legend has it, they were medieval warriors. In the sixteenth century, family members living along the Rhine in Bavaria made a dramatic switch to pacifism when they became followers of Menno Simons, who founded the Mennonite movement.

Having renounced militarism and materialism, the Eisenhauers were among many Mennonites whose farms and villages were destroyed during the Thirty Years War. For religious freedom and peace, they fled to Switzerland and then Pennsylvania.

The Eisenhowers who lived in the Susquehanna Valley were members of a religious group called the River Brethren (or Brethren in Christ), who practiced forward baptism in the name of the Father, Son and Holy Ghost, anointing the sick with oil, covering the hair of women in church, wearing plain clothes, avoiding profanity and refraining from bearing arms. They were similar to the Quakers in their beliefs.

Clear evidence exists that the grandparents of Dwight D. Eisenhower—Jacob Frederick and Rebecca Eisenhower—and their children had a strong faith in a personal relationship with Christ and in being born again. Near Elizabethville, Pennsylvania, is a still-legible, weatherworn, time-blackened limestone grave marker for their daughter Lydia, who died at seventeen:

> She gave her heart to Jesus
> Who took her stains away
> And now in Christ Believing,
> The Father too can say
>
> I'm going home to glory
> A golden crown to wear
> O meet me, meet me over there.

Along with other River Brethren, Jacob Frederick and Rebecca migrated to Abilene, Kansas, where in 1878, they bought several sections of land at $7.50 an acre—black soil that went down a hundred feet. They raised wheat and had cows and chickens.

Under the stewardship of Jacob Frederick, the farm brought prosperity to Rebecca and him. They were able to launch the marriages of each of their children with a gift of 160 acres of rich land and $2000.

One of their sons, David Jacob Eisenhower (later to become Dwight Eisenhower's father), wanted no part of farming, much to his parents' regret. He enrolled in an engineering course at Lane University in Lecompton, Kansas, near Topeka.

He had no idea that he would soon make himself eligible for one of their wedding gifts. Neither did Ida Elizabeth Stover, his bride to be.

One of eleven children, Ida was born on May 1, 1862, at Mount Sidney, Virginia. During early life, she could hear the boom of cannons from the nearby Shenandoah Valley, a bloody Civil War battleground.

Some of Ida's earliest memories were of burned-to-the-ground homes and barns, devastated orchards, dynamited bridges and railways with twisted iron tracks. The ruins, which remained as she grew up, and her Christian training gave her a strong aversion to war.

When she was almost twenty, Ida taught school for a year and saved as much as she could. She had a powerful drive to attend college, but Southern tradition said, "No, it's not ladylike! The campus is a man's world."

In 1883, with savings and small inheritances from her father and grandfather, she went west, where she could find educational freedom, enroll at Lane University and be near her brothers.

David Jacob Eisenhower found basic engineering, mechanics, classical Greek and studies of the Greek version of the Bible stimulating. He also found a charming distraction—Ida Elizabeth Stover, an ever-cheerful, energy-charged, light-brown-haired girl who smiled with her eyes as much as her lips.

Even the somber clothing required by the Brethren could not

hide her luster; it only served as the dark background to set off the sparkle of the diamond.

Before the end of his second year, this distraction became a preoccupation. David and Ida were married in the campus chapel on September 23, 1885.

Now he had to find a way to make a living. He refused to farm the land given to him and Ida. He decided to start a general-merchandise store with his $2000 cash gift and an equal amount raised by mortgaging his farm.

A location such as Hope, Kansas—twenty-eight miles south of Abilene—and a partner named Good seemed a golden guarantee of the store's success.

But Hope was only a few small houses and dusty crossroads surrounded by small farms. It was a name aspiring to be a town. And Good, too, was just a name. The Eisenhowers and the Goods lived in adjoining apartments above the store.

David had to depend almost entirely on farmers for business. Many of them bought on credit for a year at a time, promising to pay after harvest. Honest and trustworthy himself, David could see only honesty and trustworthiness in the farmers and in his partner, who handled the ledger and payment of bills.

A son, Arthur, was born to Ida and David on November 11, 1886. And the business began to grow. Then harsh weather ruined the crops, and David was forced to carry accounts until next year's harvest, to pay bills with reserves and to slash the amount of money he and Good took out of the business.

Ida encouraged David. "Next year's harvest will make up for this one." Her confident smile and optimism helped reinforce his faith.

In his softly guttural speech, David passed on this reassurance to Good.

One morning, David awoke to find the cash from the safe gone, and also his partner. Soon he learned that, instead of paying bills, Good had pocketed the money.

Late in 1888, David was forced to close the store. He also lost his mortgaged property.

His pride, self-esteem and confidence took as much of a beating as his finances. All he could think of was leaving the scene of his public humiliation. From that time, Ida, without appearing to do so, assumed family leadership.

David left Ida and Arthur behind, to look into a railroad mechanic's job in Texas. During his absence, Ida gave birth to second son, Edgar Newton. David took the ill-paying job— thirty-five dollars a month—with the Missouri, Kansas and Texas railroad and sent for his wife and family.

By day and night, their tiny Denison, Texas, house along the railroad tracks vibrated with passing trains. It was a definite come down from the roomy apartment in Hope. Ida knew that David felt this keenly. Occasionally, when a train thundered by and David was in a pensive and sober mood, Ida would act out the vibration of the house, with such extreme exaggeration that she would make the solemn David smile.

When his meager salary ran out before payday, she cooked what food she had, never letting this change her happy disposition, because she had faith in God, David and herself. An expression of concern would have been a stranger on her face.

She would anticipate when David would come home feeling low—even though he never complained—and put aside her depressing River Brethren clothing to wear her most cheerful dress.

Throughout the day, as she did her housework and attended to the two boys, she often prayed a prayer of thanks: "Thank You, God, for my many blessings—a loving, kind and industrious husband and healthy sons. Thank You for the many, many things I have and for the many, many things I don't have and probably don't need."

On October 14, 1890, Ida gave birth to her third son, David Dwight Eisenhower. She insisted on the name David being first, because it belonged to her husband, and because she loved King David in the Bible. One night she said to her husband, "I'm not sure we should call him David. When he enters school, children will nickname him Dave or Davey, and that will take away the beauty of the name."

"Well, Mother, how will you prevent that?" he asked.

"Oh, we'll call him Dwight David. Then everyone will have to call him Dwight. There's no nickname for that."

Not many years after, school children had trouble pronouncing Eisenhower, so they shortened the jawbreaking name to its first syllable, *Ei*, added *ke* and called him Ike.

Many times in letters, the Abilene Eisenhowers said they wished that David, his wife and family would return.

"Fine, but what do I do for work?" David asked.

An inspiration came to Chris Musser, who had married David's sister Amanda and was foreman of the River Brethren-owned Belle Springs Creamery. New machinery for the company's expansion program called for a mechanic-engineer. They could pay more than David was making—fifty dollars per month.

In early 1891, the Eisenhower family quietly returned to Abilene, where, between 1892 and 1899, four more sons were born: Roy, Paul (who died of diphtheria), Earl and Milton, whom Ike often referred to as "the brains of the family." He said repeatedly in later years that Milton should be president.

At a White House stag dinner, President Eisenhower once confided to me, "I was glad the family moved back to Abilene. Abilene's colorful past was one of the main reasons I became so enchanted with history. Rubbing elbows with history in Abilene directed the course of my life into the army and the presidency."

Old Abilene, Hannibal and Ike

Dwight and Ed didn't dare tell their mother that they picked up tidbits of Abilene history from graybeards who pipe smoked, chewed and reminisced their last days away on the wide veranda of the wooden, paint-flaked, general-merchandise store.

The oldsters lived in the past. As they told and retold their stories, the good old days kept getting better and better.

As Dwight and Ed listened bug eyed with fascination on the steps, they learned how their hometown started innocently and became a sin city, with saloons, gambling establishments, painted women and the wild West's most notorious gunmen and sheriffs.

Abilene had had its beginning in 1857, when a surveyor from Illinois, Tim Hersey, and his wife, Elizabeth, staked a claim on the plains within a wide bend of Mud Creek.

"We need a name for the town," Hersey said.

Elizabeth opened her Bible to Luke 3:1, where there is mention of Lysanias, the tetrarch of Abilene (a province of Judaea), which, in Greek, means "meadow" or "plains." So Abilene became the "city of the plains."

When the Kansas Pacific Railroad laid track from Kansas City as far west as Abilene, a promoter, Joseph G. McCoy, saw a way to make himself a fortune by serving as the connecting link between two needs.

Texas stockmen had a surplus of four million cattle, worth only three to four dollars per head in the Lone Star State. Large eastern cities required more beef and would pay thirty to forty dollars per head. McCoy persuaded Texans to drive their cattle along the Chisholm Trail to the Abilene railroad.

Hard-riding, hard-drinking, pleasure-seeking cowboys, flush with pay, turned the Bible-named city of the plains into another kind of city: Sodom and Gomorrah.

Abilene citizens fought for law and order, even hiring two-gun Wild Bill Hickok, who could shoot in opposite directions at the same time and hit moving targets, as sheriff. Finally, the problem solved itself. The railroad laid tracks farther west, closer to Texas.

By the time the grandparents and father of the Eisenhower boys arrived in Abilene, the town had become a peaceful farming center. Yet its history as a cow town lived on in the minds of many and was transferred to the next generation, including Dwight Eisenhower, who for the rest of his days loved to read and see westerns.

Although not accredited teachers of history, the graybeards on the general-merchandise store veranda opened and excited the mind of Dwight D. Eisenhower to the conflict, color, and spectacular happenings of former times.

Outside of the baseball diamond and the football field, no place in Abilene attracted Dwight as magnetically as the private library of Joe Howe, publisher-editor of the *Dickinson County News.*

Never had Ike seen so many books in one place. And Joe invited him to borrow whatever looked interesting. A few pages into the *Life of Hannibal*, and he was lost to the young twentieth century.

Dwight followed no special reading plan. His heroes were George Washington, general and president; frugal and thrifty Benjamin Franklin, inventor, wit, diplomat and founder of the

Saturday Evening Post (which Dwight and his brothers fought to read first); and men on both sides of the Mason-Dixon Line: Abraham Lincoln and General Robert E. Lee.

As he studied the pages, he was not just a reader about Washington. He *was* Washington in the bitter cold of Valley Forge, suffering with freezing, hungry, ragged troops, some without shoes, leaving blood prints in the white snow.

Dwight had no way of knowing that some four decades later, troops under him in the command of General George S. Patton, in their forced winter march to contain the Germans in the Battle of the Bulge, would also have worn off their shoes, leaving blood in the snows of the Ardennes Forest.

And, yet, Washington's soldiers marched obediently, patiently, never complaining.

When his soldiers suffered, Washington suffered. The personal interest he took in his troops was something Dwight never forgot as an officer in two world wars.

Many times I observed General Ike in the chow line with GIs, waiting his turn, questioning the troops about their food and, as he reached the steam tables, being served and testing to make sure it was satisfactory for his men. He watched cooks work, checked to make sure conditions were sanitary and noted the food quality, variety and method of storing.

Dwight was also a great follower of Lincoln. Somehow, Lincoln's mother reminded him of his own mother. He admired Lincoln for many things, especially his honesty, his deep faith, the Gettysburg Address and how he dealt with troublesome people like cabinet members Chase and Seward.

Behind Lincoln's back, Chase had written a letter to undermine him. He discovered that Lincoln knew what he had done, apologized and offered to resign, but the president refused to judge him on any ground except whether or not he was doing good work as secretary of the treasury, and asked him to stay.

In handling Seward, who wanted to run the presidency while Lincoln held the empty title, Lincoln firmly set him down and changed him from an enemy into a cooperating cabinet member.

He couldn't get over how Lincoln, by understanding, firmness, turning the other cheek and never holding a grudge, kept his cabinet from tearing apart. During World War II, as a commander in chief of Supreme Allied Headquarters, Dwight kept Allied cooperation from blowing up by dealing in the same way with Field Marshal Bernard Montgomery, who was attempting to undermine him, and his temperamental friend, General George Patton.

When Dwight opened Joe Howe's books on ancient Greece or Rome, the distant yesterday became today. Hannibal, Caesar, Leonidas, Pericles, Socrates and Themistocles thrilled him as much as Wild Bill Hickok.

A man born more than two-thousand years before him, Hannibal, a Carthaginian general—a genius at the surprise attack and unorthodox tactics—strongly influenced Dwight's interest in a military career. He committed the major moves of Hannibal's battles to memory, and could recall each one with perfect accuracy.

He always tried to find a quiet spot at home, or even in the huge barn, where he could read ancient history undisturbed. Dwight disliked dreary household duties rudely intruding upon the romance, pageantry and epic battles of the past. It was just like his mother to interrupt the Carthaginian wars to have him put baby Milton to sleep.

Ike refused to let drudgery interfere with history. He would place Milton into the baby carriage and lie on the floor on his back with legs spread widely apart. Then, while reading, he would shove the carriage forward with one foot until it hit the other foot, draw it back and automatically repeat the operation until baby was asleep.

Even as Milton slept, the battle raged on.

Sometimes Ida Eisenhower grew weary of having to pry Dwight away from his history books to do a simple task, but she always had a patient way of being impatient with him.

"Dwight, there are times when I can't figure out where you

end and the history book begins. Now, for a while, I'm going to lock up all your history books in the closet."

She carried out her gently spoken threat.

But Dwight did not relish life without history, so he planned his counteraction. He observed his mother carefully, until he figured out where she had hidden the closet key. Then he would read while she was away from home. When she learned what he had been doing, she took her own counteraction. She carried the key with her, but even that did not stop the determined Dwight. He learned how to open the lock with a stiff piece of wire.

And so, the flow of history continued.

So Little, So Much

Now and then, ex-president Eisenhower would glance into the rearview mirror at his life as a boy and wonder how his family managed to live so happily on such a modest scale. I am pleased that he shared his nostalgia with me.

"In one respect, my mother reminded me of the nursery-rhyme woman who lived in a shoe and had so many children she didn't know what to do. Well, there really weren't *that many* of us children, and we didn't live in a shoe, but, believe me, Mother always knew what to do.

"The thing that puzzles me is how Mother did it. There were eight of us in a home with eight hundred and eighteen square feet. Quite a full house, but, in some mysterious manner, Mother fitted us all in.

"She was amazing. Not only could she get the most out of the available space, but also out of Father's moderate income and the boy power around the house.

"We were so busy with schoolwork, chores, athletics, Bible reading (I read the Bible all the way through twice as a boy) and jobs to earn extra money that we didn't have idle time to think whether or not we were better or worse off than our neighbors. Working hard together to make ends meet made us a tightly knit family," he said.

During the boyhood of Dwight Eisenhower, the frontier had already surged westward, but some of the pioneer spirit still remained in Abilene—especially in the Eisenhower household.

What the family lacked in money, they made up in ability to adapt, in inventiveness, thrift and extra work. Their two-story, white frame house, with its three fertile acres, provided not only shelter but a major part of their food. They raised vegetables and fruit and kept cows, horses, chickens, ducks, rabbits (Belgian hares) and pigs.

Ida always bought the best and most-durable clothing for David, because it had to last through the hand-me-down route to the boys nearest his size, until threadbare sleeves and trouser cuffs could no longer be turned under.

The family couldn't afford to buy kindling wood to ignite coal in the cooking stove and the potbellied front-room stoves, so the boys gathered up discarded wooden boxes behind stores, plus fallen tree twigs and branches.

When this job took too much valuable time from football or baseball, Dwight and Ed created an excellent substitute. They collected corn cobs. When needed, they soaked them in coal oil and then rolled them in ashes to keep them from burning too fast.

Like most frontier women, Ida Eisenhower could do just about any job. She had to—particularly while the boys were small.

Twice each week, she baked a kitchen tableful of glorious, round, brown-crusted loaves of bread. She cooked plentiful, enticing food for everyone to eat heartily (but never waste), made her own dresses, retailored or patched everyone's old clothing, cut and saved squares of good material from worn suits and dresses to be sewn into colorful patchwork quilts or bedspreads.

Ida painted and papered walls, carpentered, scrubbed floors, washed windows, beat rugs, did the family wash by hand with strong yellow soap, performed first aid for assorted boy bruises, cuts and scratches, nursed and doctored. She tutored her sons, discussed the Bible with them, guided their conduct within the foul lines of the Ten Commandments, served as in-house policeman and as judge. She passed sentences, to be carried out by David with corrective words or the hickory switch when he finished his sunup-to-sundown job at Belle Springs Creamery.

The mother and father never disagreed in front of the boys, especially when one of them had passed judgment and announced a punishment.

Ida pressed her growing boys into service early in life—at first with simple tasks. She needed help and had a strong conviction that the Bible was right about hard work being good and important for everyone.

Jobs gave each family member a sense of responsibility, a feeling of belonging and a sense of accomplishment. She knew that character traits developed in boys would remain with them as men.

Even in his latter days, General Ike could not quite understand how his bubbly, affectionate, easy going mother could get "top-sergeant results out of natural-born goldbrickers who would rather have been playing baseball or football than working."

So that nobody would be stuck with the same boresome chore, Ida rotated tasks weekly: milking cows, feeding the animals and chickens, cleaning up after them, tending the garden, picking vegetables and fruit, mowing the lawn, beating rugs, washing windows, floor scrubbing, dusting, washing clothes and doing dishes.

She once instructed Dwight, "Don't sweep everything from the center of the floor into the corners. Start with the corners and sweep everything to the center, then pick it up with the dustpan."

Dwight enjoyed growing things: alfalfa, green beans, berries, cabbage, carrots, celery, sweet corn, field corn and kafir corn (milo), peas, potatoes and tomatoes. Something that always thrilled him was seeing the first hint of green in the rich, black soil. It was like a miracle. Not so thrilling was picking ugly potato bugs and gooey, well-camouflaged, green tomato worms off the vines.

"I enjoyed milking cows," he said. "It was fun hearing the first spurt of milk chime in the galvanized pail and seeing the fluid foam."

Although always particular about his own cleanliness and personal appearance, he never relished cleaning things: the chicken coop, hutches, pens, stalls or stable. He reluctantly washed clothes, particularly when Milton was in the diaper stage.

Dwight even learned how to patch trousers, let out clothing and darn stockings. "You know how to make holes in them," his mother said. "Now learn how to fill them in."

"Mother's system of rotating jobs had merit for me," he once told me. "After a week at some disagreeable task, I actually began to like doing the more-pleasant work."

Although self-sufficient in the kitchen, Ida once found herself desperately in need of a pinch hitter. Young Milton became seriously ill with scarlet fever, and she had to live with him in an upstairs bedroom during the contagious stage. She asked Dwight to cook and bake, shouting instructions to him.

"Was I a good cook and baker at that time?" asked Dwight. "I don't know, but the family survived. My mother's compliments encouraged me to try new things."

On Sundays, when his parents spent the day in church, he usually cooked the evening meal. When young Earl and Milton helped him, he had to have everything his way, according to Ida. "He got practice being the commanding officer."

Ida also said that Dwight could cook just about anything—stews, chops, roasts, vegetables and fruit dishes. He prided himself on his delicious apple pie. Dwight's other specialties were cornmeal mush and a delectable spread to put on top of it: puddin', a masterpiece from Pennsylvania Dutch cookery that made a little meat go a long way.

The thought of puddin' spread on hot, butter-fried cornmeal mush coaxed the sleep-loving Eisenhower boys out of warm beds in the darkness of winter mornings that were so cold they could see their breaths. Right at five o'clock, their father, from the foot of the stairs, would call out, "Okay, boys, time to get up!"

That meant that, within ten to fifteen minutes, they would have to be washed, combed, dressed and downstairs for breakfast. It also meant that David Eisenhower had started the kitchen-stove fire, and had set the cornmeal mush and puddin' on.

Little heat would find its way upward by the time the boys, in their long underwear, with teeth chattering, tugged out trousers and shirts that they had neatly placed under the blankets on the previous evening, to keep warm enough to wear.

Because David was due early at the creamery, everybody was expected at the table *on time!* Dwight learned punctuality. If he ever arrived in the kitchen after his brothers, his father would remain standing, looking sternly ahead.

"Only when I raced into the kitchen and seated myself did his resolute facial expression soften. He would sit down, and our day would be officially underway. He would bow his head, and we would bow our heads and observe at least a minute of silence to become attuned to talking to God. Then, in his soft, guttural, German-flavored speech, he would say something like this: 'God, we ask You to bless the food which You have graciously and plentifully given us. Thank You for this good food. May it strengthen us all in body, mind and spirit to do Your will. Amen.' "

Prayer was never mechanical with David. There were never "vain repetitions." His deep sincerity and gratitude showed in each word.

In the long period between breakfast and school, the boys did most of their chores and homework, to allow more after-school time for sports.

During summer vacation, they played more baseball and made money to help support the family. Dwight sold freshly picked corn, tomatoes, pears and berries, stacked on his red wagon, to Abilene residents on the north side of the tracks.

He would set what he felt was a fair price for his produce. If someone haggled, he would simply say, "I'm sorry, but my price is fair. I cannot sell it to you for less and make any money."

As he pulled his wagon away, the customer would usually call out, "Come on back." He would make the sale at his original price.

Autumn meant the end of door-to-door selling for all south-side boys except Dwight Eisenhower. The change of seasons wasn't going to put *him* out of business. He cajoled his mother into teaching him how to make tamales. Dwight built a vigorous trade, selling tamales at three for five cents.

No matter how busy the Eisenhowers were in the material world, they never forgot the spiritual world. Every evening, David and Ida would read from the Bible and all family members would interpret the passages. To Dwight, the high point was reading in the Old or New Testament. If he stumbled on a pronunciation, that was the end. The Bible would then go to one of his brothers until he made a mistake.

Soon after the Eisenhowers returned to Abilene, David and Ida left the River Brethren faith to join an informal group called the Bible Students.

Weekly meetings rotated from home to home. When hosted by the Eisenhowers, Ida played her ebony piano and everyone sang. Dwight watched with curiosity. Members spoke directly to the Lord, as if He were a person who was there. They also talked about their close relationship with Him and about Scriptures.

Sunday changed the Eisenhowers' routine. While the boys attended Sunday school, David and Ida spent most of the day in church services. So that the family could prepare for Sunday, Saturday night became a special time, particularly in winter. That was bath night. Without running water, indoor plumbing, an automatic hot-water heater and a bathtub, a bath was not merely a bath. It was a project.

First they had to haul in pail after pail of icy well water, without sloshing on the kitchen floor. The coal stove had a holding reservoir of only five gallons. Repeatedly, this had to be filled for heating and draining. Water was also heated in an array of iron pots on the stove's hot surface.

Only then could family members have the privacy of the kitchen, to lower themselves into the soothing, warm water.

Frequent one-hundred-degree temperatures of Abilene summers made more-frequent baths necessary. On nearly every morning, Dwight and his brothers prepared for evening baths by setting many washtubs of water under the torrid sun.

In baths and other home projects, the Eisenhower boys cooperated, but, at other times, Ed and Dwight squabbled, wrestled and pummeled each other frequently. Ed won the battles, because he was a superior athlete—larger, heavier and stronger. Dwight never gave up the idea that someday he would whip Ed. To keep them apart, their mother assigned them to widely separated beds. David and Ida set a pattern for harmony.

"In all my years at home, I never saw or heard my parents fight," Ike informed me. "They never even showed a trace of annoyance toward each other. I can't say that they ever outwardly showed love for each other, either, but their devotion was unquestionable.

"We loved both of our parents, but in different ways," he said. "It was natural that we felt closer to Mother. We were with her during the day. She was warm and understanding. She could

see something funny in almost everything except a boy's disobedience.

"Father showed interest in our problems, but his long work
schedule gave him little time. Then at night he would read the
Bible or study an International Correspondence School course
in engineering. He was not as approachable as Mother. He had
a sense of humor, but it had to be mined.

"Mother had a most unique way of teaching. Who else would
have taught children to be fair by pie cutting?

"I'll never forget my first attempt at cutting an apple pie for
the family. She said, 'Dwight, cut the pie in eight even pieces.
The cutter must wait until the last piece.' I did my best to make
them even, but I ended up with a small piece. That sort of
result will make you learn accuracy and fairness fast.

"It was easy to cut an even number of pieces, but not so easy
to divide a pie into seven or nine pieces. Soon, we got so good
that it would almost take a micrometer to measure the differences in size."

As General Ike thought about life with his father and
mother, he realized that he and his brothers were happy in a
low-income home because they didn't know or think they were
poor. They made the most of what they had, squeezing the
most possible fun out of every work or play situation.

One incident that he told me about never failed to make him
smile.

With his parents at church on Sunday, Dwight prepared the
main course for dinner and asked Ed to make dough for two
large apple pies. Dwight then sliced apples.

Ed playfully picked up the giant blob of dough and heaved it
from hand to hand, like a shot put. Too large for one hand, the
lopsided dough tilted and, before he could catch it, plopped
and flattened on the floor.

Dwight was aghast.

Ed broke into laughter. "The floor's clean," he said.

"So is the dough," replied Dwight.

Then they laughed hilariously.

Ed scooped up the mass, rounded it, and started playing

catch with Dwight. Several more times, the unshapely dough ended up on the floor, like a gigantic hotcake. Suddenly Dwight glanced through the window and saw his parents' carriage pull into the yard.

"They're home," he cried in alarm.

Quickly Ed gathered up the dough, dropped it on the board and hurriedly flattened it with a flour-dusted rolling pin. He slapped the dough into the bottom of the pie tins and trimmed the edges. Dwight threw in the apple slices and showered them with white sugar and cinnamon. Ed placed the second flat of dough over the apples. Dwight serrated the outer edges with the tines of a table fork and stabbed in a few air holes.

"Probably the fastest-made apple pie in Abilene history," Ed announced.

Dwight opened the hot oven of the coal stove, and Ed slid the tins inside just as their parents entered the kitchen. Soon after, the family assembled at the table.

Following David Eisenhower's moment of silence and grace came the main course. The seductive aroma of apples and cinnamon pervaded the house and piqued the appetites of only six of those at the table. Neither Dwight nor Ed felt in the mood for dessert. As far as they were concerned, the apple pie wasn't going to get to home plate.

Everybody else seemed to enjoy it. Mother Eisenhower thought it unusual for Dwight and Ed to skip dessert and commented that "The crust of this pie is a little tough."

Why shouldn't it be? Dwight thought. *It was worked so hard, it has muscles.*

She directed an inquiring look at Dwight, who began studying the napkin in his lap.

At that very moment, Dwight Eisenhower learned the value of no comment.

6

Baseball, Prejudice and a Girl

Usually the darkness of Fourth Street, near home, didn't give Dwight an uneasy feeling, but tonight he sensed he was being followed.

He didn't look back, but he thought fast. Why wait for someone to jump him? Why not attack first? With fists clenched, he whirled around.

Instead of having to fight, he had to laugh. The big threat was a small, white terrier pup, with a black face and a band of white flowing down from between its eyes and fanning out like a river delta around its mouth.

Dwight squatted down, cradled the pup in his large, caressing hands, and asked softly, "Hey, little fella, are you lost?"

The tiny dog wagged its entire body, showing Dwight that it was less lost than found. The "little fella" turned out to be a little girl—a most happy one.

Introduced to Dwight's parents, brothers, food, drinking water and a warm, soapy bath, she had no problem wagging her way into the Eisenhowers' hearts and home for good.

Flip and Dwight became inseparable. He taught her to shake hands, sit up, dance on her hind legs, roll over, play dead, crawl under the sprawling legs of potbellied stoves to sleep, and stay when he couldn't take her along.

When he had to leave for school, Flip would follow him to the end of the property, sit and watch him until he was out of sight. Then, promptly at 12:15 P.M., as if an alarm had gone off inside her, she would wait in the same place for him to come home for lunch.

Flip seemed to understand more than the spoken word. Intuitively, she knew when she could go with her master. And he took her on some unusual missions, such as raising money so that the Abilene High School baseball team could buy bats, balls, gloves and catcher's equipment.

There were some business places where Flip wasn't welcome. Then she would lie down outside and wait. In stores where the owner wouldn't give Dwight attention, let alone money, he would put Flip through her repertoire of tricks.

Who can resist a clever little dog? he asked himself.

Most of the time, Flip and Dwight succeeded in collecting funds.

Selling was easy for Dwight. He analyzed what he had to sell and the people to whom he had to sell it and presented his message in simple terms.

Abilene High School had little money for athletic equipment. It was important to develop the bodies of students, as well as their minds. Could Abilene afford to lag behind neighboring cities that provided athletic equipment for their teams to compete?

If everything else failed, Dwight had the clincher: After all, the parents of Abilene High School students—and students themselves—support local merchants. So local merchants should support the team, whose games provide community entertainment for students and parents.

Completely businesslike, Dwight gave receipts to every contributor, whether a store owner or one of his house-to-house customers for vegetables, fruit and tamales.

As the money raiser who made it possible for an Abilene High School team to exist, Dwight was elected president of the athletic association. As the leading hitter, with a robust .500 batting average, and the best outfielder, who made sensational catches, he was inevitably named team captain.

Dwight always looked for athletic talent on the playground, and one day, he discovered a real winner, John F. "Six" McDonald, a fireball thrower, who later became a professional pitcher and just missed the major leagues.

Six got his nickname through a strange carom of events. Each week, copies of famous paintings were shown at Garfield School, among them Raphael's *The Sistine Madonna*. Some nutty kid got the idea that *Madonna* sounded like McDonald. In time, *Sistine Madonna* got warped into "Sixteen McDonald" and then shorted to Six.

As Six informed me, "I liked Dwight Eisenhower, who was known as Ike to many students. But, sometimes he felt a puff of self-importance."

One day Ike was swaggering around the Abilene High School grounds when he spotted Six. "Hey, Six, come here," yelled Ike.

Six came over. "What do you want?"

"I'm president of the athletic association, and we're going to start baseball soon," replied Ike. "Why not go out for the team?"

"I think I can make it as an outfielder."

Ike shook his head. "You're going to be the pitcher."

"Pitcher?" Six was surprised. After all, he was a left-hander, and that didn't seem too good. "I can field and throw, but I'm no pitcher."

"I think you are," replied Ike sharply. "I've watched you on the playground. You have the best arm in school."

Ike turned out to be right. Behind Six McDonald, Abilene High won many games and was good enough to play against a fine Kansas University freshman team and just about score an upset.

Abilene High led, one to nothing, up to the seventh inning. With a runner on first base, a KU player named Bill Moore hit a low cannon shot that almost carried Six's ear into center field, where Ike was playing. Ike raced in, and the ball climbed screaming over his head. It was a home run, and KU won, two to one.

Ike Eisenhower was low. "Six, I lost the game for you."

"It's my fault as much as it is yours," replied Six. "I never saw a ball hit harder in my life."

"I lost you an athletic scholarship," Ike insisted. Several longtime residents of Abilene told me that Ike never could forget about the misjudged fly ball.

Shortly after Six McDonald became a star, a prejudiced coach nearly broke up the Abilene High School team. He never seemed to like Jack Briscoe, a black youth who played first base.

One afternoon during fielding practice, Jack let a sizzling ground ball go between his legs.

"Keep your legs together, stupid," yelled the coach.

His florid face became even more red during batting practice a few minutes later. Briscoe swung at a fastball and shattered the team's best bat.

"That's it, black boy!" shouted the irate coach.

Jack stood at home plate, puzzled, holding the bat handle. Sure, there was always a shortage of baseball equipment, but he hadn't broken the bat on purpose. It was an accident.

"Don't stand there, Briscoe! Go home. We don't want niggers on this team!"

Downhearted, Jack dropped the bat handle and started to leave.

Playing shallow right field, Ike could hardly believe what he was hearing. He sprinted toward home plate. *Anyone can make an error or break a bat,* he thought. *Jack has been fired just because he's black. He's a good player. The team needs him.*

Ike was getting mad. "Coach," he said, trying to control himself, "I don't like what you just called Jack. I don't like seeing someone fired from the team just because his skin is black. I want you to reinstate Jack."

"Not a chance," the coach retorted.

"All right," shouted Ike, "I'm quitting the team."

He walked off the diamond.

"Hey, wait!" Edgar called. "I'm quitting, too."

Others began to follow them.

When the coach saw his team vanishing, he called out: "All right, Eisenhower—and the rest of you—come on back. Briscoe's on the team again."

When Ike wasn't playing baseball, he was reading about it in exchange newspapers. Even a small publication like the *Dickinson County News* exchanged newspapers with the nation's metropolitan dailies.

These were thrown into the street-side display window in disorderly piles that soon became a sun-yellowed cemetery for swatted flies.

Ike met his special baseball hero in the sports pages: Honus Wagner, the 200-pound, bull-chested, bowlegged shortstop of the Pittsburgh Pirates.

A punishing hitter, who led the National League regularly, a thrilling base stealer and an incredible fielder, Wagner, despite his bulk and awkwardness, turned sure base hits into sure outs.

With either of his huge hands—the bare one or that wearing the form-fitting infielder's glove—he would dig out skidding grounders and rifle them (dirt, pebbles and all) to beat the runner to first base.

In the wild hyperbole of one eastern sportswriter, Honus Wagner's artillery arm could throw a baseball through a battleship. When Ike daydreamed, he daydreamed about stealing bases, hitting and playing shortstop like Honus Wagner.

As much as athletics dominated his thoughts, Ike never neglected his studies. Inside or outside of school, he was always probing, inquiring, learning.

And, strangely, one of his best teachers never saw a classroom, was illiterate and could hardly spell his own name.

Yet fisherman, hunter and guide Bob Davis, a spindly tall, stoop-shouldered, quiet bachelor in his fifties, was a professor in the art of living next to nature, as far as Ike was concerned.

On occasional weekends from the time he was eight until his high-school years, Ike, with his mother's permission, camped out on the Old Smoky River with Davis.

Davis taught him how to catch the wiliest of fish, how to clean and then broil them on glowing coals, how to shoot his shotgun (a sixteen-gauge, 1897 model, Winchester repeater, which he had bought from Ed), how never to get lost in the woods and how to play poker.

After a day in the woods, he and Bob would start a campfire, clean and cook freshly caught fish, eat heartily, and settle down by firelight for a game of poker with a greasy deck of cards. Bob taught Ike the odds of drawing to a pair, a straight, or a flush and trained him to play only by percentages, not by emotions.

"If you let emotions come in, you'll be a loser. If the odds are not in your favor, always drop out," he insisted.

Each of them started with a box of matches, instead of poker chips. Soon the student equaled and sometimes surpassed his teacher.

Ike Eisenhower never stopped calculating the odds. During World War II, he always tried to develop an unbeatable "hand" before he attacked.

Through the corridor of the years, Ike remembered with excitement one special part of camping out: quiet nights, lying on his back under the clear Kansas skies with Flip pressed against his side.

The overwhelming beauty of the heavens—silver stars, painted in a scene that spun out into infinity—thrilled him. He recalled something from Job about the stars singing together.

What a work of art! It was too magnificent, too immense, too orderly to have happened by itself. There had to be an Artist. He almost broke into prayer. Then it was as if he himself *were* a prayer. How good God had been, to make him a part of His universe!

He did not know how long this thought held him, but suddenly he sensed a breeze whispering to the cottonwood trees, and the cottonwoods whispering back. This soothing sound stirred him like a familiar daytime sight: a field of wheat, golden in the sun and rustled by a gentle breeze.

Never did he want to leave the plains of Kansas, even though the big cities promised excitement and new experiences. If ever he should go away, he would someday return and spend the rest of his life here. Then he was asleep.

As much as he learned from Bob Davis, Ike never forgot that he needed a full education. He didn't want the kind of job that would wear him down and never make him enough money for marriage, a family and security.

Well before Ike and Ed entered the Seelye Theater for the high-school-graduation-class commencement exercises on May 23, 1909, they had agreed to go into higher education. Ike hadn't selected his university or course of study, but Ed knew he was going to the University of Michigan to pursue law. Neither had any idea how he would manage financially.

Commencement speaker Henry J. Allen, editor of the Wichita *Beacon,* gave them added determination with jolting advice: "I would sooner begin life over again with one arm cut off than attempt to struggle without a college education." [1]

Both Ed and Ike laughed uproariously when they read Cecilia Curry's prophecies about them among those for the thirty-four graduates in the school yearbook, *The Helianthus.*

Ed was going to be a two-term United States president, and Dwight would become a Yale history professor.

If they were ever to end up in the White House or the halls of ivy, they would first have to scramble to earn every possible cent to get through the university. Maybe if they combined earnings, one of them could at least get started.

"You enroll, Ed," insisted Ike. "You're older than I am."

"Sure, but. . . ."

Ike cut him off. "Look, Ed, let's consider priorities. The White House should get the call over Yale, anyhow."

Ed grinned. "Okay, but let's make one change. After my first year, I'll drop out and work to support your first year. We can alternate school and work, even if it takes us eight years."

Summer vacation was anything but a vacation. Ike did chores at the Bryan farm near Abilene, then moved into a better-paying job, assembling and cold riveting grain bins. Ed pulled and stacked giant ice cakes at Belle Springs Creamery until September.

Ike moved into Ed's vacated job for still-higher wages. From there, he took something paying even more: the boiler-room fireman's job. Wearing faded blue denim overalls covered with neat rectangular patches, and a train engineer's cap, Dwight looked like a mechanic. As he shoveled fine coal into the blazing furnaces, the uniform became sopped with sweat and turned a soggy, darker blue.

Occasionally friends would visit him on Sunday—Guy Tonkin, Chick Gish and sometimes Six McDonald. They would sit on wooden boxes, as far away from the furnaces as possible, and read paperback *Nick Carter* and *Frank Merriwell* books.

One Sunday, Chick, Guy and Six wanted to try shoveling.

"I can't take a chance," said Ike. "If you don't spread the coal evenly, it will send black clouds up the chimney. My father will see them and rush over to check up."

Chick snorted with contempt. "I can do it as well as you can."

"Me, too," responded Guy and Six.

And the shovel went from hand to hand, while Ike read *Frank Merriwell* and enjoyed a tremendous game-winning home run off the bat of Frank, with two strikes and two outs in the last half of the ninth inning.

When an opening developed in the creamery's ice-making plant, Ike was promoted from the hottest job to the coldest—second engineer, a night-shift position, seven days and eighty-four hours a week (6 P.M to 6 A.M.) at ninety dollars a month. The money appealed to Ike. The hours didn't. They made dating difficult. But he never confused the difficult with the impossible.

He sometimes got a day-shift worker to pinch-hit for him, so that he could spend an evening with his favorite girl friend—beautiful, sandy-haired, stately Gladys Harding, daughter of a wealthy drayage-company owner.

When Ike couldn't be at the Harding home on evenings, he visited Gladys during the day. It seemed to Mr. Harding, who wanted his daughter to marry a well-off young eligible, that Ike Eisenhower was there night and day. Once Mr. Harding told Gladys, "I'm tired of that Eisenhower fellow hanging around here so much. Get rid of him. He'll never amount to anything."

Good-bye to Yesterday

Launched with enthusiasm, Ike and Ed's eight-year university education crash-landed after the first year. It was no one's fault, Ike felt.

He had kept his promise to Ed, sending him $200. Then Ed had lined up spare-time work and also a full-time summer job—enough to sustain himself. When he considered Ed's fortunate developments, Ike couldn't ask him to interrupt his education to work for a year. At the same time, Ike became restless. He loved his home, parents, brothers, Abilene, the open country, friendly people and, yes, its pretty girls: Gladys Harding and her lovely musical friend, Ruby Norman.

Yet it was hard to make himself work an eighty-four-hour, seven-day week on the night shift, in a job that bored him and offered no future.

Something else made it even more difficult to continue wearing his rut deeper. After graduating from high school several years before, his brother Arthur had started a banking career in Kansas City. Arthur knew exactly what he wanted and how to get it. Beginning as a messenger for the Commerce Trust Company, he intended to learn every job on the way to the top.

He shared a boardinghouse room with a Union Trust bookkeeper who ushered at the Grand Theater for extra money—a friendly fellow named Harry S Truman.

Pleased with Arthur's rapid rise, Ike was disturbed that he himself was only going around in circles.

Also, Ike missed his brother more than he could have imagined. While he had often fought with Ed, he had also enjoyed playing baseball and football with him.

Then one of the girls closest to him, Ruby Norman, left for Chicago, to study at the famed Art Institute, and still another important part of his life seemed gone for good. He cared about both Ruby and Gladys Harding, but he knew he could never become serious about either of them, on his wages. Ike could not help feeling left out.

Everett "Swede" Hazlett, Jr., whose father was a prominent physician on Abilene's wealthy north side, changed that. He and Swede had attended Abilene High together. Swede was not much of a fighter, and some south-side boys bullied him. Ike, slenderly built but solid, and possessing a pile-driver punch in both hands, threatened the tormentors. "Lay off Swede, or I'll beat your brains out!"

They had enough brains to lay off.

Swede never forgot Ike's help, or his special scholastic ability in certain areas where he himself was weak.

Ike knew that Swede had received an appointment to the United States Naval Academy at Annapolis, but had failed the entrance exam. Between customers at his father's gas-fixtures store, Swede was studying to take another exam.

Once I asked Ike if he had ever thought about trying for West Point before his friendship with Swede Hazlett.

"It wasn't even on the rim of my consciousness until Swede excited my mind. Actually, Swede didn't talk to me about West Point. He interested me in Annapolis. 'Imagine, you can win an appointment to the Naval Academy, get a free education, and even play on nationally recognized football and baseball teams,' he told me.

"I was then more fascinated with advancing myself as an athlete than in an education for a specific career. Swede convinced me that by studying with him, I could win an appointment to Annapolis. The idea of West Point came later."

During the days, Ike and Swede mixed studying in the gas-fixtures store with the pleasures of eating. Occasionally, they locked up and went out for a nickel hamburger—a generous, browned, ground-round patty with pickles and mustard on a crunchy-crusted bun—and a ten cent, sixty-pound Kansas watermelon, huge enough to have come from Texas and delicious enough to have come from heaven. Ike never forgot the delight of sinking his teeth into the deep, red meat of the melon and the spurt of the cool, sweet juice.

During the nights, they studied at the creamery, between Ike's tours to check on ice-making equipment. At approximately 11 P.M., they hosed the coal dust off a boiler-room shovel, dried it, tossed on a generous gob of butter and thrust the shovel over glowing coals until it made a golden sputter. They fried a half-dozen eggs and washed them down with a quart of creamy milk.

Swede told Ike that appointments to Annapolis and West Point were made by United States senators. Ike wrote to Senator Joseph L. Bristow, because he lived in nearby Salina and supposedly selected on merit, not favoritism.

Nail-biting weeks passed. Ike found nothing from Washington in the mailbox. How could he get the attention of a busy senator? Then it came to him. Newspapers help elect and defeat candidates and should have some influence.

Ike persuaded newspaper publisher-editors Charles M. Harger and Joe Howe, and other prominent citizens, to write letters of recommendation for him.

Those of the thirty letters he saw before mailing to the senator made a deep impression on him. They mentioned his good qualities, but also stressed those of his father: honesty and conscientiousness (paying cash for everything and complete dedication to his work).

That should do it, thought Ike.

Three weeks dragged by, and nothing with a Washington postmark arrived. Would he be ignored again? Then unexpected hope came. A story seemed to leap off the front page of the local newspapers at him. There was soon to be a competitive exam for an appointment to Annapolis and West Point.

Ike rushed a letter to Senator Bristow. If the senator did not see fit to appoint him outright, could he give him permission to take the exam?

Within less than a week, Ike was invited to compete in Topeka.

On October 4, 1910, Ike took exams for both Annapolis and West Point and scored the highest of all contestants—87.5—first among those for Annapolis and second among those for West Point. He let out a shout of joy, but his happiness didn't last long. He learned he was several months too old to qualify for Annapolis.

Now he would have to make new plans for college. Or would he? Cheering news came through. The winner of the appointment to West Point had dropped out. Senator Bristow notified Ike that he had been selected for West Point.

Although proud of Dwight's achievement, his parents were secretly sad. All of their sons had been trained in the River Brethren doctrine, opposing war and violence. How, then, could Dwight choose a military career, in which pacifism was impossible?

Not once did David or Ida try to change Dwight's mind. He had a right to make such an important decision for himself. Ida was in agony.

She prayed that God, in His infinite wisdom, would influence Dwight. An unexpected answer came to her: She had used prayer to deny Dwight his God-given free will, and God does not intrude on our free will, just as He does not force us to obey His commandments or to accept Him.

Late in spring of 1911, Ike quit his job to prepare for West Point. He sorted through belongings, deciding which should go to which brother, which should be stored and which should be thrown out.

Each one sparked memories. As he fondled the brown stock of his Winchester repeater shotgun, he had a wave of regret at having to leave. He remembered times past—times that would never come again—Bob Davis, his teachings, the fun of outdoor living, but, most of all, his thoughts under the stars.

Ike said good-bye and thanked every person who had given him support. On his last visit with Gladys, he didn't want to stay too long. It was too painful. On the dark front porch, in the still of the evening, he held her tightly, kissed her and promised to write.

"I've asked my good friend Six McDonald to look after you," he told her, and Gladys cried.

On the evening before Ike's departure, Guy Tonkin, Chick Gish, the three Lucier boys—Big, Little and Middle Frenchy— and Dave Brightbill staged a farewell party for him.

Guy, with Ike in the front seat, delivered all participants to the Gish home, in his father's new rubber-tired surrey with the let-down top, which was pulled by the family's favorite trotting horse, a freshly curried and proud Sunday School Bill.

After a heavy meal, they attacked the formidable dessert, Mrs. Gish's large, yellow layer cake, with chocolate frosting thick enough to have been troweled on.

If Ike found it hard to say good-bye to his lifelong friends, it was even more difficult on the next day with his mother and twelve-year-old Milton, the only ones at home when he left.

Farewells made him self-conscious and sad. It had never been easy for him to show his feelings. He wanted to thank his mother for everything, and could find no words to thank her for anything.

How convenient it had always been to have her near for advice. How often he had taken her for granted. How comforting she had been in his most troubled times! No one in the world knew his faults better than she and loved him anyway.

In the awkward silence, he thought he saw a mist come over his mother's eyes—eyes that usually sparkled with joy. It was he who had brought this on, but what could he do about it? Quickly, he held and kissed her, shook Milton's hand, picked up his suitcase and started away.

No one had to tell Flip that he was leaving. Her usually

straight-up ears lay flat against her head, as if she had been abused. She followed him to the end of the property.

One more good-bye!

Ike put down his suitcase. The white terrier placed her forefeet on his thigh and raised her head to have her neck stroked. Ike obliged, as he studied the black face.

How could he ever forget the dark night when she had followed him home? How could he ever forget her star performances that helped him raise money? But, most of all, how could he forget the times they had camped with Bob Davis under the stars?

He patted her and said, huskily, "Good-bye, girl!"

As Ike started downtown toward the train station, Flip remained still, watching. So did Ida and Milton on the west porch.

"Mother stood there like a stone statue," says Milton. "And I stood there right by her, until Ike was out of sight. Then she went to her room and bawled like a baby. . . . Of course, I cried too."

Ike realized that soon all the old, warm and familiar things of Abilene would fade away and he would be in a new, cold and unfamiliar place. The past and future tugged at him.

Then, through some unknown alchemy, the uncertainty suddenly became mystery and challenge. He wanted to reach West Point in a hurry, to find out what was going to happen to Ike Eisenhower. He was ready for the great adventure.

Rebel At West Point

An almost-belligerent hiss of steam escaped the train that had braked to a stop at the small West Point station on the hot and muggy morning of June 14, 1911.

Cadet candidates spilled out of the railroad cars. After claiming their suitcases, they labored up a long, steep hill to the administration building—as if on a strange pilgrimage.

These cadet candidates, and others of the 285 already arrived—tall and lean, squat and stocky, medium height and weight; fair-skinned, swarthy, freckled; clad in everything from cheap, ill-fitting, loud, travel-rumpled suits to fine, tailored, conservative woolens—looked miscellaneous. How could they ever become standardized, by uniforms and training, into even a mediocre class, let alone the most celebrated in West Point history, with so many general officers (59) that it was called "the class the stars fell upon"?

The initiation process was not calculated to fortify the fearful, the weak or the easily discouraged. It was bedlam, pandemonium and chaos, multipled by bedlam, pandemonium and chaos.

Upperclassmen barked and shouted orders apparently intended more to confuse than to direct or inform candidates:

"Pick up your clothes!"

"On the double!"

"Shoulders back!"

"Come on, move it!"

"Eyes up!"

"Chin in!"

Many of the bewildered, browbeaten and exhausted cadet candidates—the elite of their home states—would have given anything to be back home.

Ike didn't entertain that thought for a minute. He refused to let the frills distract him from the fundamentals; he had come for a free college education, and that was exactly what he was going to get.

Near day's end, the noisy scramble, disorder and confusion gave way to a welcome contrast: a quiet, dignified and solemn ceremony for swearing in all the assembled candidates as cadets of the United States Military Academy.

As right hands were raised in unison and voices repeated the official oath, Ike experienced a strange, new sensation. Gooseflesh raised on his arms. Never before had he reacted this way to the words *the United States of America* and to the American flag, which seemed almost alive in the breeze. "It was the proudest moment of my life up until that hour," he once told me.

From this instant forward, he would be serving that nation, that flag—not himself. His life now belonged to the United States of America.

Ike had no idea how many fellow cadets responded in the same way, but he knew that he reacted differently from many of them to West Point on the Hudson River, with its somber, massive granite walls, buildings like unassailable fortresses and tight discipline. He did not let it depress him. It only ignited good cheer and optimism in him.

Hazing by upperclassmen amused, rather than intimidated him. "I had had tough bosses before." After learning that it was more a nuisance than threat, Ike and a classmate, Tommy

Atkins, sometimes got back at their tormentors.

Once Ike and Tommy violated a minor regulation, and Corporal Adler, of their division, ordered them to report to him in full-dress coats. Obviously he meant them to be in complete uniform, but Tommy said, "Hey, Ike, let's take him literally and show up wearing only our full-dress coats—not a thing underneath."

At the required time, they rapped on Corporal Adler's door. Cadets Eisenhower and Atkins were reporting as ordered.

"Seeing our hairy legs and incomplete uniforms, Adler bellowed at us, while his roommate roared with laughter," Ike told me. "The commotion attracted other upperclassmen, who joined in the laughter. Although Adler forced us to go through disciplinary action—pulling our shoulders back, sucking up our stomachs, pulling in our chins, and other punishment—we won that round."

But Ike wasn't superior to West Point in every respect. Once he saluted the most-decorated officer he had ever seen, without receiving a return salute. The fellow turned out to be a drum major!

Despite Ike's coordination in athletics, he could not march in time to the military band, and was assigned to the Awkward Squad until he, his feet and the music could get together. This indignity gave him new understanding and later increased his effectiveness as an officer.

From his first days at the academy, Ike rebelled against strict discipline in what he considered nit-picking regulations. Records from 1912 show the type of infractions that made him stand one hundred twenty-fifth in his class in conduct: "Late to gym formation; alcove not in order; dressed improperly in room; failure to execute a right into the line properly; shoes require polishing."

Ike continued to excel in subjects that interested him most: English, military history and math. His roommate, Paul A. Hodgson, also a Kansas native, envied Ike's ability to turn out sparkling essays in thirty minutes, that were often read to the class and rated the highest grades.

The first Christmas at West Point was not a time for celebration by all Plebes. Difficult courses and the way of life itself had caused fifty candidates to leave. Within the next three and one-half years, seventy-five more dropped out.

During his year as a Plebe, Ike lost no time in trying to impress the football coach that he was varsity material. The coach had little use for a lanky, rawboned, Kansas kid only five-eleven and weighing a mere 152 pounds.

During the next year, a twenty-two-pound heavier Ike, by smashing tackles and slashing runs, made the varsity as a linebacker-halfback and was mentioned as a potential All-American.

"I always played as hard as I could. I gave all I had on every play. This made up for my lack of weight," he once told me.

Two closely spaced occurrences ended his football playing and threatened his military career.

In a game against Tufts College, he plunged through the line and, when tackled, sustained a twisted knee and torn ligaments. He underestimated the seriousness of the injury. Discharged from the hospital, he took part in exhausting horsemanship exercises in the riding hall. As he vaulted to the hardwood floor, he felt a sharp pain and dismounted awkwardly.

"Very poor, Mr. Eisenhower," called out the instructor. "Do it again."

"Sir, I've had a football injury. . . ."

"Let's not goldbrick," shouted the instructor. "Go through the exercise until you dismount perfectly."

Again, Ike dismounted. The injured knee buckled, he collapsed in agony and was carried to the hospital.

Dr. Charles Keller, the chief surgeon, examined his knee and gave him an answer that brought on the depression of his life: "Mr. Eisenhower, we can put your knee back together, but never again will it be sound enough for you to play baseball or football."

A death sentence could hardly have been less welcome. Ike's first impulse was to resign from the academy. *That's ridiculous,* he told himself. He and a friend, Omar Bradley, also eliminated from athletic competition with a football-injured knee, discussed their problem. *Small consolation,* Ike thought. *It won't put either of us back on the field.* A light smoker, he began smoking almost incessantly. This habit dominated him for many years.

When his knee permitted, he tried gymnastics and strengthened his arms so that he could chin himself three times with one hand. He also mastered the giant swing, which only outstanding gymnasts could accomplish. But he was still unhappy. Gymnastics could never replace football.

If he couldn't play, he could coach. Under Ike's direction, the junior varsity won three victories. Ike taught the players game strategy and how to enhance their natural abilities. He developed several excellent players for the varsity and made a name for himself as a coach.

From competing and coaching, he saw, over and over, the inestimable value of teamwork on the playing field and how it related to the battlefield.

Despite his best efforts, Ike couldn't stay away from varsity football. If he couldn't be in the lineup, he could at least be on the sideline, as a cheerleader.

He did that and more. He got a brainstorm that brought color and showmanship to football games. Ike designed black and gold capes to be worn by certain cadets over their gray uniforms. He arranged their seating in the stands in such a way that they spelled out the word *Army*. His innovation was the model for today's card stunts. His capes also were the forerunners for the World War II Eisenhower battle jacket.

Few cadets had more friends and enjoyed academy social life more than Ike—poker, dances and bull sessions. Already he was noted for his spontaneous, broad grin.

Like most West Pointers, Ike Eisenhower looked forward to the end of his second year, and furlough time, when he could spend almost two and one-half months in Abilene with his family, Gladys Harding and friends.

Brimming over with things to tell about West Point, Ike arrived in Abilene early one morning. On the edge of the

Eisenhower property, as if she had received a letter from him, was Flip.

She leaped three feet in the air, pounced upon him and barked so shrilly that she woke up the entire household. After greeting everyone, Ike ran from room to room, making sure all the furniture and bric-a-brac were just where they had always been.

His visit was not quite what he had planned. Often, before his knee injury, he had visualized a triumphant return to the Abilene baseball team, smashing home runs and making incredible, somersaulting, circus catches that would dazzle Gladys.

Instead of playing in the informal league that included cities such as Chapman, Herington, Junction City and Salina, he had to be satisfied with the unglamorous umpiring of Abilene home games at fifteen dollars each—welcome money for an ever-broke cadet. Local men invariably officiated at home games.

Therefore, Ike was surprised when the Chapman manager phoned him. "Eisenhower, we would like you in Chapman, to umpire our game this morning."

"Did I hear you right?" Ike asked in astonishment.

"Yes, we want you to umpire our game."

"But, you're playing Abilene, and I'm from Abilene."

"No matter," replied the manager. "You are always fair."

The manager even sent a Model-T Ford to Abilene to pick him up.

"When I showed up to umpire, the Abilene team members couldn't believe their eyes," said Ike. "The team was so stunned that they played poorly for several innings."

During the summer, Ike missed Six McDonald, who was playing professional ball for Omaha. Six never corresponded with Ike, and had no idea he was in Abilene.

True to Ike's requests, Six had looked after Gladys Harding. He had taken her to several movies and had grown to care for her, but baseball season had taken him away from the area. During the previous February, he had been on twenty dates with her.

Often, as he traveled with his team, Six thought about Gladys. He longed to be with her. After pitching a hard game, Six made an unheard-of request to his manager, asking for two days off. He didn't think he would get it, because even after a game, the pitcher was sometimes needed in the bull pen, but the manager said okay.

Six ended up in Enterprise, not far from Abilene. He paid a man a dollar to drive him there. As they bumped down the dirt Enterprise road to the south side of Abilene, Six could hardly control his excitement. Soon he would be with Gladys. He asked the driver to slow down as they approached the Harding house.

Just as he was about to say, "Stop," he glanced out of the car window, and there on chairs in the center of the green, neatly cropped front yard sat Ike Eisenhower, spectacular in his West Point uniform, and Gladys, always beautiful, holding hands.

Six felt his heart sink. Suddenly he was empty and depressed. He couldn't intrude. "Take me right into Abilene," he told the driver.

Six played pool all night with the guys and then got on next morning's train to rejoin the team in Lincoln.

Ike didn't understand why Six hadn't called at his home. They never saw each other again.

Shortly after Ike had gone halfway through West Point, he was nearly all through. Even many years later, he felt a chill when recalling how close he had come to being kicked out of the academy.

Although he had a special aptitude for integral calculus, he occasionally failed to apply himself. In the midst of an Ike Eisenhower daydream, the captain instructor announced, "Tomorrow's problem is going to be one of the most difficult we have ever had."

With a mighty effort, Ike pulled himself down from a cloud.

"The head of the mathematics department has asked me to explain the approach to the problem and the answer. So pay close attention."

Ike copied the answer and followed the explanation, until he realized that the instructor had only a shadowy idea of what he was talking about. He was parroting the solution step-by-step from a paper on his desk.

Why bother listening? Ike asked himself. *In a class of twelve, the odds of my being called upon are eleven to one.*

That morning's odds shortened dramatically the next day, when the instructor said, "Mr. Eisenhower, demonstrate the solution to the class."

Ike's panic did not show through his poker face. How could he possibly use the instructor's solution? He hadn't listened. All he could do was make a wild stab at it.

To gain time, he rose and slowly walked to the blackboard. As he picked up a piece of chalk, he felt silly. What could he possibly write?

"I didn't even know how to begin. Somehow I remembered the answer and scribbled it in one corner."

Disturbing thoughts raced through his mind. If he failed to do at least something to solve the problem, he would get a zero. Even worse, he would be cited to the disciplinary department for neglecting duty, because he had no defense for ignoring the explanation.

He prodded his memory, but it refused to cooperate. All he could do was attempt solutions by trial and error.

Minutes sped by, and he could feel the eyes of the instructor and the class on him. Suddenly, in desperation, a solution came to him that followed the lines of the instructor's, and the chalk whirled across the blackboard.

His approach actually led to the right answer. Amazing! Relieved, he sat down. The instructor studied the untidy figures and asked for an explanation of the method.

Hardly had Ike finished detailing his simple solution when the instructor angrily declared, "Mr. Eisenhower, you know nothing about this problem. That is obvious. From the known answer, you have set down totally meaningless figures and steps, just to try to deceive me."

Ike flushed in anger. He had been called a cheater! More

than anything, he wanted to smash the officer in the face. He jumped to his feet. "Sir, you have accused me of cheating. . . ."

At that very moment, a sharp command rang out from near the doorway. "Captain, hold on a minute!"

Ike and the instructor instantly recognized the voice of Major Bell, the associate professor of mathematics, and turned. The major had dropped into the class unannounced, on an inspection visit.

"Captain, I would like to see Mr. Eisenhower go step-by-step through his solution."

Still seething, Ike went through his explanation.

Major Bell, who had nodded during each step, beamed when Ike finished.

"Mr. Eisenhower's solution is much more logical and simpler than ours. It surprises me that none of us—and we're supposed to be good mathematicians—has ever discovered it. We'll scrap the old solution and use Mr. Eisenhower's."

Ike breathed a silent prayer of thanks. If Major Bell hadn't visited the class exactly when he did, Cadet Eisenhower might have punched the instructor and been booted out of West Point in disgrace.

The instructor never again gave Ike a good grade.

Not long before graduation, Ike was asked to report to Colonel Shaw, head of the medical department. A suspicion crossed his mind. Colonel Shaw was probably going to talk about his bad knee, which had hospitalized him periodically since the football and horsemanship injuries.

Would the colonel tell him he would receive his degree, but not a commission in the army? He had heard rumors that such things happened.

The peacetime army in early 1915 had roughly 120,000 men and little room for newly graduated second lieutenants, other than those who rated highest in their class. The also-rans were commissioned, but labeled "additional second lieutenants."

West Point authorities made sure they didn't commission men with physical disabilities, who couldn't serve in any or every branch of the army, or who might be forced to retire early on a disability pension.

Colonel Shaw dispensed with preliminaries. "Mr. Eisenhower, your recurring knee problem may make it necessary for me to recommend that you not receive a commission." He studied Ike's impassive face. "Of course, you will be graduated and receive your diploma," he hastened to add.

Ike thought about his knee injury. It had happened in the line of duty—in football—and been aggravated in the horsemanship drills. Why should he be penalized?

"Well, Mr. Eisenhower. What is your reaction?"

Ike considered the question. He had come to West Point for a free education, a college degree and to play baseball and football. He had accomplished these things.

"That's all right with me, Colonel," he replied cheerfully. "I just may go to Argentina, to see what it's like."

No one could have been more surprised than Colonel Shaw. He had expected strenuous resistance. Instead of following his original tack, he said, "Mr. Eisenhower, I want to think this matter over."

Several days later, he asked Ike to report again.

"Mr. Eisenhower, I may have a way out of this dilemma. You could apply for the Coast Artillery. Then I could justify recommending that you be commissioned."

Ike reflected on the Coast Artillery's do-nothing role: keeping giant sixteen-inch guns oiled and greased for an invasion that would never come in his lifetime.

"No, thank you, Colonel," Ike replied, not masking his contempt.

Colonel Shaw reacted visibly. Ike had no way of knowing that the Colonel had once served in the Coast Artillery. "All right, Mr. Eisenhower," he said curtly. "That's all I can do for you."

Ike began writing for travel literature about Argentina. Before his inquiries drew responses, he received another call from Colonel Shaw.

"Mr. Eisenhower, in reviewing your entire service record, I

found that your knee injury had been aggravated by an exercise in horsemanship."

"That's right, Colonel."

"You will soon be required to sign a card to indicate your preferred branch of the service. If you don't designate mounted service, I will recommend that the academic board commission you."

"Colonel, I have no interest in the cavalry. The infantry is for me."

Colonel Shaw brightened. "Good! I'll recommend that you be commissioned, but you must agree not to request any branch of army service than that on your preference card."

"I agree, Sir!"

On his preference card, for first, second and third choices, Ike wrote, "Infantry, INFANTRY, *INFANTRY.*"

In the final days before graduation, Ike learned that academically, he had finished sixty-first in his class of one hundred sixty-four and one hundred twenty-fifth in conduct.

His records neither embarrassed nor discouraged him, and he felt that they reflected his performance quite accurately. Yet he was confident that he would make a better soldier than student.

Did West Point faculty members who rated him realize that Eisenhower, despite his good, gray mediocrity in scholastics and superiority in earning demerits, would someday become an outstanding officer?

They knew that he excelled in subjects which seemed to equip him best for military accomplishment. His ability to write well-organized, clear and concise papers, his creativity in mathematics and his phenomenal grasp of military history and strategy—although he disapproved of the unimaginative way in which it was taught—were revealing indicators. His spirited performances in athletics, his ability to work in harmony with teammates and coaches, and his initiative, leadership and imagination in coaching and cheerleading did not escape notice.

Many years later, when Ike was a five-star general, he learned that one instructor had referred to him as an uncommon man, who would enjoy army life and give fair value to duty and recreation, although he could not visualize him as "a man who would throw himself into his job so completely that nothing else would matter."

A second officer saw him another way: "Dwight Eisenhower was born to command."

Soldier Takes a Wife

Surely there are more important historical dates than June 12, 1915—such as October 12, 1492, and July 4, 1776—but the former ranked high to Ike, because it was liberation day from West Point. Now, instead of playing soldier, he could be one.

So he thought.

Ike had requested duty in the Philippine Islands, and all the odds seemed in his favor. He was so certain that most army men would shun the steamy hot, equatorial, crawling-with-insects land that he bought only tropical uniforms—field-service khaki and dress whites—from the fund that he, like all cadets, had accumulated from pay deductions of fifteen dollars per month.

Tropical uniforms cost much less than conventional military clothing—olive drabs for garrison service and dress blues, which he felt he wouldn't need. With the balance of a few hundred dollars, he would take a leisurely vacation in Abilene.

Before Ike and classmates could become full-fledged second lieutenants on the army payroll and receive assignments, President Woodrow Wilson had to sign their commissions. Ike knew his commander in chief had other things to do, such as keeping a wary eye on the war in Europe and on the Mexican border raids of Pancho Villa, but he didn't think it should take anyone three months to sign his name.

Ike's savings dribbled away for room and board at home and for fun. Suddenly, one day he received his commission with President Wilson's autograph and an assignment to Texas.

Why not to the Philippines? Mainly due to warlike action along the entire border of Mexico, from Brownsville, Texas, to California. When President Wilson recognized General Carranza's government, Pancho Villa, leader of opposing forces, began raids into United States territory. No one knew where he would strike next, so the army had to be prepared.

Shipment to Texas meant a disappointment and financial crisis. Already in debt to his father, Ike now had to buy a full officer's wardrobe for continental duty. He talked a quality military tailor into making his required olive drab and blue uniforms, a full-dress coat and full evening dress, on credit.

Upon joining the Nineteenth Infantry Regiment at Fort Sam Houston in San Antonio, Texas, Lieutenant Ike received his three months' back pay, made a dent in his debts and added to his $141.67 per month pay with poker winnings.

To Ike Eisenhower, being a soldier meant going into combat. International developments made him think he would see military action. Fierce fighting in Europe had taken place for almost a year, when on May 7, a German U-boat off Ireland sank the *Lusitania,* a British passenger ship. One hundred twenty-eight Americans were lost, and the United States moved closer to war in Europe.

Shortly after Ike reported to San Antonio, another development intensified border hostilities. President Wilson gave General Carranza special permission to move troops over United

States territory to bolster the garrison at Agua Prieta, directly opposite Douglas, Arizona. This advantage made possible a Carranza victory. Infuriated, Villa increased over-the-border attacks, killing and wounding innocent Americans and destroying property.

Yet Ike got no closer to combat than training National Guardsmen. But something exciting did happen. He met a girl—not just a girl, but *the* girl.

On a bright, clear, Sunday afternoon in October, Ike, in ODs, campaign hat, blouse and sidearm, came out of the bachelor officers' quarters. He hardly paid attention to the small group on the sidewalk across the street, until someone called out, "Ike."

It was Lulu Harris, wife of Major Hunter Harris, a much-loved lady at Fort Sam. She invited him over to meet some friends.

"Wish I could, Mrs. Harris, but I'm on guard duty and have to make an inspection tour."

In an aside to a young girl in the group, she remarked, "Humph! The woman hater of the post!" [1] The girl, in turn, suggested something to Mrs. Harris, and she tried again. "We didn't ask you to come over to *stay*. Just come over and meet these friends of mine."

"Sure," replied Ike.

Lulu introduced him to the Doud family, of Denver, who were wintering in San Antonio. As he glanced at youthful Mamie Geneva Doud, his eyes stopped there. They could see no one but her.

Was he *actually* seeing, or just imagining? Had this lovely vision just stepped from within the gold-leafed frame of a masterful oil painting, or floated down from an ethereal pink cloud?

An olive-shaped face, large, round, saucy blue eyes and a petite body were accented by a straw hat whose band featured pink roses. She also wore miniature coral earrings shaped like roses; a white, fine silk, embroidered blouse; a pink cretonne skirt, and a broad cummerbund decorated with pink roses.

"The most beautiful girl I had ever seen—and the best dresser—with poise beyond her years and the most gorgeous, clear blue eyes that were full of impertinence," was the way he thought of her then and many years later, as he confided to me during World War II in his offices at the Saint George Hotel in Algiers.

Ike invited Mamie to inspect guard posts with him. As they walked and talked, he became more intrigued.

Like a good military man, he had located his objective and immediately planned a campaign to capture it. From Lulu Harris, he learned that Mamie was eighteen, on the verge of nineteen, one of the daughters of John and Elvira Doud. Eleanor was their eldest daughter, followed by Eda Mae and Mabel Frances (nicknamed Mike).

A student of Miss Wolcott's School, a Denver finishing school, Mamie was a pampered darling at home, called Miss Mamie by servants in the giant, Victorian house, custom-built by John Doud, who had launched a meat-packing firm in Boone, Iowa, at twenty-eight. Within eight years, he was making more money than he, his wife and family would ever need.

Now that Ike planned to date Mamie, he was pleased he had accepted a coaching job for the Peacock Military Academy football team. This meant an extra income of $150 for the season. It also eventually meant a way of selling the Doud family on himself—*eventually*, because he had trouble finding an opening on the calendar of the popular Mamie.

The fact that Mamie was dating every night did not discourage Ike. It made her all the more irresistible, and him all the more determined.

On many evenings, Ike sat on the broad front porch, chatting with Mr. Doud until Mamie came home. Ike out-persisted the competition and scored a major victory by luring the Douds out to watch football games of the team he was coaching. Soon all family members were lobbying for him.

Ike happened at the right time in Mamie's life. She was fed up with pale fellows and their oily, slick pompadours—"lounge lizards with patent-leather hair." From the start, Mamie felt proud to walk beside Ike. He was so tanned, handsome and powerful, with broad, strong hands, a spontaneous and infectious grin, and he made such fascinating conversation.

On a typical date, Ike and Mamie would ride into downtown San Antonio on a jitney bus—a large automobile that charged a jitney (nickel) per person. They would dine at the Original, a Mexican restaurant near the Alamo, where chili, enchiladas and tamales for two ran about $1.25 with tip, and then attend a movie or a vaudeville program.

Ike was extremely kind to Mamie, spoke softly to her, always pinned a corsage on her dress before they attended a dance, and insisted on having every dance. He never taxed her physically, because he knew that in childhood the valve on the left side of her heart had been badly damaged by rheumatic fever, and she tired easily.

Ike's first important gift to Mamie was his West Point portrait, inscribed, "to the dearest, sweetest girl in the world."

Still paying on his military clothing and the debt to his father, Ike strained his personal exchequer by purchasing a silver jewel case that he presented to Mamie on her nineteenth birthday (November 14). When she accepted this expensive gift, her parents knew she was serious about him.

Shortly after Christmas, Ike asked her to marry him, and she accepted. For their engagement, he presented her his West Point class ring on Valentine's Day, 1916.

Mr. Doud warned Mamie that marriage to a military man would involve hardships, many household uprootings and forced moves, many periods of separation, friendships made and broken, and living on an income far below what she had ever experienced. But she was deeply in love.

John Doud thought he had the trump card. He told her that Ike could become a casualty in the European war, which would soon draw the United States into its vortex.

It failed to work. Mamie became even more determined, and Mr. Doud gave his consent. The wedding was set for November 14, Mamie's twentieth birthday, but Ike almost blew it.

Some months earlier, he had applied for Army Aviation Section service. Pilot training and getting a 50 percent pay boost appealed to Ike, concerned about supporting two on a salary that had failed miserably to support one.

Surprised with an acceptance notice, he almost flew to the Douds', to share the good news.

An icy silence froze his enthusiasm. Finally, Mr. Doud spoke, deliberately, firmly: "I'll come right to the point. Flying is a dangerous experiment. . . . "

Not at all, thought Ike. *It's a new, exciting military offense!*

Mr. Doud continued: "If you are so irresponsible that you would risk your life when you are planning to be married, Mrs. Doud and I will be forced to withdraw our consent."

For several days, Ike lived under a black cloud. He wanted *both* Mamie and flying. Obviously, he had to select one, and that one was Mamie. "As upsetting as it was to give up flying, the crisis worked for good," Ike once confided to me. "I got a new perspective on myself. I had been living the typical bachelor's life, doing more or less what I pleased, responsible only to myself and always in debt. It was time to view myself and my career seriously. Now I determined to become the finest army officer, no matter in what branch I was asked to serve—to do every duty assigned me to the absolute best of my ability."

The international situation also sobered Ike. Increased indignation at sinkings of more American ships by Germans, and killings of Americans by Pancho Villa's troops made military action seem about to explode.

Ike and Mamie decided to move up their wedding date. He wangled a ten-day leave and now had several other problems. It was Sunday, he was broke, had no wedding ring and couldn't afford to waste a day of his precious leave.

Adversity seemed to bring out the best in Ike. He woke up a friend, an officer of the Lockwood National Bank of San Antonio, explained his predicament, and got him to open the bank to make him a $250 loan.

He convinced another friend, who managed Hertzberg's jewelry store, to come down and sell him, on credit, a seventy dollar wedding ring that he and Mamie had previously chosen.

The wedding was set for noon, July 1, 1916, in the music room of the Douds' multistoried Victorian home in Denver.

Slender and fragile, a swirl of light-brown hair covering much of her forehead, Mamie looked almost luminous in a delicate, white-lace wedding gown with tiers of embroidered scallops on her skirt and bolero jacket of the same material. Ike, finally wearing a tropical white dress uniform bought for the Philippines, nervously led her down the aisle. The two were married by a Dr. Williamson, a minister from England who was temporary pastor of the Central Presbyterian Church.

To preserve the creases in his trousers, Ike refused to sit down, Mamie remembered. Guests at the reception gasped in surprise as Ike cut the wedding cake with his sword.

Later the newlyweds posed before a tall window in the music room, Mamie without her wedding bouquet, because Ike, to preserve it, had doused it in hot, melted candle wax and ended up with French-fried flowers.

A bit of good news came through from the army on their wedding day. Ike had been promoted to a first lieutenant, with pay of $151.67 per month—a raise of $10.

After a weekend at Eldorado Springs, a nearby mountain resort, the Dwight D. Eisenhowers stayed for a few days at the Doud mansion and then went by Union Pacific to Abilene, arriving at four o'clock in the morning to find David Eisenhower waiting in a deserted railroad station. They could stay for only a few hours before boarding the train for San Antonio. The Eisenhowers unanimously loved Mamie—particularly Milton and Earl. Ida cooked a fried chicken dinner for breakfast.

A surprise overwhelmed the couple at Ike's Fort Sam bachelor quarters. Mamie's blue eyes widened in wonder. "Look," she cried.

On every inch of floor—living room, bedroom, bathroom— were brightly ribboned packages of useful gifts: a percolator, toaster, chafing dish, broiler and small electric cooking stove. These items would help them to avoid the culinary atrocities of the officers' mess.

After the *oh*s and *ah*s of gift unwrapping, Mamie slowly

began to see the reality of her "functional" apartment: the cheap living-room pieces and the bedroom furnished only with a bed and a small, paint-nicked dresser. Ike could not wait until her elegant walnut bedroom set and Oriental rug—a wedding gift—arrived to remove the GI appearance.

In accordance with Eisenhower family custom, Mamie was given responsibility for money and all purchases.

A severe test of the marriage came early. Ike rolled up his bedding to go on a two-week maneuver. Mamie, who had never spent a night alone, pleaded, "Please don't leave me so long."

Ike grimaced. He had to be firm. "I can't tell you where I'm going, and one thing must be clearly understood between us. Much as I adore you, I have to answer the call of duty first. The army has first call on my time, and my first duty is to the United States of America. It always will be. I have no choice."

Mamie tried to understand, but the hurt, although it diminished with the years, never healed completely.

Improvisations

Nothing since their wedding brought Mamie and Ike closer together than the information, early in 1917, that she was going to have a baby.

A first lieutenant's income did not permit buying a new wardrobe to accommodate Mamie's increasing dimensions. She knew nothing about sewing, so Ike, drawing upon his Abilene home experience, expertly let out her clothing.

It would be great if he could be with Mamie, at least until their child was born, but the military did not operate for the convenience of its personnel.

After leading a military-police detail in San Antonio, Ike became supply officer for the Fifty-seventh Infantry Regiment at Leon Springs, Texas, about twenty miles away as the buzzard flies: wide-open sagebrush spaces, without a building and only one fresh-water well. Few places he had seen would have been more hostile to life—especially to that of the 3,000 rookies that the War Department suddenly thrust upon him.

As Ike, now a captain, started from scratch to requisition, borrow, buy or scrounge tents, food and water, trucks and infantry equipment, he wondered which master bungler in Washington had contrived this mess—the first of many impossible situations which made him comment that the War Department "moves in mysterious ways its blunders to perform."

As he solved these problems, those on the international scene built to a crescendo. On April 6, 1917, the United States declared war on Germany.

Despite concern for his Mamie, Ike now felt driven to go into combat. He applied to the War Department for overseas duty and was turned down. Instructors seemed more needed than combat officers, and his coaching had tagged him an instructor. He was transferred to the Officers' Training Camp at Fort Oglethorpe, Georgia, to teach candidates the *how-to*s of becoming second lieutenants.

For days on end, he and his trainees lived in trenches and dugouts like those on Europe's Western Front.

Meanwhile, Mamie, in the final stages of pregnancy, was joined by her mother at Fort Sam Houston. Then, on September 23, Doud Dwight Eisenhower was born. Three days later, the Ike Eisenhower who had gone into the trenches as a mere husband emerged as a father. It was painful not to see his boy at once.

Before Christmas, he was transferred to the Army Service School at Fort Leavenworth, Kansas, to train new second lieutenants. He arranged a few days' leave to see Mamie and his boy in San Antonio.

Ike was awestruck. Doud Dwight, nicknamed Icky, was not merely a son; he was a miracle. As Ike held him in his arms, Icky gurgled, cooed, kicked and smiled. Warmth and joy suffused Ike. Never before had he felt such happiness.

Before leaving for Fort Leavenworth, Ike reported to Fort Sam Houston and learned that a friend, Captain Gilbert Allen, was organizing a machine-gun battalion for overseas duty. Ike asked to join his outfit. Allen teletyped a request to Washington for Eisenhower's transfer. The War Department tartly replied that Captain Eisenhower had special ability as an instructor. That was how the army intended to use him.

Even that wasn't the end. At Fort Leavenworth, the post commandant, Colonel Miller, read him a scathing letter from the adjutant general.

The War Department frowned on young officers requesting special duty. Officers were supposed to obey orders and let the War Department run the war.

> This made me furious and when the Colonel proceeded to add several reprimands of his own, I reverted to the old, red-necked cadet. I was asking nothing, after all, except to go to battle.
>
> "Sir," I said, "this offense—if it is an offense—was committed before I came under your jurisdiction. If there is punishment to be given out, I think that it should be given by the War Department and not added to by yourself, with all due respect."
>
> Strangely enough, I heard him say, "Well, I think you're right. And I respect you for standing up to your convictions." The Colonel sent me out in a friendly mood toward him, although my views of the War Department continued to be beyond easy conversion to parlor language.[1]

An unexpected benefit soon materialized: the chance to study in a new military field—tank warfare. He was excited with discussions and analyses of experimental tank usage in the war in Europe. Ike chafed for combat duty. With seven years of training to lead fighting men, he was bogged down in routine.

Then, in February 1918, his experience in training and organizing new outfits, plus the course in tanks, made a surprise opportunity for him at Camp Meade, Maryland, forming a tank corps for overseas duty.

As Ike organized and equipped the 301st Tank Battalion (Heavy) for combat, he found that small tanks were rarities. Heavy tanks were even more so. It seemed to Ike that large tanks would be the ultimate weapon for overcoming no-decision trench warfare, for smashing down wire entanglements, spanning trenches and rolling over machine-gun nests.

One day in mid-March, Ike received thrilling news. The 301st would soon ship out for France. Now his outfit could help bring the stalemated war to a dramatic finish. Ike examined the New York City harbor embarkation point and talked at length with port authorities, to eliminate the possibility of unforeseen problems.

Then his world crashed.

Instead of shipping out with the 301st, Ike was made commander of troops left behind, with orders to take them to Camp Colt, an abandoned military base in Gettysburg, Pennsylvania, the locale of a great Civil War battle and the hallowed ground on which President Abraham Lincoln made an address that earned him distinction in history and literature.

The organizational setup of the Tank Corps was unorthodox. It was directed from Washington, D.C., by Colonel I. C. Welborn and commanded by Eisenhower, the only regular army officer in camp.

Soon Ike's frustration was displaced by heavy responsibilities: a steady flow of volunteers to equip, organize, train and ship overseas.

Camp Colt was a typical example of the nation's unpreparedness for war: with swarms of volunteers and inadequate facilities and equipment, it was a camp for training troops in tank warfare with no tanks.

Captain Ike improvised for lack of facilities, equipment and even training directives. He had enough tents for his five-hundred men, but no wood flooring or heaters. He ordered tents to be pitched on bare ground.

An early-spring, heavy snowfall almost buried the camp, and Ike trembled at the thought of men suffering undue exposure and dying of pneumonia. He ordered troops to shovel a swath wide enough for an army truck to drive into town, where he bought every available stove in Gettysburg and was still short.

For tents without stoves, Ike had to improvise. He had men build fire pits from accumulated rocks. An all-night patrol fueled and monitored the fires.

Suddenly Ike had a new headache. The need for overseas tank troops shut off temporarily, and trainees kept pouring into Camp Colt. After basic training and tank instruction, what could he do to prevent idleness and keep morale from plummeting?

Ike, promoted to temporary major in June 1918, wanted useful follow-up training to prepare men better for combat, but there was little feedback on requirements from the battle fields—a shortcoming that Eisenhower corrected in World War II.

Ike and his aides kept the troops occupied with new courses: telegraphy (on the premise that poor communication can lead to defeat or disaster in battle) and mechanics.

How could he possibly train men for tank service without proper weapons, backstops and tanks? Only one way—by using his imagination.

Three-inch swivel guns and machine guns were not available in the army, so Major Ike, through Colonel Welborn, finagled them from the navy.

One of his men improvised tanks by mounting machine guns on flatbed trucks to fire at targets against a natural backstop, Big Round Top, a famous Gettysburg battle site.

Later Ike received a surprise: three small (seven ton) Renault tanks from Europe. Finally, someone "over there" or in the War Department saw the worthiness of giving the Tank Corps armed tanks, like the ones they would someday operate! Ike examined the tanks, and his joy faded. The Renaults had come without guns! Yet they did include something of value: two British tank-officer instructors. It was Ike's first sample of Allied cooperation. The officers lauded a man named Winston Churchill. This government leader had championed tanks for seven years and urged their production in quantity. Ike wished he could meet Churchill, but he was one war too early.

While Ike had had many disagreements with the army, he still was objective enough to commend the War Department for one thing: a special program for "civilian" troops—men seemingly untrainable due to lack of coordination, concentration, mental quirks, physical limitations or other handicaps.

Development battalions received special instruction in marching—Ike recalled his initial lack of coordination at West Point—and in any other deficiencies.

Under a Captain Randolph, who was selected by Ike, success was phenomenal. Most of the seemingly incompetent men were soon transferred back to their regular organizations. Many became noncommissioned officers, and twenty-one were enrolled in officer's training school, with eighteen winning commissions.

"I am inclined by nature to be optimistic about the capacity of a person to rise higher than he or she has thought possible once interest and ambition are aroused. If I were not, the experience of watching Randolph with the Development Battalion would have made me so. . . ." Ike wrote in *At Ease.*[2]

Colonel Welborn, aware of Eisenhower's accomplishment against severe limitations, promoted him to a temporary lieutenant colonel on his twenty-eighth birthday. Later, he recommended him for the Distinguished Service Medal, an honor rarely given officers serving in the United States. Ten years separated the recommendation and the actual award. Colonel Welborn's comment about the long delay appealed to Ike's sense of humor. "At least the award was not posthumous."

When the war ended on November 11, 1918, so did Ike Eisenhower's hope of ever being in combat. The army faced wholesale demobilization. Millions who had volunteered and been drafted in a hurry had to be discharged in the same way.

Lieutenant Colonel Ike received orders to close up camp and

move all men and records to Fort Dix, New Jersey, to prepare his troops for discharge, before tidal waves of overseas troops would inundate Fort Dix for the same purpose.

Then he and several hundred remaining Tank Corps members were ordered to Fort Benning, Georgia, until the War Department could find a permanent base for them.

Many times before and after March 1919, when the Tank Corps was transferred back to Camp Meade, Ike lived in suspense about his outfit. What would be the future of tanks and the Tank Corps?

Many top infantry officers regarded tanks as an experiment that had failed. As far as they were concerned, the future of tanks was already behind them. Tanks were bulky, heavy, slow and clumsy—mechanical and steel brontosauruses—which malfunctioned at critical times, cost too much and deserved abandonment to mystify future archeologists.

In contrast, Ike Eisenhower had a visionary's outlook on tanks. If they had a fault, it was that they were too new to be old enough for acceptance by ossified minds. True, the present versions were riddled with faults, but, after all, they were only infants. As a tactical weapon, they had a dazzling future.

In the midst of helping demobilization, Lieutenant Colonel Ike found more than the tank's unpopularity to discourage him.

> I had missed the boat in the war we had been told would end all wars. A soldier's place was where the fighting went on. I hadn't yet fully learned the basic lesson of the military—that the proper place for a soldier is where he is ordered by his superiors . . . .
>
> As for my professional career, the prospects were none too bright. I was older than my classmates, was still bothered on occasion by a bad knee, and saw myself in the years ahead putting on weight in a meaningless chair-bound assignment, shuffling papers and filling out forms. If not depressed, I was mad, disappointed, and resented the fact that the war had passed me by. . . .
>
> There was, after all, a brighter side. For an officer graduated from West Point less than two years before the United States entered the war, I had been singularly fortunate in the scope of

my first three and a half years of duty. How to take a cross-section of Americans and convert them into first-rate fighting troops and officers had been learned by experience, not by textbook. Not to overstate the fact, I had a feeling for the military potential, in human terms, of the United States. My education had not been neglected.[3]

Learning From the Fox

He couldn't possibly have seen it.

The breathless pace of the present left no time for Ike Eisenhower to look at his past long enough to see the unfolding of a specific plan for his life.

He was moving toward becoming one of the world's greatest generals, and two persons he was about to meet would have a tremendous influence in nudging him in the right direction.

With my 20/20 hindsight, I can see the working out of this plan, starting with people, events, interests and characteristics from his boyhood: the Halloween incident; his enchantment with history and leadership in athletics; his friendship with Swede Hazlett; his appointment to the United States Military Academy; his experience as a coach, learning strategy and motivating men; his decision to be the finest possible officer; his open mind toward new weapons (aircraft and tanks); and his deep interest in military tactics.

Now, at Camp Meade, he met Colonel George S. Patton, Jr., an expert and already a legend in tank warfare, fresh from the European battlefields.

Supposedly, Patton, riding on top of a tank, had charged the enemy, flourishing his sword. Tall and straight—as if drawn with a T-square—a dominating figure in an impeccably tailored uniform and boots buffed to a blinding polish, Patton surprised first-time acquaintances with his high-pitched voice. His delicate hands featured long, slender fingers, adorned with a number of colored rings.

The wealthy, dashing, sensation-seeking Patton and Eisenhower differed in most respects. They became instant friends, because neither could get enough of tanks and military history. Patton and Ike originated a new method for using tanks with infantry.

Tanks on the Western Front traveled a little faster than three miles an hour—the walking speed of infantrymen—and moved about fifty yards ahead of them, to knock out machine-gun nests. The two men foresaw faster, more-versatile tanks, for swift surprise attacks on defensive positions. Their armor had to be heavier, to withstand light field-gun fire, but not so heavy that it reduced maneuverability.

One day, Eisenhower and Patton's exercises with small Renaults and ponderous, powerful Mark VIIIs almost cost them their lives. When two Renaults became bogged down in a muddy ravine, they tried towing them with a Mark VIII, by means of a long, inch-thick steel cable attached on each side. Patton and Ike, upslope from the Mark VIII, watched the huge tank labor slowly, its engine roaring, pulling the two cables taut.

Suddenly the tension became too great. A cable broke, cracking like a whip in a slashing semicircle, cleanly cutting off underbrush and whining past Patton and Ike, inches from shearing off their heads.

Like scientists in trial-and-error experiments, they became

convinced that their idealized tanks could revolutionize warfare. They even took a tank apart and put it back together with no leftover parts.

Ike came up with a way of selling tanks and their strategy to War Department skeptics. He placed an article with the *Infantry Journal*. George did the same for the *Cavalry Journal*. Once Ike's article hit print, he was called before the scowling chief of the infantry.

"I was told that my ideas were not only wrong but dangerous," Ike wrote, "and that henceforth I would keep them to myself . . . I was not to publish anything incompatible with solid infantry doctrine. If I did, I would be hauled before a court-martial." [1]

Patton got similar treatment.

"With George's temper and my own capacity for something more than mild irritation, there was surely more steam around the Officers Quarters than at the post laundry," he wrote.[2]

Many times, although absorbed with exciting tank strategy, Ike longed for Mamie and Icky. He became tired of being an absentee husband and father, but Camp Meade provided no family accommodations.

Just when he began to think he would need a reintroduction to Mamie and Icky, he got a lift. Officers were given permission to remodel two-story barracks into family apartments and furnish them at their own expense.

An overjoyed Mamie came back to her Ike and started redesigning part of the barracks for—she hoped—a permanent home. She and Ike were eager to complete the work and bring Icky home from Boone, Iowa, where he was staying with Mamie's aunt.

Patton and Ike socialized, not only as individuals, but also with their wives. George and Beatrice invited Ike and Mamie to a Sunday dinner party for Brigadier General Fox Conner, who had been General Pershing's operations officer in France and was one of the army's sharpest brains. Conner was so intrigued with Patton and Ike's tank experiments that the three talked in the tank shop until dark. Ike was not sure that Conner could do anything to advance the cause of tanks, and soon forgot about the afternoon.

Stuck with an additional duty coaching the camp football team at the request of Commanding General Samuel D. Rockenbach, Ike conditioned his men with proper nutrition and exercise and taught them game strategy. He used the forward pass, a new weapon, to field winning teams for two years.

But Ike's greatest satisfaction did not come from winning football. It came when Mamie brough Icky home from Iowa. When he thought in terms of "my son," he felt warmth and tenderness such as he had never before known.

Seeing and hearing Icky react to wonders of the world around him, Ike relived many of his own early days. Icky enjoyed watching the monster Mark VIIIs caterpillar up hills and hearing the eardrum-shattering roar of tank engines. He would clap his hands as the tanks reached the top.

Enlisted men and noncommissioned officers of the Tank Corps bought Icky a complete tank uniform, including a thick overcoat, so he could be with them and be one of them in winter and summer. Icky's soldier friends often persuaded Mamie to dress Icky in full uniform and let him ride in a tank.

He liked to range the sidelines during football practice as his dad coached, especially when the ball bounced toward him and he could pick it up without fumbling. Ike had a secret hope that someday Icky would accomplish in football what his bad knee had kept him from doing.

Military music thrilled Icky. He would never miss a parade.

What a natural his son was to be a soldier!

During this period, the Eisenhowers finally climbed out of debt, and, in a family council, Mamie and Ike decided to hire a local girl to release Mamie from household duties.

Neither of them ever stopped regretting this decision.

Before Christmas, Ike and Mamie bought an evergreen tree and a fire-truck-red kiddie car. As they decorated the tree, Ike could not remember a happier preholiday season. Now, at last, the family was together! Then Icky came down with what seemed to be a cold.

"He'll be well soon," the post doctor assured Ike. But he wasn't. Icky's fever rose high, and the doctor examined him again. "He has scarlet fever," said the physician.

Ike shuddered. He remembered how critically ill Milton had been with scarlet fever. "I insist you call in doctors from Johns Hopkins Medical School," he said. The physician agreed.

Then the Eisenhowers got a shock. They learned that their hired girl had had scarlet fever and was a carrier of the disease.

Doctors refused to let Ike in Icky's hospital room. Scarlet fever is highly contagious. He could spread it throughout camp. Ike was permitted to wave to his son through a porch window.

"His condition is no better," the doctor told Ike, who rarely left the hospital, pacing, daring to hope, never failing to pray.

Recovery never came. Icky died on January 2, 1921.

It couldn't be true, Ike told himself. This *couldn't* have happened. And yet, he knew it had. Somehow—he could not remember how—he got home from the hospital. He and Mamie sat in a daze. In their grief, they could hardly talk to each other.

One thought persisted: He would never again take Icky to tank exercises, never again watch his eyes light up along the sidelines of football practice or along a parade route.

Now he faced a dreaded prospect. He and Mamie would accompany Icky's body by train to Denver where the boy would be buried in the Doud family plot. Sometimes Ike's mind played tricks. Icky was not gone. He would be back home in a little while, Ike told himself.

Ike opened the closet to select clothing for the trip. There, in plain sight, was Icky's tank uniform. He tried to hold back tears.

On the day of their departure, the Tank Corps came out for a last salute to their junior member. Icky would never again ride in their tanks, but he would never stop riding in their memories.

Every year, for the rest of Ike's life, he presented Mamie with a bouquet on Icky's birthday.

To dull the pain, Ike plunged deeper into his military career. If he were going to move upward, he would have to show stronger initiative, War Department opposition or not. He applied for Infantry School as a stepping-stone toward the Command and General Staff School. It would have been nonsense to think ahead to the ultimate—the War College—the training school for generals.

The War Department stayed consistent, turning him down. Initiative was expected in an officer, yet the War Department did everything possible to discourage initiative.

Then came an unexpected development. General Fox Conner, now in command of the Twentieth Infantry Brigade in Panama, asked Ike to become his executive officer.

General Rockenbach refused to let Ike go. Eisenhower persisted, and the general sent his application to the War Department.

Another turndown!

Stoically, Ike put the prospect out of his mind. He hadn't reckoned on General Conner's influence and ability to pull political strings with Conner's old friend, General Pershing, now Army Chief of Staff. Several months later, the War Department transferred Ike to Conner's command.

Nothing about the Panama Canal Zone appealed to Mamie: the steamy, suffocating, tropical heat; the endless drip or downpour of rain; their ramshackle jungle home, her "double-decked shanty"; the ever-present smell of mildew and the armies of crawling and flying things.

The makeshift house had been slapped together. Floors bowed under walking feet, and a sheet-iron roof often let in nearly as much rain as it kept out.

To Mamie Eisenhower, the first night in Panama (which was almost her last) was a terrifying nightmare: wild animal screams; rats, scratching and gnawing at the bedroom door; cockroaches too numerous to exterminate; legions of bedbugs—thwarted only by the pans of kerosene in which the legs of the bed were set—and an indefatigable bat that dive-bombed them.

A survival school would have been more appropriate preparation for Panama than Miss Wolcott's.

Julie Eisenhower, in her book *Special People,* described what happened next: "Mamie told me proudly how her hero, Ike, stood on the bed, unsheathed his sword and swung wildly at the bat, 'just like Douglas Fairbanks.' She laughed when she described that night, but at the time it was not at all amusing. In fact, life in Panama was as alien to Mamie as life on Mars. Within a few months, she was back in Denver again, where John was born." [3]

Despite the many unwelcome guests in the house, the frequent rain and the sticky, night-and-day jungle heat that robbed sleep, Ike tolerated the Panama Canal Zone to be with General Fox Conner—a tall, spare, relaxed Mississippian, who became his one-man faculty.

As they casually talked about military strategy, Conner was pleased with Ike's observations and penetrating questions. He handed him several absorbing and well-documented historical novels. These fascinated Ike. Then General Conner gave him nonfiction books describing Army tactics.

Conner would ask him questions about the books—especially about why commanders made certain decisions. "What would have happened if opposite decisions had been made?"

More books followed, and more questions and answers. Ike Eisenhower became a star pupil of this master of strategy.

Conner preached that the Treaty of Versailles carried dragon seeds that would germinate into a greater war than the one so recently finished. He told Ike to be prepared and, someday, to try to be assigned to a Colonel George C. Marshall.

"In the new war we will have to fight beside allies and George Marshall knows more about the techniques of arranging allied commands than any man I know. He is nothing short of a genius." [4]

Whether in Conner's office, his library at home, riding patrols on horseback (often for a day at a time) or around the campfire, the general and Ike reconstructed Revolutionary War, Civil War and Napoleonic War campaigns. To keep his protégé from becoming lopsided in his learning, Conner introduced him to the great philosophers and welcomed discussion.

On a more prosaic level, one of Ike's unfailing daily duties was composing a field order for the operation of Camp Gaillard.

A few years later, Ike became restless for new duties.

Mamie, worn out from the rains, muggy heat, combat with rats, cockroaches and bedbugs, longed to return to the United States with Ike and young John, who resembled Icky.

Mercifully, a transfer to Camp Meade came through. The pleasure of returning to the temperate United States was spoiled by Ike's assignment—coaching the football team. He was back at the dead end!

Once more, General Conner pulled a behind-the-scenes maneuver. Ike was transferred out of the infantry and, after brief duty in Denver, assigned to the next class of the Command and General Staff School at Fort Leavenworth—a breakthrough opportunity.

The yearlong course was for majors or above. Realists in the regular army knew that there was little chance to rise higher than a lieutenant colonel without this prestigious training.

Now Ike was moving across the unique blueprint for his life. Glowing with enthusiasm, he reported his good fortune to the office of the chief of the infantry.

An aide in the office almost extinguished Ike's glow. "The Command and General Staff School is no place for someone who hasn't graduated from Infantry School."

"The guy was full of encouragement," Ike once mentioned to me. "He said, 'You'll probably fail.'"

On that cheery note, Ike began thinking ahead to August, when he would start the course.

Family of David Jacob and Ida Eisenhower photographed in 1902. Between his parents is Milton ("The brains of the family," according to General Ike). Second row: Dwight, Earl and Roy. Rear: Edgar and Arthur.

Ike Eisenhower (top row, second from right) was the star outfielder and hitter of the Abilene High School baseball team. Ike had ambitions to play the game like Honus Wagner, Hall of Fame shortstop for the Pittsburgh Pirates. Photo was taken in 1909, when Ike was almost nineteen.

Dwight D. Eisenhower, at graduation from West Point in 1915, was a member of "the class the stars fell upon." More general officers came from this class than from any other. Only one West Point official saw the leadership qualities in Eisenhower. His evaluation of him was "Born to command."

Tanks such as this one at Camp Meade, Maryland, in 1918 gave Ike Eisenhower and George Patton a common bond that endured problems and conflicts until Patton's death by accident after World War II.

On July 1, 1916, Second Lieutenant Dwight D. "Ike" Eisenhower married Mamie Geneva Doud in her father's custom-built Victorian mansion in Denver. He bought the wedding ring for seventy dollars on credit. In addition to gaining a wife that day, he received a promotion to first lieutenant.

Seated on the steps of the Abilene, Kansas, home where he spent his boyhood and youth is Major Dwight D. Eisenhower, on leave from the United States Army. The family portrait was taken in 1925.

The brilliant strategy of Ike Eisenhower as chief of staff to Lieutenant General Walter Krueger in the nation's largest war games earned him a promotion to temporary brigadier general and transfer to the Operations Division of the War Department. On January 23, 1942, this photo was taken. Left to right: generals Robin Crawford, Eisenhower and Leonard Gerow.

Old "Blood and Guts," General George S. Patton (left) and his World War II commander, General Dwight D. Eisenhower, study a map relative to the Allied campaign in North Africa. Photo taken at Patton's headquarters in Tunisia on March 16, 1943.

General Eisenhower, commander in chief of the North African war theater, and General George S. Patton, Jr. (third from left), commander of an American task force, receive the salute of a sentry (right) on General Eisenhower's tour of the Tunisian front. (Wide World Photos.)

President Roosevelt presents Ike with the Legion of Merit in 1943. The presentation was made during the president's trip to Cairo and Tehran. (Wide World Photos.)

Eisenhower talks with Prime Minister Winston Churchill in front of 10 Downing Street after a luncheon. (Wide World Photos.) *Below:* General Eisenhower and General George C. Marshall discuss the North African campaign at Allied headquarters in Algeria.

A Time of Uncertainty

Doubts nibbled at Ike's self-assurance. Could he believe the aide? Would he be less qualified because he hadn't attended Infantry School? If so, how could he correct his deficiencies?

Ike quickly wrote General Conner, asking which studies to pursue to prepare himself for Fort Leavenworth.

Conner shot back a reply:

> You may not know it, but because of your three years' work in Panama, you are far better trained and ready for Leavenworth than anybody I know.
>
> You will recall that during your entire service [with me] I required that you write a field order for the operation of the post every day for the years you were there. You became so well acquainted with the technics and routine of preparing plans and orders for operations that included their logistics, that they will be second nature to you. You will feel no sense of inferiority. . . .[1]

Ike didn't.

Most of the course consisted of case-method instruction — war games, such as General Conner and he had played endlessly. Ike scored first in the class. Colonel George Patton, one of the school's instructors, congratulated Ike and said prophetically, "Someday I'll be working for you."

Transferred to Fort Benning to command an infantry battalion, Major Ike instantly learned that the distinction he earned at Fort Leavenworth had not broken the War Department mold for him. There, he was assigned as one of the coaches for the soldier football team and hoped that something would come up to deliver him from coaching forever.

Shortly before Christmas, he got his answer—a chance to transfer to General John J. "Black Jack" Pershing's American Battle Monuments Commission in Washington. Fox Conner had recommended him.

The American Battle Monuments Commission beautified cemeteries of American soldiers killed in France. The first assignment planned for Ike was to write a guidebook to battlefields where Americans had fought. Another desk job!

Mamie urged him to accept. Hadn't General Conner always steered him right? He took the job. Within six months, he had reduced tons of directives, maps, reports and statistics to readable form.

General Pershing lauded him for his work. Simultaneously, Ike received notice that he had been accepted to attend War College in Washington, D.C., the army's leading postgraduate school, dealing with problems handled by generals: grand strategy, supply, transportation of armies and integration of commands with allied nations.

A year later, on June 30, 1928, Ike graduated from the War College, again number one in his class. This record excited the attention of War Department officials, and Ike received two offers: an opening on the War Department general staff and the opportunity to rejoin the American Battle Monuments Commission and visit the battlefields of France before revising the guidebook.

The Eisenhowers selected France for the chance to travel and for the special educational advantages that would be available to young John at the McJanet School for American children.

Neither Ike nor Mamie made it over the language barrier. Mamie ended up communicating with shopkeepers and her cook in a mixture of English, French expressions from a dictionary in hand and desperate gestures.

Ike observed the major battlefields and more. He constantly surprised Mamie with his spongelike ability to soak up even minute details about the topography, highway systems, railroads and harbors.

France was another unfolding of the plan for Ike's life. When he was supreme commander of Allied forces in World War II, he could still squeeze that mental sponge to understand the harbors, beaches and terrain of France for invasion.

When the Eisenhowers returned to Washington in November 1929, the nation was down in the dumps, financially and emotionally, from the great stock-market crash in August and the subsequent depression. While the United States was taking inventory of itself and not enjoying the results, Ike Eisenhower was doing the same thing.

A major at thirty-nine years of age, he had spent much of his military life being trained and training others. Now the state of the small, peacetime army was giving him no cause for optimism. The depressed economy was forcing the entire federal government to reduce expenditures, so the army, too, had to cut back.

Would he ever get a command of his own? Would he ever use his extensive knowledge with troops in the field? A field assignment would be his only hope for promotion. Would he ever become a permanent full colonel? There seemed to be an outside chance, if he lived long enough.

Now he was assigned to the United States assistant secretary of war, to interview executives of manufacturing companies for their expertise on ways to mobilize industry in the event of war.

To Major Ike, the project seemed fascinating. To industrial firms, it seemed ridiculous. The only enemy the United States would be fighting in the foreseeable future was the depression.

Data from interviews with industry, with Bernard Baruch (who headed the War Industries Production Board during hostilities in Europe), with government officials, and his own military experience convinced him that an outside agency was needed. Otherwise, competition by the army and navy for materials and weapons would interfere with production.

Both services rejected the plan for two reasons: price controls and the thought that the army and navy would not cooperate without pressure from an outside agency.

Near the end of 1930, General Douglas MacArthur was made army chief of staff and backed the plan, which was presented to a congressional committee formed to study ways of taking excess profits out of war production.

The plan created a favorable impression in the committee and also served to upgrade the status of military supply, technical services and production, which until then were regarded as inferior services by combat officers. The army and navy began assigning better students to the Industrial College, and the college expanded.

Shortly before Franklin D. Roosevelt's inauguration as president, on March 4, 1933, Ike Eisenhower was officially added to the MacArthur staff, to supervise the office and write the general's directives, reports and letters.

MacArthur—patrician, imposing, autocratic—overwhelmed mere mortals by his awesome reputation, achievements and equally awesome presence.

Number one in the West Point class of 1903, with the highest grades ever earned up to then, MacArthur distinguished himself as chief of staff of the celebrated Rainbow (Forty-second) Division in France, and wore half a chestful of medals and ribbons. Appointed superintendent of the United States Military Academy, he modernized methods of instruction and elevated scholastic standards. In 1930, at the age of fifty, he was named army chief of staff by President Herbert Hoover; the youngest man to reach this office.

An eloquent orator, with occasional diamond sparkles of brilliance, MacArthur, frequently archaic in expression, had one area of never directly admitted mediocrity: communicating through the written word. Ike's economical and unexcelled writing gave MacArthur camouflage to continue his illusion of perfection.

Eisenhower knew his own temperament and MacArthur's. There would be problems, but he could not expect to be fully compatible with every commanding officer. MacArthur had chosen him. He had not chosen MacArthur. Ike was grateful that his brother Milton was in Washington as his safety valve, confidant, proving ground for ideas, source of understanding and morale builder. Yet it was in Milton and Helen Eisenhower's Falls Church, Virginia, home on a frigid, snowy night in 1934 that Ike's morale was almost annihilated. His brother Edgar, whose law practice in Tacoma, Washington, was one of the state's most successful, had come to the nation's capital as counsel for lumber interests and helped initiate a reunion of Eisenhower brothers. Earl, a well-established electrical engineer in Pennsylvania, joined Milton, Ike and Ed. Roy's pharmacy in Enterprise, Kansas, and a critical business conference for Arthur kept them from coming.

Ike listened quietly, wistfully, in sublimated frustration to his brothers' enthusiastic exchanges about their careers. Talk of Arthur's dizzying ascent to the rarefied atmosphere of banking and Milton's references to his White House visits to represent Secretary of Agriculture Henry Wallace to the president, accented Ike's career stagnation. He hadn't had a promotion in ten years, was making only $3000 a year and going nowhere at the age of forty-five.

His guidebook had established him as a writer, and when a group of newspapers offered him almost $20,000 annually to be its military editor, he was tempted. Should he resign from the army? If he did, and there were another war, he would be left out. He decided to stay in service.

Somewhat later, when MacArthur lauded Ike for unusual adeptness in coping with complex and sensitive problems, he felt less frustrated. The president then asked MacArthur to be chief military adviser to the Philippine government, and he invited Ike to be his chief assistant.

Ike firmly resisted.

After West Point, he had been desperate to go to the Philippines. Now he was almost desperate to stay away. He wanted a field assignment, not another desk job. Further, Mamie, John and he did not relish a second tropical experience.

When Ike dragged his feet, MacArthur turned his invitation into an order.

MacArthur Plus Eisenhower Equals Trouble

Two military men could hardly have been intentionally designed to be more incompatible than General Douglas MacArthur and his senior aide, Major Dwight D. Eisenhower.

It even surprised Eisenhower that persons so totally different could get along tolerably well for almost ten years—four in the same suite of offices in the Philippine Islands.

MacArthur's cold, iceberg isolation—his pompous, austere manner—contrasted with Eisenhower's melting warmth, friendliness and instant compatibility.

General MacArthur, who had arranged for President Quezon to make him a field marshal in the Philippine army, against Eisenhower's well-intentioned advice, played the imperial role with a theatrical flair.

Few have painted him in words as well as Stephen E. Ambrose: "Strikingly handsome, MacArthur wore flashy, nonregulation (self-designed) uniforms that reminded observers more of a Latin American dictator or a comic-opera general than an officer of the United States Army." [1]

Major Ike wore civilian clothes or conservative military uniform.

MacArthur was seldom visible before 11:00 A.M., was hard to see and, on occasion, failed to treat President Quezon with the respect normally accorded to the head of a sovereign state.

Major Ike, always in the office early, accessible, courteous and cordial, filled the MacArthur vacuum.

Differences between the two started early in their relationship. Nothing would remove the bad taste in Ike's mouth from MacArthur's handling of the Bonus Marchers in July 1932.

During the Great Depression—with one-third of the nation unemployed, many without food and homeless through foreclosures—veterans of the war in Europe converged on Washington, D.C., to exert pressure on Congress to pay them immediate cash for bonus certificates redeemable in 1945.

Roughly 20,000 men camped across the Anacostia River, in tents and huts made from packing boxes, scrap lumber, tin and even cardboard, cooking bought (or begged) food over open fires. They had no sanitation or health facilities.

Picketing disrupted the Capitol's business. Conservative President Herbert Hoover and Republican congressmen thought the veterans' action a threat to law and order—possibly the nucleus of a revolution, even though demonstrators were, with a few exceptions, orderly.

Major Ike saw no peril in their actions and believed veterans should be treated with respect. MacArthur relished the order of his commander in chief, President Hoover, to clear the marchers from Washington. The Communist revolution had to be crushed, and he was going to do it personally. He ordered Ike to join him in full battle dress.

Ike objected. It upset him that the army would risk injury or death to veterans. MacArthur overrode his subordinate and made the event a big show, posing for dozens of photographs.

I'll never forget the humiliating scene. I was then covering Washington for United Press. Six hundred troops, with guns and fixed bayonets, supported by noisy, clanking tanks, confronted the marchers, some armed with bricks and ready. The tension was explosive.

Pelham Glassford, Washington chief of police, called through a megaphone to the veterans: "We've all been through messes like this before. Could I ask one request of you men? If you throw bricks, please throw bricks with round edges, instead of the jagged ones. *They* really hurt!"

A roar of laughter went up from the veterans. The tension was broken. Troops slowly moved toward the marchers, who, in retreat, jeered, booed, swore and spat toward MacArthur. It was the first time I had seen Eisenhower, who was red-faced with mortification.

Hoover had forbidden army troops to drive the veterans across the Anacostia bridge, but MacArthur followed his own plan, his first insubordination to a president's directive.

Fire broke out in the marchers' camp, sweeping from shack to shack. Major Ike stated that no troops were near enough to have started the fire. He was incorrect. I saw soldiers with torches running from shack to shack.

The hungry, ragged, discouraged—and now shelterless— veterans slowly dispersed. The contest was over. All they had left to do was ride the rails, hitchhike or walk the long distance home.

That night I attended President Hoover's press conference in the White House. Hoover pulled aside the curtains of his office. As the last glow of burning shacks was dying, he commented, "A good job well done."

Just when Major Ike felt he couldn't stand another day with MacArthur, the general would do something human and warm. Before their departure for the Philippines in 1935, the general lauded Ike's loyal, efficient, critically important service, despite his desire to have a troop command. MacArthur said that many requests had been made for Ike's services, due to his reputation as an outstanding soldier, which is how MacArthur regarded him.

Many years later, when Eisenhower had been nominated for the presidency, MacArthur demeaned him as "the apotheosis of mediocrity," and "the best clerk I ever had."

When asked for his reaction to serving under MacArthur, Eisenhower commented in 1965, "I studied dramatics under him for ten years."

For better or for worse, MacArthur and Major Ike, later made a lieutenant colonel, had a monumental mission. The Philippine Islands, by congressional action, had been made a commonwealth for ten years, to prepare them for independence, self-rule and self-defense. Rumblings from the warlike Japanese indicated that the Philippines would be one of their first targets.

Realistically, Ike could not see the building of an army capable of defending the islands properly before 1945. Even this timetable presupposed United States air and naval protection. The initial, bare-bones military budget worked out by Eisenhower was sliced in half by President Manuel Quezon and the dictates of his modest treasury, but Ike enjoyed immediate respect and acceptance by Quezon.

After a year in the islands, Ike was able to bring out Mamie and John, who had finished eighth grade and was enrolled in the Brent School, part of an Episcopal mission in Baguio. Baguio, the nation's summer capital, was five-thousand-feet high, in the cool, pine-covered mountains of central Luzon. Baguio's temperate climate—about seventy degrees year-round—contrasted with that of sweltering, muggy Manila, where John's parents stayed in the Manila Hotel.

Largely due to the erratic office hours of Field Marshal MacArthur, most of the work ended up with Ike. When President Quezon could not reach MacArthur, he discussed problems with Eisenhower, who soon became his close and trusted friend. They breakfasted together almost every day at the Malacanang Palace, discussing everything from military defense to world history, labor unions, education, foreign trade, youth, integrity in government and personal philosophy.

Eventually, President Quezon asked Ike to draft portions of the Philippine constitution. When I was a guest of a later president of the Philippines, Ramón Magsaysay, in the Malacanang, he told me that much of the constitution for the republic had been written, directly or indirectly, by Eisenhower. Quezon and others had simply inserted statements, outlooks, and recommendations from Eisenhower.

Further, Magsaysay said that Eisenhower wrote the Defense Act for the Commonwealth of the Philippines. When these islands became independent, the Defense Act was adopted and made the opening part of the constitution.

Although MacArthur and Eisenhower disagreed on many small matters, their major difference came one day when MacArthur decided to stage a mammoth military parade down Dewey Boulevard in Manila, to demonstrate progress in forming an army. When Eisenhower learned that the parade would cost the Philippine government $15,000, money sorely needed for defense, he was horrified. He had assumed that, in a matter of such importance, MacArthur had obtained Quezon's approval.

As Ike entered the inner sanctum, he nodded to MacArthur's physician, who was reading a newspaper near the open door. The doctor reported the fireworks that followed to Ira Eaker (later an important air-force general).

"Field Marshal," Ike said, "I have checked into costs. If we hold the parade, it will syphon away fifteen thousand dollars badly needed for weapons and ammunition."

Affronted with Eisenhower's challenge to his judgment (an unpardonable sin) MacArthur glared at him: "Eisenhower, I asked you only to check into costs, not to go behind my back to report on our conversation to President Quezon in one of your daily secret meetings."

The color rose from Eisenhower's neck to his cheeks, and a prominent blood vein over his right eye rounded up from his skin. Standing at attention and giving a sharp salute, he shouted: "Field Marshal, you could accuse me of almost anything except treason and I might accept it, but no living man can tell me that I have carried on secret discussions and gone behind his back. I will not take this from you or anyone else. I will resign from the service first!"

MacArthur's dark countenance looked like a thunderstorm ready to break. Then he almost smiled. "That's one thing I like about you, you Dutchman. You have a short fuse—a magnificent temper. Perhaps I was too strong in my statement, so why don't we forget it?"

They did, the parade was canceled and Ike mulled over MacArthur's response. It was the closest thing to an apology he had ever heard from his commander.

Lieutenant Colonel Ike's stature continued to grow. Lucius Clay, a prominent general in World War II, and Ira Eaker revealed to me that the Filipinos were aware that most of the army organizing and defense planning was being accomplished by Ike Eisenhower.

There was talk of replacing MacArthur with Eisenhower. When Ike heard about this, he became angry. "I won't be a party to or accept such an arrangement," he erupted. "If such talk doesn't stop at once, I will resign and return to the United States!"

Ike found it necessary to make many trips to widely separated parts of the islands. Tired of time-wasting, slow travel by army vehicles or boat, he took pilot training early each morning, before going on duty. He earned his license, logging 350 hours of flight, and later became the only president ever licensed to fly.

Then, in early September, Germany invaded Poland. By transoceanic radio, Ike heard British Prime Minister Neville Chamberlain announce a state of war with Germany. Suddenly the future became clear to him.

"This time, I don't want to miss combat," he told MacArthur.

Neither MacArthur nor President Quezon could change his mind, although the latter prepared a new contract and asked Ike to write in the salary and any other benefits that would induce him to stay.

Quezon held a farewell party for the Eisenhowers, awarded him the Distinguished Service Star and said to the group: "Among all Ike's outstanding qualities, the quality I regard most highly is this: Whenever I asked Ike for an opinion, I got an answer. It may not have been what I wanted to hear; it may have displeased me; but it was always a straightforward and honest answer."

After return to the United States, Ike had assignments at Fort Ord, California, and Fort Lewis, Washington, before going to San Antonio, where (as a temporary colonel) he was made chief of staff to Lieutenant General Walter Krueger, commander of the Third Army.

Now Dwight D. Eisenhower's course and mine were not far from intersecting.

Peace and War

The explosion of a Luftwaffe bomb could not have shocked me ut of sleep more effectively than the normally subdued voice of Lord Kinross, head of Royal Air Force Intelligence.

In the blackness of the North African desert, I had been enjoying the womblike warmth of my sleeping bag under an

RAF lorry eighteen miles southeast of Tobruk.

The light of Kinross's electric torch showed me that no view is quite as ugly as the sand-crusted bottom of a truck.

Why would he bother me, when he knew I needed rest to cure a heavy cold?

"Virgil," he shouted. "Mind the Jerries and Ities don't bag you, because now you'll be a prisoner of war. The Japs have bombed Honolulu. Virgil, *you* are in the war!"

Fully awake, I jammed on my shoes, without shaking them to dislodge crawling things, and rushed with Kinross to the battle-headquarters tent.

Randolph Churchill, son of the prime minister and major in charge of public-relations officers in the Middle East, commented; "The old boy and Roosevelt together couldn't have drawn up a better blueprint. Now America is in the war on a full-time basis, thank God."

Then he added quickly, "What I have said, Virgil, is strictly off-the-record as long as I'm alive. If you ever repeat it, I will be the first to deny and the last to confirm it."

The off-the-record reference captured the attention of those listening to a vivid account of the bombing over BBC: Sir Walter Monckton, the prime minister's representative in the Middle East; Jock Campbell, in charge of the Eighth Army Armour; Kinross and several other officers.

Randolph continued: "Recently I called on the prime minister at 10 Downing Street. The old boy was shaving. He had his braces [suspenders] hanging down, and his underwear was tucked in around his throat. As he shaved, he said, 'Randolph, my boy, I have never been so tired in all my life, but now I can begin to see a faint light at the end of the tunnel.

" 'With America's manpower, America's riches and the ability of the United States to produce tanks, airplanes, lorries and other tools of war, there is no doubt about the final outcome. We no longer stand and fight alone. We have the strongest nation in the world as our close ally now. Thank goodness I have established the relationship I have with President Roosevelt!

" 'We have a long way to go, and the road will be extremely rough. There will be setbacks and even defeats. It will probably take us three or four years to achieve final victory in Europe, although this could come a little sooner if the Russians stay in the war and continue to fight as valiantly as they have been. It will probably take another year to clean up the war in the Pacific against the Japs.'

"He continued to lather his face and shave, and he slumped, indicating how tired he really was. . . ."

As Randolph talked on, I remembered that his father had always been an accurate prophet.

Although Winston Spencer Churchill had no position in the government at the time, he periodically warned the House of Commons about the covert German-war-machine buildup. Deeply disturbed by Commons' indifference, apathy or unwillingness to see what it didn't want to see, he in turn raged, pleaded, bullied and persuaded, with elegant Churchillian prose, emphasized by extravagant histrionics.

After one of Churchill's inflammatory speeches, Stanley Baldwin, the Conservative Party prime minister, scornfully commented, "He was like an Abyssinian run amok in the House of Commons."

Yet Churchill was not overreacting to harmless shadows. He was reacting to substance: German glider clubs, cover-ups for training Luftwaffe pilots; the German Rocket Society, a respectable front for horror weapons; youth brigades that "marched better than the United States Marines," carrying out long hikes with full military packs and developing the ability to knock down and put together a machine gun in two minutes.

While the German army had been limited to 30,000 under the Versailles Peace Treaty, all of these men had been carefully selected and vigorously trained to become officers in the new German army.

Within battle-headquarters tent, there was more talk about Americans supplying the tools of war. Randolph Churchill put his arm around my shoulder, but it was more than just a warm gesture toward me. It was as if he were embracing all Americans, for he knew that soon we would also be in the war with manpower *and* materiel.

About the same time that Randolph Churchill had made me of symbolic importance to the outcome of World War II, someone of real importance to it had also been shocked from a sound sleep with the news of Pearl Harbor's bombing.

Temporary Brigadier General Dwight David Eisenhower, who had already climbed a notch higher than the colonelcy which he felt would be the peak of his peacetime military career, had given strict orders on the afternoon of Sunday, December 7, 1941 "not to be wakened for anything."

After a light lunch in the officer's mess, he had felt heavy with fatigue. Cigarettes and black coffee had left him letdown, irritable and jittery.

Nothing but a long nap could dispel his weariness from the greatest peacetime war maneuvers in the nation's history—400,000 troops and officers—and its hectic aftermath. As chief of staff to Lieutenant General Walter Krueger, he had been responsible, to a large degree, for the strategy that had enabled the Third Army to score a smashing victory over the Second Army of Lieutenant General Ben Lear.

Eisenhower collapsed on the bed, too tired to take off his clothes and shoes, savoring the thought of a two-week leave that he and Mamie would take over the Christmas holiday with John, a Plebe at West Point. After ten minutes' sleep, the news of Pearl Harbor burst into his consciousness.

The bombs that devastated Pearl Harbor blasted the United States from peacetime to wartime.

West Coast residents studied the skies for enemy bombers. None were there, but they saw many, because they looked, not with their eyes, but with their fears. Telephone calls and wires frantically demanding help against invasion jammed the lines to Washington, D.C.

Orders from the War Department fanned out to army headquarters throughout the nation. Teletypes of the Third Army headquarters clacked on a twenty-four-hour basis: . . . transfer antiaircraft units and troops to the West Coast . . . estab-

lish the means to counter sabotage . . . begin immediate reconnaissance of southern borders and the Gulf of Mexico
against the entry of spies.

Although army moves are generally empowered by paperwork, the emergency permitted orders to be issued by telephone. One phone call could start an infantry unit rolling
across the continent.

On December 12, a single telephone call from the War Department moved Brigadier General Eisenhower into the
rarefied atmosphere of the top army hierarchy.

The caller, Colonel Walter Bedell Smith, came right to the
point: "Ike, the Chief says for you to hop a plane and get here
right away. Tell your boss that formal orders will come through
later."[1]

Of course, the chief was General George C. Marshall, but the
news did nothing to cheer Eisenhower. He wanted battle action,
not war against paper work.

"If that's an order, I will naturally obey it," responded
Eisenhower. "But if General Marshall will grant my wish, I will
remain as chief of staff of the Third Army and work with soldiers in the field."

It *was* an order!

After World War II, when I interviewed General Marshall,
he told me what happened when Eisenhower reported to the
War Plans Division. "When I met him on Sunday morning,
December 14, he saluted sharply and said, 'Sir, I am reporting
for duty as you ordered, but I left my heart in Texas, where I
was working with troops, something I have always wanted to
do. As chief of staff with General Krueger's Third Army, I had
a chance of becoming a permanent general. Here, at forty-
seven, I will be too old ever to reach that level."

Marshall only smiled.

Ike asked himself, *Why does Marshall want me?*

The answer seems obvious. He had completed a long tour of
duty in the Philippines and knew the islands, the people and
their defenses. After Pearl Harbor, the Japanese had turned on
the Philippines.

Marshall summarized what was occurring in the western Pacific. The crippled Pacific Fleet would not be in operation for months. There was a good chance that the Japanese would invade Hawaii—notoriously weak in defense—and possibly even the mainland United States. Both the army and navy departments favored reinforcement of Hawaii as a first priority.

The Philippines were weak. Many of the thirty-five B-17 bombers and two-hundred-twenty fighters there had been destroyed or inactivated. Cavite Navy Yard had almost been destroyed. Probably, Japanese would soon swarm over the Philippines.

Marshall suddenly turned to Ike. "All right, Eisenhower. Those are the facts. What should be our line of action?"

Ike tried not to show surprise. What Marshall wanted was war strategy for the entire Pacific area! "I'll need several hours, Sir."

"Go ahead," replied Marshall.

Intuitively, Ike realized that Marshall would require more than just military considerations. Marshall would have no patience with literary fluff or cotton candy. He wanted hard facts.

Few bright spots appeared in Eisenhower's analysis and recommendations, but he boldly presented his report to Marshall: Without a secure Pacific base, the crippled surface fleet could only be defensive and keep out of Philippine waters. Hawaii had to be reinforced with ground and air defensive strength. Major reinforcements could not come to the Philippines until the navy had been rehabilitated.

Yet it was imperative to prolong defense of the Philippines, to slow the sweep of the Japanese into the South Pacific. Critically needed military and medical supplies could be shipped in by submarine and blockade runners.

Some air transports might be able to get through enemy interception, but this depended upon having a fairly near base from which to operate. Australia answered that requirement. Islands from there to the Philippines could serve as stops for refueling, maintenance and repair, stepping-stones or springboards.

To make Australia a base for defensive and, eventually, offensive operations, a free line of communications to it had to be assured. Hawaii, Fiji, New Zealand and New Caledonia had to be strengthened and saved from the enemy. Even Australia, in line with the ever-broadening thrust of Japanese conquest, had to be fortified.

Possibly resource-rich Dutch East Indies could be saved. If so—and such efforts should be made—an oil supply necessary for further Japanese offensives could be cut off and used by the Allies. Only if the Allies could keep the Japanese out of the Dutch East Indies, could short-range fighter aircraft essential to the Philippines' defense be flown from there.

One of Eisenhower's most telling points was psychological and political. No matter how unprepared the United States was for war or how difficult the task, no matter how many risks and whatever the competition for available war materiel and supplies, no great nation could coldly desert the Filipinos and thousands of Americans there. Everything possible should be done—by submarine, blockade runners and air.

"General, it will be a long time before major reinforcements can go the Philippines, longer than the garrison can hold out with any driblet assistance, if the enemy commits major forces to their reduction. But we must do everything for them that is humanly possible. The people of China, of the Philippines, of the Dutch East Indies will be watching us. They may excuse failure but they will not excuse abandonment. Their trust and friendship are important to us. Our base must be Australia, and we must start at once to expand it and to secure our communications to it. In this last we dare not fail. We must take great risks and spend any amount of money required."

Eisenhower paused for a breath, and Marshall replied, "I agree with you. Do your best to save them." [3]

Eisenhower did his best, but it was already too late to save the Philippines. Yet his Pacific plan proved to be successful, not only for the Allied cause, but also for himself.

Marshall had found a man who could make sound military-political decisions!

An exhausting schedule kept Ike at his desk seven days a week. Bolting hamburgers and gulping endless cups of black coffee for lunch and dinner, he continued to prepare for every eventuality.

Although pressed for time, he kept updating a little black notebook that he had started in the Philippines. It was his secret weapon in the event that he would get a command and need outstanding men. He scribbled in a brief entry on Colonel Walter Bedell "Beetle" Smith.

As he riffled the pages, there were write-ups on Lucius Clay and Ira Eaker—who had served with distinction under MacArthur—and on Alfred Maximilian Gruenther, his ingenious Third Army deputy during the war games—a man with a computer memory, who was nationally famous for his championship bridge playing.

Ike's long hours of fruitful service and decisiveness impressed Marshall. Eisenhower emphasized throwing most of the nation's forces into defeating Germany rather than dividing them equally between both war areas. Marshall was also impressed with his plan for overcoming Germany after successful invasion of Europe: "Eisenhower's plan for Germany was to cross the Rhine on a wide front to expose the German armies so that they could be attacked and destroyed and to encircle the Rhine and the Ruhr and take away Germany's ability to produce tools of war.

"That is why I brought him to Washington. His imagination, initiative and resourcefulness led to my promoting him, within three months, to head of the War Plans Division."

Ike's cheerful and dedicated service in a desk job, which he actually disliked, made Marshall groom him for greater responsibility and authority beyond anything that his wishful thinking could have fashioned.

Eisenhower Takes London

It was a twist he hadn't expected.

Temporarily assigned to London with General Hap Arnold, to observe the use and effectiveness of German airpower, Eisenhower had no idea he himself was to be observed and evaluated by the British.

"I wanted to learn how the British would react to Eisenhower in the event that he would later be put in command of American troops there," General Marshall once informed me.

Before Eisenhower came to 10 Downing Street for a meeting with Churchill and the top British officers, they decided to have some fun with "this country bumpkin from Kansas."

After World War II, Lord Louis Mountbatten told me the story, in the spacious library of his country estate outside Southampton.

In World War I, when General Pershing initially came to Britain, they tabbed him, at best, a colonial. *Now another of the same type*, they thought.

Around a huge mahogany table, with Prime Minister Churchill at its head, sat an imposing array of admirals, air chiefs, generals and field marshals—most of them with sleeves completely covered with gold braid.

Conspicuous, by contrast, in his plain United States Army uniform without decorations and only the two stars of a temporary major general, Eisenhower was placed opposite Lord Louis Mountbatten, to whom, by oversight, he had not been introduced.

The British asked Eisenhower a number of pertinent questions, which he answered crisply and well. But much of the time, he sat quietly, listening to the others.

Then one of them asked, "Would you be willing to serve under a British supreme commander?"

"In view of your experience, it would be wise to have the top man come from one of your forces," answered Eisenhower.

Someone asked him if he knew anything about Lord Louis Mountbatten, and would he be willing to serve under him?

"Certainly," replied Eisenhower.

"Have you ever met Lord Louis?" asked Lord Alanbrooke, head of the Imperial War Staff.

"No," responded Eisenhower, "but I understand he is a tremendous leader of men, highly imaginative and ingenious."

"Why don't you shake hands with him?" asked Lord Alanbrooke. "He's seated opposite you."

As Lord Louis and I drank tea in his library, he told me the sequel to the story. "When the meeting was over, the prime minister walked out with me. Taking me by the arm, he said, 'That fellow Eisenhower is a born gentleman. He is a man sent to us by God in this great hour of trial and need.'"

Eisenhower returned to the United States, not even aware he had been tested and had passed. He was made commanding general of American forces in the European Theater of Operations. Something record-shattering had happened: He had been promoted over 366 other well-qualified generals!

On June 23, 1942, Eisenhower, now a temporary lieutenant general, Captain Ernest "Tex" Lee, his aide, and Sergeant Michael "Mickey" McKeogh, Ike's orderly, flew from Bolling Field to England.

Immediately he changed the character of the United States Army offices in London. They had been used for observing the war and as a listening post. About all the listening done there was to the tinkle of ice in cocktail glasses.

Now they were in gear with the war, preparing a buildup of men, arms, munitions, supplies and landing craft, and working toward becoming a truly Allied command, such as generals Marshall and Conner had visualized.

"Allied unity was a passion with General Ike," I learned from Lionel "Pug" Ismay, Lord Hastings, Churchill's liaison with the armed forces. "He was one of the few top officers ever to come to me for advice about improving Anglo-American relations. What a master of tact and diplomacy!"

My first meeting with Eisenhower was in the red-brick United States embassy offices in London's Grosvenor Square. He had called in four press-bureau heads and top correspondents, as a committee to lay down ground rules for coverage of United States operations.

Having covered a number of wars—Italian-Ethiopian, Spanish Civil and some Axis operations in the early phases of World War II—I had met and talked with many generals, but never had I met one quite like Dwight David Eisenhower.

An aura of warmth and friendliness lit up the office better than the electric lights. His quickly erupting grin seemed as broad as his home state of Kansas. A high, tanned forehead had not a single wrinkle. If I had ever seen brighter and clearer blue eyes, I couldn't remember where. He was as comfortable as an old pair of house slippers.

Never once was there a desk between him and us. He sat next to me, on a brown leather couch, and talked as if he had always known us, occasionally pacing up and down, slightly favoring the leg whose knee had been smashed in a football game.

It was not so much his factual information that impressed us, as his understanding of our requirements for news, our obligation to our bureaus, newspapers and readers, and of his obligation to supply us with all the facts, within limits of security, so that fighting men, their relatives and friends and every tax-payer funding the war could be properly informed.

Some American troops already were landing in the United Kingdom, and prospects for many more were imminent. With this steady buildup, whose secret name was Bolero, Britain would become the base for carrying the war to the Germans and Italians.

"General, do you expect serious difficulty in integrating American objectives and military structures with those of the British and Free French?" I asked.

His grin became even more broad. "First of all, will you please call me Ike?"

His answer was frank: "Yes, Virgil, we expect difficulties, but none that can't be overcome. We are here with full appreciation that the British, virtually alone, have kept freedom and Allied hopes alive with their brave stand against tremendous odds.

"We are here not as competitors or rivals, but as cooperators toward our common goal. Both we and the British respect each other. I will do all in my power to see that this attitude continues as we work more closely together. The Allies must remember that we are fighting the Germans, Italians and Japanese—not one another."

I asked whether American GIs would fit into the British scheme without making tidal waves.

"Again, we anticipate problems: the higher pay of our armed forces, an attitude in some that what is American is always the best, and the fact that there are only so many girls available for an increasing number of men. I intend to meet with 'Pug' Ismay and Brendan Bracken for suggestions as to possible solutions."

Eisenhower was coordinating something he couldn't mention to us—a buildup of troops and supplies for a surprise invasion of North Africa (Operation Torch).

Every week or two, we met with General Ike or someone in his offices: General Mark W. Clark, his chief of staff, Colonel Al Gruenther, who had arrived on August 2 to serve as deputy chief of staff, or Captain Harry "Butch" Butcher, a naval-reserve officer, former head of the Columbia Broadcasting System in Washington, D.C., and a close friend of Ike. Butch had been selected to develop better army cooperation with the navy and to handle press relations.

Late in October, General Ike had supposedly gone to the United States to see Roosevelt and Marshall. All sorts of rumors circulated among us.

"Roosevelt is going to involve American troops somewhere in Europe."

"My bet is it's going to be with the British Eighth Army in Egypt."

"Not a chance! Americans won't fight under a British commander."

"I think it will be in North Africa."

"Why there? Who knows whether the French would desert the Vichy government? There are too many factions on the infighting there. How could anybody in his right mind depend upon the French?"

"North Africa is a dangerous place. An invasion in the western part could tilt the balance and bring Spanish Morocco and Franco into war on the Axis side."

"I heard Churchill and Roosevelt promised Stalin a European front to take pressure off the Ruskies on the Western Front."

"What better place to hit Europe than from North Africa, after the base has been established? And American troops could get combat experience before fighting the Jerries on the continent."

Those of us who bet on North Africa turned out be right.

Intrigue With French Dressing

High tension! That was what General Ike felt, in the catacomb-type offices inside the Rock of Gibraltar.

On August 14, 1942, by secret order, he had been named commander in chief of the Allied Expeditionary Force soon to invade North Africa.

How many years he had agonized for a combat command! Now he had one so gigantic—the largest in military history — that the responsibility staggered him: four hundred warships, one thousand airplanes and hundreds of thousands of men, including a battalion of paratroopers about to make the first combat jump of the war.

Being on the Rock of Gibraltar, an insurance company's symbol of security, brought little security to General Ike. It was a dismal setting. Carved into the rock were block-long, dank, smelly dark tunnels, in which feeble electric bulbs tried valiantly. These led to musty, cavelike offices with arched ceilings, from which came the steady drip, drip, drip of seeping water.

Many concerns gnawed at Ike. American soldiers were green and untested. Combining British and American troops to fight as one was not going to be easy. Landing craft, arms, munitions and supplies were short. Then the big question mark: Would the French permit a peaceful invasion, or put up a bloody resistance?

Those in the underground could be counted on. Others secretly rooted for the Allied cause, but wouldn't dare commit themselves. Much of the population remained loyal to the Vichy French government and faithful to terms of the 1940 armistice with the Germans. If the French did not oppose the Germans militarily, the Germans would not occupy southern France, which, like North Africa, was under leadership of the aging, white-haired Marshal Pétain, who was controlled by Adolf Hitler.

A dozen times, Ike had reviewed the invasion plan and its three objectives: Casablanca, on French Morocco's west coast (forces led by General George S. Patton, Jr.), and, through the Straits of Gibraltar, farther east—Oran and Algiers, on the Mediterranean Sea.

Once the invasion was accomplished, the greatest prize was still farther east: the seaport of Tunis. If the Allies—and it was a giant *if*—seized this city, they could cut off supplies for Field Marshal Erwin Rommel and wipe out Axis resistance in North Africa.

Already, convoys were cleaving Atlantic swells off North Africa. The one destined for Casablanca had shipped out of the United States. The other two, from Great Britain (Americans and British), neared Gibraltar, ready to sail into the Mediterranean, hoping to avoid Nazi U-boats and surprise Oran and Algiers.

Eisenhower's brow furrowed for an instant. Casablanca could be rough in two ways. Viciousness of the Atlantic Ocean could turn beach landings into a hazardous nightmare. The French of Morocco would probably resist stubbornly. Yet Casablanca had to be taken, because at any time, Spanish Morocco—directly opposite Gibraltar—might enter the war on the Axis side and block Allied warships, troops and supplies from the Mediterranean. If Casablanca were secure, British and American troops could at least move eastward by land.

But more than military problems made Eisenhower feel uneasy. An undercover political effort to eliminate French resistance to the invasion could backfire.

Two months earlier, the United States State Department's Robert D. Murphy, who was also President Roosevelt's personal representative in North Africa, had received an intriguing proposition from Jacques Lemaigre-Dubreuil, a wealthy processor of salad oil and other vegetable oils, with operations in Algiers, Oran, Dakar and Dunkirk.

"Guarantee me a major American invasion of North Africa, and I can assure you of internal cooperation to overthrow the Vichy government here," he had said.

For almost two years, Lemaigre-Dubreuil had dangled similar bait before Murphy; but until now, neither the fisherman nor the fish had appeared ready for action.

Murphy was troubled. "It is your reputation as a German Fascist sympathizer that bothers me."

Lemaigre-Dubreuil laughed, as if Murphy were a not-too-bright child. "That is easy to explain."

"Explain it," demanded Murphy.

"I . . . how do you Americans say it? . . . trumped up the case against myself. I had the police arrest me and seize documents which I had prepared to show I am a Nazi sympathizer."

"Why?"

"To permit me to travel freely to Vichy and German-occupied France. While carrying on business, I was able to start an underground network for French liberation."

Lemaigre-Dubreuil's plan was to smuggle France's great war hero, General Henri Honoré Giraud, out of hiding in southern France and bring him to North Africa.

"He will persuade the French to lay down their guns before the liberators."

Murphy promised to discuss the matter with Washington, which passed it to Eisenhower for decision.

"Any arrangement that might spare lives—Allied or French—should be tried, " responded Eisenhower.

General Giraud's integrity and dedication needed no one's

validation. He had thrilled the world with two imaginatively executed escapes from German prisons. Indeed, Giraud was a living legend, fortunate he was alive to be a legend. During World War I, he had been seriously injured in battle. After one look at his mangled leg, a German prison doctor said he would be fortunate ever to walk—even on crutches. He didn't know Giraud. Still weak from wounds, Giraud escaped from the hospital by hopping away on one leg. Posing as a Belgian, he talked himself into a job with a carnival destined for Brussels. There he convinced nurse Edith Cavell to help him get to Holland. It was easy for him to ship to London and then back to France, where, though lame, he rejoined his regiment and fought the Germans until the Armistice.

During the Battle of France, on May 19, 1940, near Le Catelet, Giraud, now a sixty-one-year-old five-star general, was captured again by the Germans.

The Nazis took no chances this time. They locked him in a prison from which "No one can escape—least of all, an old, lame man."

Giraud couldn't go along with that.

Yet the forbidding gray stone fortress of Königstein, set on a sheer cliff 150 feet above the bank of the Elbe River in Saxony, was indeed a challenge! Two armed guards patrolled each gate twenty-four hours a day. Every ten minutes, armed sentries paced by on the walk below.

Giraud worked for two years to escape. As a general officer, he was permitted to write letters and to receive them and packages from home. One day he learned that an invalid prisoner was to be returned to France.

Here was his chance!

Through this man, he sent code words to his wife. It took him twelve months to communicate his escape plan through innocent-looking code words in letters.

His wife then sent him food packages wrapped with stout cord, which he hid and later wove into lengths of rope. Concealed in the false bottom of a package was a Tyrolean hat and 150 feet of strong wire to reinforce the rope. This, with his raincoat and acquired civilian trousers, would make him look like a German.

On a bright morning in April 1942, he strapped a parcel of food and disguise clothing to himself and waited for the guards to march out of sight. He tied one end of his rope to the balustrade and the other end to his waist. Another prisoner fed out the rope as Giraud, feet against the rock wall, painfully worked himself to the ground.

He escaped to southern France, a refuge from the Nazis.

Murphy relayed to Eisenhower the terms for cooperation that Giraud had given to Lemaigre-Dubreuil. A United States invasion would have to be substantial, and he would have to be in command.

Eisenhower shook his head. "No. The command has to wait. Shortly, the Allies will have a half-million troops in North Africa. We can't live with a force that size under French command. We can only promise that French troops will remain under a French general who reports to an Allied commander in chief."

One day, exciting information reached Murphy. Nazi collaborator Admiral Jean François Darlan, the Vichy government's vice-premier, foreign minister and successor-designate to Marshal Pétain, would consider defecting. But first, the United States would have to mount a major invasion and then place him in control of North Africa.

Murphy cabled the news to Washington and filled in Eisenhower. A quick reply from the office of President Roosevelt told him to coordinate with Eisenhower and let him make whatever decision might help the military. FDR left many key decisions to Ike.

"This could be a real opportunity to shorten invasion time and save lives," Eisenhower told Bob Murphy.

When Churchill got the word, he saw the possibility of instant advantages. "If I could meet Darlan, much as I hate him, I would cheerfully crawl on my hands and knees for a mile if by doing so I could get him to bring the fleet of his into the circle of Allied forces." [1]

General Ike and Murphy began to sweat. They already had a commitment with Giraud, a confirmed anti-Nazi. How could they make a similar offer to Darlan, a Nazi collaborator, unless the two could share the command?

That would be like bringing fire and gasoline together. Could it be done without an explosion?

Perhaps Darlan would be important in the Allied future, but right now, handling negotiations with Giraud was enough of a job for Bob Murphy.

In a blunt letter, Giraud had made two impossible demands: that he be placed in charge of the Allied command within forty-eight hours after the Americans landed, and that the United States guarantee an invasion of southern France shortly after North Africa.

Murphy grimaced. Ike had already ruled the command out. It had been a horrendous task rounding up shipping and landing craft for the North African invasion. He couldn't promise Giraud anything, but he had to promise him something. In diplomatic double-talk, he wrote: "Everything can be arranged to your satisfaction."

Even the travel arrangements did not come out the way the general had expected.

It had been agreed that Giraud was to be smuggled out of southern France by skiff, rendezvous with a submarine and transfer to a flying boat. Because Giraud insisted on an American submarine, and none was available, Eisenhower borrowed a British sub and placed an American in command; the first time this had ever happened.

In the dark of night, a small skiff set out from a secluded French harbor near the Spanish border, to rendezvous with the submarine 1,000 yards from shore. Accompanied by a small staff, General Giraud, limping markedly, lost footing on the craft's slippery gangway, fell and was shaken up.

Giraud thought the flying boat was on its way to Algiers. Instead, it ended up in Gibraltar. Eisenhower wanted to make sure he would operate according to Allied plans before putting him on his own.

Eisenhower's first exposure to Giraud was less a meeting than a head-on collision; "one of the most excruciating times in World War II for me," as General Ike once told me. "It was also one of the most frustrating, because I had to work through interpreters."

Giraud didn't request; he demanded. First, he must be made commander of the Allied Expeditionary Force. Then there must be an immediate invasion of southern France.

Eisenhower studied him.

Rumpled civilian clothing could not conceal the proud, soldierly bearing of the six-foot-three-inch General Giraud. War, imprisonment, escapes—nothing quenched his spirit.

"For the present, an American must be in command—myself," responded Eisenhower patiently.

Giraud frowned, drew himself up stiffly. "In that instance, I withdraw from the operation."

That was the last thing Eisenhower wanted. He was prepared to give Giraud everything, within Washington's and London's ground rules.

"General Giraud, please do not be hasty. You must try to understand our position."

"And you must try to understand *mine*," Giraud responded. "My status with other French generals would be seriously compromised if I agreed to place French troops under American command in a campaign on French territory."

"General," replied Eisenhower, "I can certainly understand that, but at present, with almost one-half million Americans about to land and with the strategy already established, it would be impossible to make such a move."

The same arguments, in slightly different words and shades of meaning, bounced back and forth for several hours, until Giraud's temper flared. Eisenhower's warm blue eyes became icy, and a large vein on his forehead enlarged. Redness crept up his neck.

Giraud pointed to the three stars on General Eisenhower's shoulders, reminding him that he was a mere lieutenant general. "I have five stars. You should be reporting to me."

Eisenhower bolted from his chair. He paced to control himself.

"The number of stars has nothing to do with who is in command. Our plan is for you to go to Africa—as soon as we can guarantee your safety—and take command of French forces which choose to fight under you."

"I can participate only as Allied commander in chief," retorted Giraud.

"There is no legal basis on which any subordinate Allied commander could accept orders from you," responded Eisenhower. "There is not one Frenchman in the Allied command at present. In fact, the enemy, if any, at the moment is French."

"You have heard my conditions," Giraud replied.

"And you have heard ours," said Eisenhower.

Sitting proudly in his chair, Giraud tried again. "General Giraud cannot accept a subordinate position. His countrymen would not understand, and his honor as a soldier would be tarnished."

Eisenhower clung tenaciously to his position, but at the same time, he felt sorry for Giraud. This brave, patriotic and determined man had risked every precious possession in the world to help his nation. His family in France would likely be persecuted, captured and imprisoned. He was laying his own life on the line.

The discussion was going nowhere. Eisenhower called a recess and talked privately with political advisers from the United States State Department and the British Foreign Office.

"Why not put General Giraud in nominal command, while you direct the campaign?" they asked.

"Look, I won't agree to subterfuge," bristled Eisenhower. "Unless Giraud contents himself with commanding North African French forces that he influences to our side, we'll go on without him."

With General Mark W. Clark interpreting in flawless French, the sparring continued exhaustively and exhaustingly until midnight. Neither side budged from its position.

Giraud rose from his chair with finality. "General Giraud will be a spectator to this affair," he said, and walked out of the room.

A night's sleep—or insomnia—favorably influenced Giraud. He would, after all, participate as the Allies wished.

The Darlan Affair

Shortly before twilight on November 7, German intelligence agents and many French in Algiers had noted a gigantic convoy steaming eastward. The British had carefully planted the information that its destination was the island of Malta, not far from Sicily.

German U-boats swarmed off the coast of Sicily, and fighter airplanes remained on the alert for the precise time to smash the convoy.

In the blackness, part of the long line of ships headed for Algiers to implement Operation Torch. Just before midnight, the landings began. At the same hour, Lemaigre-Dubreuil's crew went to work: 400 aggressive young Frenchmen, many employed in his vegetable oil plants, all trained in groups of twenty-five for specific assignments. Clad in civilian garb, wearing arm bands and carrying rifles, they dispersed throughout Algiers, taking over all communications: the telephone and telegraph offices, radio station, airport, power stations, police and military headquarters and transport centers.

Lemaigre-Dubreuil informed Robert Murphy that all was going well. "We still hope Algiers can be captured without a shot fired."

Murphy was mystified. Giraud had not shown up, and he could get no response to numerous radio signals, asking "Where's Giraud?" He could delay no longer. Lives could be lost needlessly, unless he informed the most-influential French Army officer in North Africa—General Alphonse Pierre Juin, commander in chief of the ground forces—that the Allied invasion was underway.

Juin was stunned at this news and also that Giraud would soon be in Algiers. Murphy asked him to support the invasion or, at least, not resist.

"I would be with you," Juin replied, "but, as you may know, Admiral Darlan is in Algiers. He outranks me. No matter what decision I might make, Darlan could immediately overrule it."

Now there was no choice. Eisenhower and he had agreed that the first consideration had to be sparing Allied and French lives—not the politics of Darlan, as odoriferous as they were.

Murphy couldn't push out of his mind the two years of anti-British and anti-de Gaulle radio broadcasts of Darlan from Vichy. They were all strictly Nazi party line. To counter him, the British and Free French had branded him a traitor to his own people and the Allies.

Grave repercussions could result from dealing with Darlan, but Bob Murphy had no way of knowing that, before it was all over, even General Eisenhower's command would be threatened.

Admiral Darlan, described by General Mark W. Clark as "a small man, with watery blue eyes and petulant lips," became furious when Murphy told him the news.

"If you Americans had waited only a few weeks, you could have received effective French cooperation: simultaneous military operations in France as well as North Africa."

He was so agitated it took thirty minutes for Murphy to calm him down. Then Murphy said, "Admiral, it is your responsibility to arrange that no French blood will be shed by senseless resistance to the American landings."

"I cannot violate my allegiance to Marshal Pétain!"

"Well, then get his authorization."

Darlan promised to cable him immediately.

Meanwhile, Eisenhower was down in the dumps with reactions of Frenchmen to radio appeals from General Giraud to lay down their arms. They were ignored, received with irritation or contempt, or resented. It was as if a nonclub member were meddling in affairs that were none of his business.

Most Frenchmen wanted to be rid of the Germans, but they still respected the Vichy authority and chain of command. General Giraud was not Vichy sponsored and, therefore was illegitimate.

Eisenhower's first report from Casablanca revealed that Patton and his landing party had experienced smoother surf than expected. General Ike sank to his knees to thank God for that. But Patton's forces and those invading Oran were meeting with resistance.

Around nine o'clock in the morning, Darlan heard from Pétain: "Act freely."

As American troops swarmed into the city, Admiral Darlan issued a cease-fire for Algiers. This was obeyed.

"I cannot make the order apply to all of French North Africa until I meet with General Eisenhower," Darlan told Murphy.

Murphy hurriedly cabled Ike news of the Darlan development. Eisenhower grimaced. What he had feared had come upon him. Now he had two French leaders for North Africa. He had to make official the commitment to Darlan, whose authority over the French had been conclusively proved in Algiers, and he had to keep his commitment to Giraud, although his radio messages had proven futile.

Eisenhower sent General Mark W. Clark and, later, Giraud, to North Africa. He wanted Clark to hammer out the preliminaries of the formal arrangement with Darlan, to keep the latter in line, and to try to work out a way of Darlan accepting Giraud as his second in command.

Adolf Hitler went into a frenzy with Admiral Pétain for making a deal, through Darlan, with the Allies. He coerced Pétain into opening Tunis airport for German aircraft and giving permission for German troops to help the French defend this territory against the Allies. He even threatened the bulk of the French Navy, in anchor at Toulon harbor in southern France.

Eisenhower counterpunched. He cabled Clark to put the squeeze on Admiral Darlan to order Tunis commanders to "destroy Axis planes and resist Axis invasion."

Too late. Darlan had already transmitted Pétain's order. Murphy and Clark could not persuade the resolute Darlan to rescind the order.

Next morning (November 10) in a hot and stuffy room of the Hotel Saint George, Clark, before perspiring American and French officers, told Darlan that Eisenhower expected his full cooperation to further Allied interests.

"We want a cease-fire at Oran and Casablanca."

The tiny admiral stalled. "I must await orders from Marshal Pétain."

Clark looked as if he were ready to explode. "Look, Admiral, you have two choices: action or prison!"

Darlan trembled. "Nevertheless, I must await orders. . . ."

General Juin held up the palm of his hand for Clark to be patient. He led Darlan into a corner, talking rapidly: "What is the use of resistance in Oran and Casablanca?"

Darlan shrugged his shoulder, turned to Clark and said, "All right. I shall order troops in Oran and Casablanca to cease fire against the Allies, but not resist the Germans."

Then came the next Vichy move. Exposed to Hitler's fury, Pétain made a public declaration that Admiral Darlan had been removed from office.

Sadly, Darlan told Clark, "I have no choice. I must call off the armistice."

Clark scowled down at the admiral from his Olympian six-foot-four-inches. (Churchill had described him as "the American Eagle.")

"In that case, Admiral, I'm going to throw you into prison."

Darlan fidgeted nervously. He did not glance up at Clark. Without emotion, he said, "The cease-fire stands."

Events happened rapidly. On November 11, Hitler let the world know his troops were about to march into unoccupied southern France.

Darlan objected strenuously. Hitler, not Pétain, was now running southern France. The admiral announced that he had secret orders from Pétain to act independently of Vichy if the Germans violated their 1940 agreement.

Under the Nazi gun, Pétain announced that Darlan was relieved of authority. Now the North African French were confused about authority. Pétain or Darlan?

Darlan needed Allied backing. Clark, acting for Eisenhower, told Darlan that while he was to serve as high commissioner of North Africa, he had to accept General Giraud as commander in chief of French forces. The expected explosion never came about. Giraud, too, accepted.

On November 13, Eisenhower, Admiral Andrew Cunningham, and Captain Harry Butcher flew to Algiers and met with Clark, Murphy, Darlan, Giraud and generals Juin and Noguès to sign a formal agreement with Darlan.

After studying the Clark-Darlan agreement, Eisenhower felt uncomfortable. It was a tremendous responsibility, involving his nation and the British. Ike turned to Murphy, "Bob, what's your opinion of the document?"

"The whole matter has now become a military one," replied Murphy.

Surprised, Eisenhower thought for a moment. The Germans were flying more troops into Tunis and moving toward the prized French Navy in Toulon. Sure enough, there could be bad reactions to the Darlan appointment, but think of the lives, ammunition and property that would be saved. Time was too precious for foot-dragging. He had to sign *now!*

He affixed his signature. Later, he and Murphy sent dispatches to the Allied governments and the combined chiefs of staff, explaining the arrangement.

A brief lull followed the dispatch. Meanwhile, a message from President Roosevelt arrived at headquarters, congratulating General Eisenhower and the Operation Torch forces.

Immediately, Eisenhower sent copies to his commanders, to be tacked to company bulletin boards for all to share the president's commendation.

The pleasant atmosphere was not to last long.

Roosevelt Behind the Scene

A torrent of criticism about the "Darlan Deal" and Eisenhower broke loose in the United States and British press. It was called a sellout, a Judas double cross that canceled out the principles for which the Allies were supposedly fighting.

Robert Sherwood, an Office of War Information official, summarized the uproar like this: "If we make a deal with a Darlan in French territory, then presumably we will make one with a Goering in Germany or a Matsuoka in Japan?" [1]

Indignation of General Charles de Gaulle and his Free French, who had been omitted from Operation Torch, blistered Roosevelt, Churchill, the State Department, the Foreign Office and Eisenhower.

Of all bedfellows to choose—Darlan, the crawling compromiser—Neville Chamberlain with a French accent!

Various opinion makers asked, "How are our Russian allies going to react to the Darlan deal?" Every correspondent and editorial writer tried to outdo the others in original, slicing denunciations.

Particularly, reporters in North Africa viewed the Darlan deal and abuses and corruptions of the region through high-powered lenses—every bristly haired mole, wart, wen and pustule.

They were revolted by Vichy-appointed officials who cared less about ridding *La Belle France* of Nazis than about their daily graft, by openly persecuted Jews, by Arabs beaten with little or no provocation, and by Spanish Republicans, anti-Vichyites and French Fascists, who, from their pillboxes of bureaucratic security, bullied those who failed to share their sympathies. Where were liberty, equality and fraternity?

The heat became too much for Roosevelt and Churchill. They requested more detailed information about the Darlan deal.

Eisenhower sent a long cable, saying that:

> No hasty action should be taken in the United States to disturb the North African equilibrium. Only through Darlan, a part of the Vichy structure, could cease-fires have been realized. General Giraud was in complete accord with the Darlan arrangement. The French would do everything possible to assist the Allies in taking Tunisia and getting the French fleet.
>
> Unless the Vichy administrative structure were left intact, it would take 60,000 Allied troops to keep tribes in Morocco pacified. (Patton's estimate.) If Darlan was rejected, French forces would resist.
>
> The Darlan arrangement secured many advantages and eliminated disadvantages and could only be properly appraised by someone on the local scene. A mission should be sent to investigate, if the British and United States governments did not accept these statements.

President Roosevelt's unusual response to Eisenhower's message is reported by Robert Sherwood, an eyewitness:

> On November 14, Roosevelt received a long cable from Eisenhower which I heard him read aloud to Harry Hopkins. It was a remarkable statement of Eisenhower's reasons for the Darlan deal. Roosevelt was deeply impressed by it and, as he read it with the same superb distribution of emphasis that he used in his public speeches, he sounded as if he were making an eloquent plea for Eisenhower before the bar of history. . . .[2]

Meanwhile, Eisenhower remained in limbo, not knowing whether or when he would be removed from command. Often he examined past events and concluded that if he had to do it all over again, he would do it all over again in the same way. Eisenhower ruefully explained his mixed feelings about his roles:

> I think sometimes that I am a cross between a one-time soldier, a pseudo statesman, a jack-legged politician and a crooked diplomat. I walk a soapy tight-rope in a rain storm with a blazing furnace on one side and a pack of ravenous tigers on the other.[3]

Would he make it across? If so, he could think of no greater reward than a quiet little cottage "on the side of a slow-moving stream, where I can sit and fish for catfish with a bobber."

One does not twist the arm of the president to induce him to take a stand. Yet advisers of Franklin D. Roosevelt—Harry Hopkins, Samuel I. Rosenman, Robert Sherwood and Admiral William D. Leahy, the president's chief of staff and former ambassador to Vichy—did everything but that to persuade him to declare himself on the Darlan deal. Even Winston Churchill finally joined the persuaders.

Privately, FDR agreed with what Eisenhower had done. Publicly, he wanted his view to be private. Finally, he issued a weasel-worded press release stating that he had "temporarily" accepted Eisenhower's political arrangement in North Africa.

Then he sent a private message to General Ike: ". . . I appreciate fully the difficulties of your military situation. I am, therefore, not disposed to in any way question the action you have taken." [4]

Even Premier Stalin, in a message to Churchill, endorsed the Darlan deal.

Roosevelt's press statement made Darlan sad. "I am only a lemon which the Americans will drop after they squeeze it dry," Darlan told Clark.[5]

He further protested. "I am in an awkward position. I hope that the United States will not again give Frenchmen the impression that the authority of the leader which has brought French Africa back into the struggle is a diminished one."

Eisenhower relayed to Bob Murphy instructions from the president that Darlan's movements and communications should be carefully watched.

During a luncheon meeting at a private New York City club after World War II, Murphy told me:

> As it turned out, it was not necessary to live in Darlan's back pocket. The man did everything he promised, and more. I got to know him better than any other American. I grew to like him.
>
> Despite his conduct during the first few years of the Vichy government, he proved emphatically during the Allied Expeditionary Force's landing that he was, beyond question, a French patriot.
>
> Along with furthering the interests of France, Darlan vigorously promoted the Allied cause. He voluntarily invited me to listen on extension telephones to conversations with important French commanders and to read the major messages which he sent them. His influence hastened the end of military resistance to Patton's troops in Morocco. His secret order led to the French destroying their own fleet to keep it out of Nazi hands.
>
> On more than one occasion, he said to me, "Please tell your President that any time he decides I am more of a liability than an asset to him, I will gladly step down. . . ."

Frequently Murphy felt a tincture of sadness about the diminutive admiral. "He had such an overwhelming desire to reestablish his stature with the Allies, and it seemed such a futile task."

End of a Campaign

Eisenhower had little choice.

He shuddered at the thought of driving on German-held Tunis before his generals could consolidate invasion troops, but every day's delay meant additional Germans reinforcing the city.

There were more problems than solutions. How could he move thousands of men, armament and supplies with a severe truck shortage and only a single-track railroad between Algiers and Tunis—approximately the distance between Cleveland and New York City?

What could he do with aircraft mired to their wings on muddy airstrips? And how could he pull out Allied forces in French Morocco by sea or air when there was danger of a German attack through Spanish Morocco?

He gambled that speed and boldness would compensate for the handicaps and hurried the grouping of British General Kenneth A. N. Anderson's elements. But Anderson moved too slowly.

The Axis soon had 150,000 troops in Tunis. Then even a

military loss in Egypt turned into a gain for them. Fleeing German soldiers joined with divisions in Tunis, making its defenses stronger.

More than two weeks before Allied landings, General Sir Harold Alexander had launched the British Eighth Army, commanded by General Sir Bernard L. Montgomery, against Axis troops under Field Marshal Erwin Rommel near El Alamein.

Quickly, Montgomery's army stunted Rommel's offensive and sent his army retreating westward. Montgomery failed to follow up fast enough to capitalize on the stunning victory. Rommel's troops established themselves behind a near-impregnable defense called the Mareth Line.

Now twenty miles from Tunis, Anderson's troops were pushed back. A coastal linkup between Eisenhower and Montgomery was thwarted. The Allies had lost the race for Tunis.

It was Christmas Eve, a time which General Ike, from his early religious training, held in reverence—a special time of restrained joy. Chilled and head aching, he entered Fifth Corps headquarters, a plain farmhouse, and sent a message to the combined chiefs of staff, admitting temporary defeat.

Hardly had he settled at the mess table for dinner when shocking word came from Communications: "Admiral Darlan assassinated!"

With flying conditions impossible, Ike drove thirty hours, through sleet and rain, to Algiers. Darlan had been shot by a young man who had been convinced that assassination of the admiral would make him a national hero.

General Clark and Robert Murphy were deeply moved. As Bob stated:

> Many commentators in the United States and England wrote that Darlan's death was a fortunate break for the Anglo-Americans, relieving us of the intolerable burdens of the "Darlan Deal."

That was never my feeling. President Roosevelt could have had Darlan's resignation instantly, if he requested it. Clark and I, talking over matters in the hospital, agreed that Darlan had contributed as much as any Frenchman to the success of a highly speculative military and diplomatic venture.[1]

So did General Ike.

Darlan's assassination, the period when Giraud assumed authority, and preparations for the Casablanca Conference put General Ike under additional stress, and his cold became worse.

Overwhelming weariness, a severe headache, soreness throughout his body, and doctor's orders kept him in bed until noon. He didn't want Roosevelt, Churchill and General Marshall to see him in that condition. His life had no room for illness.

A personal concern also nagged him. Letters had suddenly stopped coming from Mamie. Was she ill, too?

On the previous day, he had sent a message via the new two-way teleprinter to Washington, requesting the duty officer to phone her. A cheerful answer had come through. She was chipper and had written regularly. Officers to whom she had given letters had not yet arrived at his headquarters.

That night, she was in his prayer of thanks to God. Then his mind drifted to rasping military subjects. How urgently every kind of air activity was needed. How much closer British and American armed forces would have to work, to assure victory!

German night bombings were rocking Algiers. Arabs working at the docks fled into the hills, where they stayed for days. Much of the city's population asked, "Why did you bring this war to us? We were satisfied before you came to get us all killed." [2]

Recent events upset Ike. Lack of paved runways made it necessary, in the winter rainy season, to park Spitfires close together in areas where they would not sink into mud. They were often strafed or bombed by the Luftwaffe.

He was sickened by the lack of integration and cooperation among separate branches of service. Aircraft supported ground advances reluctantly, or not at all. Limited cooperation of American and British forces appalled him.

A strong command was needed to shatter barriers between various branches of service and military organizations of Allied nations. Before he could win over the Axis, he had to win over internal Allied problems.

Eisenhower demanded British fighter aircraft, replacement parts and maintenance personnel to protect Algiers and support the drive on Tunis. The British met his demands—and more. They sent him a genius in versatile use of air power: Air Marshal Sir Arthur Tedder.

A fiercely loyal Tedder linked air with land and sea. Admiral Cunningham linked the sea with land, with General Ike providing the linkages. They and Alexander were the architects of victory in North Africa.

Eisenhower was making excellent progress in January 1943, the time of the Casablanca Conference, where Roosevelt, Churchill and the Joint Chiefs of Staff agreed upon the next Allied campaign: invasion of Sicily and Italy.

After the conference, General Marshall flew to Algiers to review war operations and stayed at General Ike's villa.

Marshall protested at General Ike giving him his second-floor bedroom, but Ike prevailed. As they and Mickey McKeogh, Ike's orderly, went up stairs, Telek, General Ike's perky black Scotty, nipped at their heels and bounced into the room before them.

Enthusiastically, Ike talked about the luxurious comfort of the large double bed, covered by a fine, maroon silk spread, as Telek jumped up on the spread and, in excitement, raised his leg and let go.

Mickey and General Ike were horrified. Marshall's surprised look indicated that he didn't think this was standard procedure. In a lightning maneuver, Mickey snatched Telek and the spread off the bed.

Ike's composure returned and he said to Mickey, "When Telek does things like that, he's *your* dog!"

Later Marshall commented to General Ike, "Eisenhower, I'm pleased with your progress in building a coordinated Allied team, but not with your physical condition. You're working too-long hours. Get more rest and take time away from war for peace of mind and exercise. I want you to ride at least three times a week."

General Ike was surprised when Marshall, supposedly a cold war machine, presented him with a box full of baseball gloves and hardballs.

"Work out every day with your commanders for a half-hour," Marshall ordered. "Then you'll all make the team."

After covering the Casablanca Conference for United Press, I stayed in Algiers, attending some of General Ike's baseball breaks with Admiral Cunningham and Air Marshal Tedder.

Ike's fastball still had zing as it smacked into the fielders' gloves. The cricket-oriented British commanders enjoyed baseball.

One day Admiral Cunningham asked me to come to his villa above the Saint George Hotel. His staff car would pick me up. On the way over, I wondered what sort of exclusive story the admiral would give me.

"Thank you for coming," he said, a twinkle in his clear blue eyes. "What I want to talk to you about is not an affair of state. General Ike has shown Lord Tedder and me how to throw curves, knuckleballs, sliders and fast ones. He teases us about throwing the ball like girls or sissies, because we use our circular, overhand, cricket-style of bowling.

"We've mastered the American way of throwing sidearm, but we need advice. Ike keeps talking about some darn thing he calls an out drop. I would appreciate your teaching me how to throw it. I want to master that pitch for Ike. I believe it would please him enormously."

Through instruction from one of my American sergeant friends, Admiral Cunningham conquered the out drop. This was not his only victory: eventually, with his fellow commanders and men, he defeated the Italian fleet in the Mediterranean.

General Ike often told me that Marshall had not only taught

him military strategy but also the necessity for regular physical exercise when under constant stress.

Several times a week, Ike would ride by himself, with a staff officer or Kay Summersby, a driver-secretary. Butch Butcher told me that he almost always stayed within the property, for security reasons.

Now the Allies were beginning to pressure the Germans from the east and west. In southern Tunisia, bold, blustering General George S. Patton attacked the flank and rear of Rommel's Mareth Line, while to the south, General Montgomery sent elements of the British Eighth Army through the desert to outflank the Axis position.

Patton disliked the cocky, bantam Montgomery, who already had adopted a black tanker's beret as his personal identification mark. Despite his differences with Monty, Patton cooperated well with him, and soon they had all Axis troops compressed into a small bridgehead at the northeastern tip of Tunisia.

Much to his frustration, Patton was ordered to relinquish his command to Major General Omar N. Bradley, so that he could prepare for the next campaign. Patton visited Ike's villa. Soon he and Ike were discussing the need for toughness, as Butch told me.

Patton admitted he faced enemy fire frequently, to set an example for his men. Ike said he had sent West Point classmates who were not equal to their jobs back to the United States.

Butch began to laugh. "Underneath it all, you're both chickenhearted."

"You know, Butch," George Patton replied, "before I left the Second Corps headquarters, I picked an armful of wild flowers to put on the grave of an aide."

Patton became sober as his mind revisited the occasion. Then his voice quavered. "I guess I'm getting to be a sentimental old fool." A tear skidded down one cheek.

One morning a message arrived for Patton from General Marshall. Marshall congratulated him on his fine work in the North African campaign and on justifying the commander in chief's confidence in him.

Butch informed me that Patton's eyes became misty, and he looked with gratitude at General Ike. "I owe it all to you, Ike."

Ike shook his head violently. "Not at all. You owe it to yourself."

Late in the North African campaign, Lord Louis Mountbatten, on his way to becoming supreme commander of the Southeast Asia theater, spent several days with General Ike. He was impressed with Eisenhower's ability to knit the most polyglot forces in the history of warfare into an effective fighting team: Americans, British, Canadians, French, Norwegians, Indians, New Zealanders, Poles and South Africans.

"Ike, I'm amazed at your ability to establish so high a degree of unity with such a diversity of nationals. I would like to duplicate your setup in India and Burma. How should I go about it?"

General Ike grinned. "Dickie, get yourself the best-possible tailor, and take him with you."

This was hardly the reply Lord Louis had expected.

"You will need a good tailor to make the uniforms and civilian clothing you will require to attend every possible kind of social event." That was all he would say.

Several weeks later, when Lord Louis was setting up his new headquarters, a large manila envelope arrived from General Ike. It was a comprehensive twenty-eight page report, sharing the important principles of a unified command that he had learned in North Africa.

Finally, in mid-April, the North African campaign was over. The Allies had brushed the continent clean of Axis resistance. The cost to the Allies: 70,000 casualties. The cost to the Axis: over 1 million casualties (including 240,000 prisoners captured in the last week alone).

Prone to fracture the facts to suit his nation's objectives, Germany's propaganda minister Goebbels honestly characterized the loss in Africa as the greatest German defeat since Stalingrad.

General Ike was already deep in planning to defeat the Axis in Sicily and Italy.

Eisenhower and Montgomery inspect men of an American unit in England after pre-invasion maneuvers in February 1944. (Wide World Photos.) *Below:* Churchill and Eisenhower reviewing American paratroopers in England before the invasion. (Wide World Photos.)

Walking along a sunny road in Normandy are, left to right: British Air Marshall Sir Arthur Tedder, Eisenhower, and General Montgomery. (Wide World Photos.) *Below:* Ike chatting with General Charles De Gaulle during an inspection of American troops in 1944 at Ike's advance headquarters in the Normandy area of France. (Wide World Photos.)

General Ike enjoyed chatting with army enlisted personnel, as with this GI in Belgium in November 1944. He made a habit of eating in enlisted men's mess halls, sampling food, observing cooking procedures and even checking on food storage.

During Inauguration Day ceremonies of January 21, 1953, incoming President Eisenhower receives congratulations from outgoing President Harry S. Truman. *Below:* Richard Nixon, Paul Hoffman, President Eisenhower and Virgil Pinkley.

President Eisenhower's first-term cabinet and other key officials of his administration posed for this picture on May 8, 1953. *Below:* President and Mrs. Eisenhower welcome Queen Elizabeth and Prince Philip to the White House on October 12, 1957.

THE WHITE HOUSE
WASHINGTON

LEGISLATIVE LEADERSHIP CONFERENCE

MONDAY, JUNE 28, 1954 --- 8:30 AM

1. Symington Amendment to the Extension of Trade
   Agreements Act   (Secretary Dulles)

2. Report on Status of Legislation in Senate Finance
   Committee (Senator Millikin)

3. Senate Report (Senator Knowland)

4. House Report (Speaker Martin)

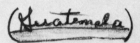

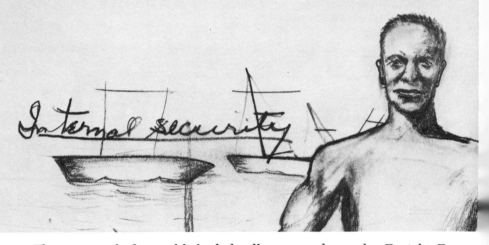

These never-before-published doodles were drawn by Dwight D.
Eisenhower at various times during his presidential terms. Most of the
doodles were penciled or penned on agendas during cabinet meetings. In one instance, Eisenhower listed, in order of preference, his
secret choices of candidates to succeed him in office. Little did he
realize that someday his private doodlings would be made public
and that curious individuals everywhere—psychologists and non-
psychologists—would have the opportunity to puzzle over them and
try to determine their significance.

Possibilities   actively   religion

a Nixon   Guenther —   or age

a+ Adams (health & age ?)   Milton E. —

a Brownell —   Adams (poverty ?)

a+ Lodge —   age)

a Case (N. J.)

a Bush   2

a+ Morton

a' Robert Anderson

a' Dillon Anderson 2 ;

a' ~~Frelinghuysen~~ 2 .

b ~~Cowper~~

a+ Hauge   2

a+ Percy   2

a Fora   2

Nixon,   Percy

Lodge,   ~~Hauge~~

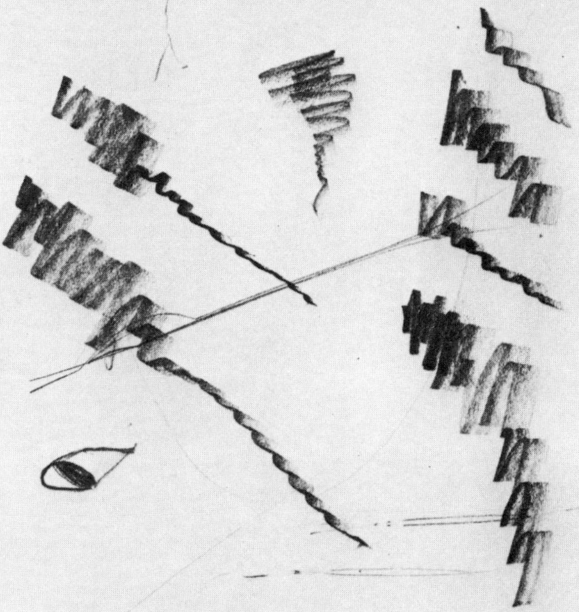

Adams,   Morton

Robt Anderson,   Bush

      ~~Frelinghuysen~~

Morton   Hauge

Larson.

American for Modern ~~Republicans~~

A. M. R.

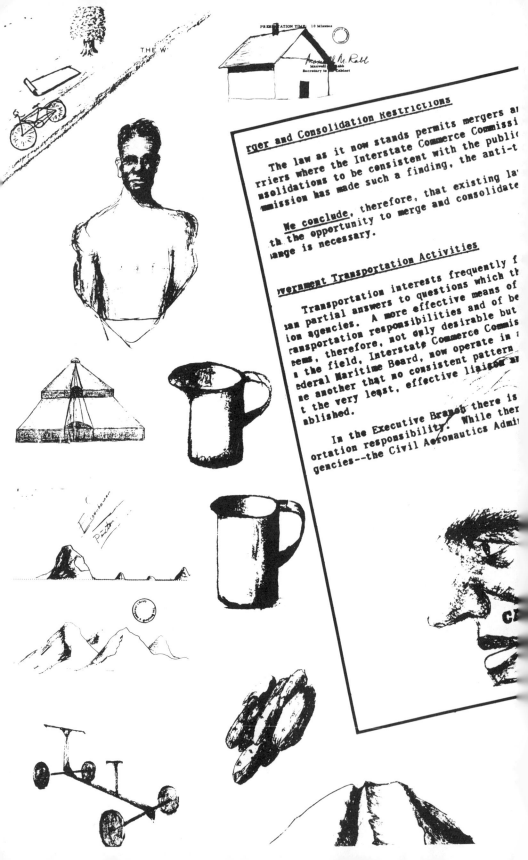

...d consolidations of common
...on finds such mergers and
... interest. Where the
...rust laws do not apply.

...w does not unduly interfere
..., and that no legislative

...nd it difficult to get more
...ey pose to Federal transporta-
... discharging the government's
...ing able to indicate its interest
... necessary. Regulatory agencies
...ion, Civil Aeronautics Board,
... manner so wholly independent of
...of Federal regulation is achieved.
...ong these agencies should be es-

...also widespread sharing of trans-
...e are three large transportation
...istration, the Maritime Administra-

...NET PAPER
For Consideration

Up the Bloody Boot—Sicily and Italy

To General George S. Patton, Sicily was more than an island stepping-stone to Italy for his Seventh Army and other Allied forces. It was a showcase under the eyes of the world, where he could expose his British counterpart, General Bernard Montgomery, as a military inferior.

Patton gloated over this rare opportunity, because he regarded the hero of El Alamein as obnoxious, overbearing, overinflated and undertalented. He would reach the major objective of Messina first, despite Montgomery's insistence upon having more landing craft, troops, tanks, mobile artillery, a greater air umbrella and a shorter distance to travel.

While Patton finalized plans for invasion, starting on July 10, 1943, General Eisenhower flew to Malta to coordinate massive Allied air, navy and ground activities. The campaign for Sicily and Italy (Operation Husky) had been planned at the Casablanca Conference, and the Allies started to prepare before completing the drive for Tunis.

There were three major reasons for Operation Husky: Conquest of Sicily and Italy could knock the Italians out of the war and secure Allied control of the Mediterranean; it would draw German divisions from the Eastern Front, which would relieve pressure on the Russians; and it would keep an Allied promise to Premier Stalin.

For Operation Husky, General Ike placed the Fifteenth Army Group under General Sir Harold Alexander—some 160,000 troops—including Patton's newly created United States Seventh Army and General Montgomery's British Eighth Army. Then he sweated out the weather.

Fair weather and calm seas were necessary for amphibious landings. Moonlight was a must for accurate inland dropping of a whole United States airborne division, sent to divert coastal defenders and to capture air bases for Allied use.

About two weeks before the invasion, General Ike called a press conference at the Maison Agriculture in Algiers. "Gentlemen, you are aware of the bombing patterns we have carried on in recent weeks on Sicily and southern Italy. . . ." [For many weeks, Allied aircraft had bombed the west coast of Sicily, to make defenders think that was their invasion point, rather than the eastern and southern coasts.] "We are going to land in Sicily, and after this campaign, which should be an extended one, we will move into the south of Italy, probably striking from Messina and the heel of Italy's boot.

"Airborne troops will go in first, to capture airfields and soften up or knock out gun positions and strong points occupied by Germans or Italians."

As General Ike paced and talked in front of us, he suddenly stopped. "Gentlemen, I am telling you everything about the two invasions, so that you will know exactly what our plans are. Knowing this, you will not write or broadcast anything which will be of assistance to the enemy.

"I am trusting each of you to see that you give no aid and knowledge to the enemy. Now, in a broad way, you know everything I do about these invasions. Yes, there might be some particular details that I have not filled you in on, but, basically, you know what our program is and why."

Intelligence reports had revealed that some 350,000 troops, mainly Italian, manned Sicily—with a core of seasoned German soldiers.

Despite this numerical strength, Magic, a project of the United States government's National Security Agency, offered encouraging top-secret information.

By breaking the codes of Japan and Italy, the NSA learned that Premier Mussolini had been quarreling with Germany over how Europe was to be divided up. He got no satisfaction.

Other messages also indicated Il Duce's disillusionment with Hitler and weakening Italian morale.

Strong winds over the Mediterranean soon became a gale. Ike and British Admiral Andrew Cunningham consulted with meteorologists, who predicted that the wind and surf would subside by sundown.

General Ike made the decision to sail, and the huge invasion armada steamed toward Sicily. Before paratroopers took off from Malta, General Ike, alone on the beach, knelt in the damp sand and prayed for forty-five minutes for success and few Allied casualties.

After naval bombardment softened defenses and paratroopers landed, the armies of Patton and Montgomery landed with a minimum of casualties.

Montgomery's Eighth Army, aided by Canadians, landed without marked resistance at the southeast end of the scalloped triangle that is Sicily, moving northward along the coast toward the narrow, rugged country near Mount Etna on the way to Messina.

To divide enemy defenses, Patton's Seventh Army struck at the south, thrusting northward through the heart of Sicily toward Marsala and Palermo on the north coast. Montgomery started less than half the distance from Messina, and it was a foregone conclusion that he would arrive before Patton, whose route promised to be circuitous and difficult. "Not a chance!" Patton vowed to himself.

When Montgomery's army met crack German troops behind

protective cover on Mount Etna, part of Patton's army supported him on the left.

Stubborn resistance and a destroyed bridge delayed Monty. Patton stormed to the north coast, bisecting Sicily and battling eastward toward Messina. Much of the road was a narrow, rocky, coastal shelf with many bridges, which the fleeing enemy bombed. But Patton refused to be stopped. He used landing craft to transport his troops beyond the blasted bridges. They carried out leapfrog amphibious landings behind the enemy.

Montgomery expected to enter Messina first, with fanfare, but standing in the main square to welcome him was the elated Patton.

Patton's lightning advance amazed British General Sir Kenneth Strong, head of G-2. When he studied the map, he turned to General Eisenhower and, with typical British restraint, commented dryly, "I do believe Monty's got himself completely surrounded by Patton's forces."

Eisenhower's greatest trial early in the Sicily-Italy campaign was Patton's flagrant misconduct, which took some luster from his dazzling victory. While visiting an American hospital, Patton slapped two enlisted men whom he suspected of malingering.

The first slapping occurred in a tent hospital near Palermo. Much misinformation has been written about this event. A captain under Colonel Arthur McChrystal, head of General Ike's censorship department, was in the hospital with a shoulder wound. He saw the entire incident.

A soldier in field uniform, wearing a helmet liner, was sitting on the edge of a bed, nervous and trembling. Patton immediately saw that he was not physically injured.

"They don't break anymore," the young man kept muttering. A member of the Seventeenth Field Artillery, he was talking about shells in trajectories too high or low to hit targets.

"What's that?" Patton testily inquired.

"They don't break anymore," the GI kept repeating.

Patton exploded. Swearing at the soldier, he cuffed him on the side of his head, sending the helmet liner spinning to the ground. General Patton pulled pearl-handled pistols from his holsters. "I ought to shoot you on the spot!"

The medical doctor and the nurse seized Patton's hands. Suddenly aware of what he had done, Patton burst into tears.

Later, Patton slapped a second soldier. It turned out that this man had had an excellent combat record in Tunis and Sicily. A medical doctor had told him to get treatment a week earlier, but he continued fighting until ordered to the hospital by his commanding officer. He was running a temperature of 102°.

General Ike was shocked by Patton's acts and assembled us correspondents for an announcement:

> I am sorry to tell you about two slapping incidents in which General George Patton was involved. He will be severely reprimanded and punished in a way which will be most humiliating for him.
>
> I am going to order him to apologize personally to the GIs he slapped, to the nurses and members of the hospital where the incidents took place, and to soldiers in a mass meeting in the square before the palace he occupies.
>
> The day will come when the Allies will punch a hole through the west wall built by Germany along the English Channel and Atlantic coastline. Then we will need the greatest open-field runner in history to take the mails to town. George Patton is that man. If he is then commanding armor in Europe, he will save thousands of American and Allied lives and shorten the war by many months.
>
> You all know that there is something more important in this war than a single story. If you want to write about these incidents, you may do so, and there will be no censorship. There will be no recriminations on my part. I leave each of you to use your conscience and do what you feel is best.

Not one of the more than sixty correspondents filed a single word!

Several days later, a congressional committee and representatives of the Sperry Bombsight Company visited the North African theater, and the Patton story leaked out. On the following Sunday, after returning to the United States, someone in one of the groups confided the information to radio commentator-columnist Drew Pearson. He revealed the Patton slapping on the ABC coast-to-coast network that night.

Correspondents and press services received blistering wires from the United States for not filing the story. United Press in New York wired me: "What's the matter with you, Pinkley? I thought you were a war correspondent, not a suppressor of front-page news. What's your lousy excuse?"

I had no lousy excuse—only a good one: General Ike's statement to the press.

Congressmen screamed to bring Patton back to Washington for a full-dress investigation. Eisenhower was face-to-face with a tough decision. If Congress got a hold of George Patton, they would reduce him to a colonel in some teaching command where recruits could learn "Squads right."

Often, Eisenhower had been an army witness in congressional hearings. He had been grilled by congressmen operating under congressional immunity and protection. Many were out to make headlines.

No! Patton was not going back for *that!*

Ike had some anxious moments. He wanted the appointment as supreme Allied commander for the invasion of France, and protection of Patton could ruin that prospect, but he knew there was only one way to go.

General Ike sent a signal to General Marshall and President Roosevelt. He described the disciplinary action taken and said if they insisted on bringing Patton back, they could accept his resignation. Let any of the numerous Allied generals who wanted his command have it.

The furor finally died down, and Patton went on to glory with his Third Army.

Shortly after the slappings, General Jimmy Doolittle, in command of American air forces in North Africa, tested out a new English Spitfire-12 fighter. Flying over the Mediterranean near Italy, he spotted a lumbering German Heinkel bomber.

Never one to miss an opportunity, Doolittle got on the bomber's tail and, with the sun behind the German, shot him down in smoke and flames. He turned back over the Mediterranean, spotted two Italian fighters and promptly shot them down. Then, on the way to Palermo, he said to himself, "I think I'll drop in on Georgie Patton. He must be awfully lonely after all the heat on him."

So he signaled the control tower that General Doolittle was approaching and would like to pay his respects to General Patton, if that was agreeable. A couple of minutes later, the tower came back to Doolittle: "General Patton would be delighted to see you. Please proceed to runway four."

What Doolittle saw as he scrambled out of the cockpit dazzled him: Patton at the wheel of a Jeep decorated enough to have come off the Hollywood assembly line.

Flags of the United States, the Third Army and a three-star general fluttered from standards above the radiator and front fenders. Everything seemed highly polished brass: rims around the headlights, rods running from roof to the front of the vehicle and a dashboard holding-bar for the general to use when he stood in parades or reviews of troops.

Patton vaulted out of the Jeep, pearl-handled revolvers in reverse, and rushed to Doolittle. He bear hugged him, and in his high-pitched, fluty voice cried out, "I didn't think anybody in the world would come and see a miserable, mean old _____ like me."

"Georgie wept so hard that, by the time he had finished, my uniform, shirt and underwear were soaked clear to my skin," Doolittle told me later. "Then I flew back to my base in Morocco, where I found a message from General Eisenhower. He ordered me to proceed immediately to headquarters in Algiers."

"What is he calling *me* for?" Jimmy asked himself.

After an uneasy flight to Algiers, he entered headquarters. "General Eisenhower, who usually had a warm grin on his face, looked bleak. I gave him my best-snapped salute, reserved for the superior commanders. Ike merely waved his hand, and I knew I was in trouble.

" 'What's this I hear about you shooting down three planes?'

" 'Yes, sir. That's correct.'

"He stared right through me. 'Look, Jimmy. You're supposed to be commanding American air forces in North Africa. If you want to play hide and seek in the skies, shooting down Jerries and Ities, I can break you back to second lieutenant. Then you can spend all your time having fun. But if you want to command the air forces, as I want you to do, get back to base and stay where you belong. Now what's it going to be?' "

Doolittle saluted stiffly and said, "Sir, of course I want to continue to command."

Despite human-relations problems, General Ike regarded the progress in Sicily satisfactory. The 10,000-square-mile island, invaded on July 10, was taken on August 17. The Germans suffered 10,000 casualties and the Italians 100,000 losses (including men captured), to 31,158 Allied casualties.

With Sicily lost, Italians overthrew the Mussolini government. Capitulation seemed imminent, and the Germans rushed troops into southern Italy to shore up the wavering Italians.

On September 2, a British force landed on the toes of the Italian boot and moved toward the airfields near Foggia. On September 8, Italy surrendered, and the Allies took over their fleet. Then the United States Fifth Army, commanded by Lieutenant General Mark W. Clark, landed on the beaches along the gulf of Salerno.

Crack German troops counterattacked and, in four days and nights, some of the war's bloodiest fighting took place. Nazi troops tried to drive Clark's army into the sea. Valiant combat by Americans and support of naval gunfire and airforces finally repulsed them.

On the next day, the British Eighth Army joined the United States Fifth Army and, within two weeks, they captured Naples and had access to its fine harbor. The Italian campaign tied down twenty German divisions. Mountainous terrain, heavy rains, seas of mud (Russian military observers couldn't believe it) and stubborn German resistance slowed Allied progress.

In October, near Cassino—a strong defense point called the

German Winter Line—expert German fighters, rain, impossible infantry conditions and a narrow access route stopped the Allies on the road to Rome.

Field Marshal Sir Harold Alexander planned to outflank the bottleneck by sea and envelope the Germans.

For this maneuver, Clark utilized the United States Sixth Corps to land at Anzio, about thirty miles south of Rome. With the remainder of his Fifth Army, he drove against the Winter Line to divert the Germans from Anzio, trying to break through to the Liri Valley toward the Italian capital.

The landing was successful. The penetration of the Winter Line was not. Now the Germans from Cassino and Monte Cassino Abbey Heights systematically shelled the Sixth Corps on Anzio beach.

In a bloody contest, the Americans held the beachhead.

Prime Minister Churchill, Eisenhower and General Alfred Gruenther, chief of staff for General Mark W. Clark, met to discuss the strategy from that point.

Near the end of the session, Churchill reviewed the British strength present in the Mediterranean to support the operation: 1,042 front-line aircraft and more than 900 in reserve. He gave totals on available British and Commonwealth troops.

"As of eighteen-hundred hours yesterday, there were three battleships, seven cruisers, thirty destroyers and twenty-nine submarines, with nine operating off Anzio and ten near Malta." The prime minister leaned back in some self-satisfaction at his feat of memory.

When he invited comments, General Gruenther spoke up. "Mr. Prime Minister, if you will recheck your figures, I believe you will find that you have credited yourself with two more front-line aircraft than you possess and three less reserves. Also, I think you will find that the submarines are just the other way around: ten lying off Anzio and nine off Malta."

Churchill almost swallowed his Havana, rolled it around on his lips several times, turned to an aide and asked him to check the figures.

A few minutes later, the aide reported: "General Gruenther's figures are correct."

As the conference broke up, Churchill grasped Eisenhower's arm. "Ike, you'd better watch that young fellow. He's a human teletype. He will have your job!"

As the Allied drive for Rome became stalemated, I entered Eighth Air Force headquarters in Caserta, Italy, one day to see my good friend, General Ira Eaker. Something in the outer office stopped me: a lifesize photo mural of the lovely, smiling Kathy Harriman, daughter of United States Ambassador to Great Britain W. Averell Harriman. Huge black lettering under the photo read, The Sweetheart of the air force.

That puzzled me. Most of the guys had pinup gals like Chili Williams, Betty Grable or Dorothy Lamour, so how come Kathy? Surely there was a story in that.

There was. Ira told me what an uphill battle he had had in trying to convince others that his plan for daylight precision bombing of Germany should be adopted. From the start of World War II, the Royal Air Force had carried out night saturation bombing of strategic areas—a much safer and more conservative approach than Eaker's.

Ira felt strongly that a two-fisted attack—the RAF by night and the United States air forces by day—would knock out Germany's war-making potential more quickly. He presented his case at the Casablanca Conference to President Roosevelt, Prime Minister Churchill, the Joint Chiefs of Staff and Eisenhower. It was shot down. The consensus was that too many precious aircraft and lives would be lost, without inflicting serious damage on Germany. Churchill raised the strongest opposition. The United States air forces should continue night bombing with the RAF.

General Eaker knew that if he could convince the stubborn bulldog Churchill, he would have his plan sold. At Casablanca, he met Kathy Harriman. Kathy casually mentioned that Prime Minister Churchill had told her, "If you ever need a favor, come to me."

Ira pounced upon her statement. "Kathy, do *me* a favor. Let me borrow *your* favor! I need an appointment with the prime minister, to present the case for daylight precision bombing. It could speed the end of the war!"

"Granted," smiled Kathy, who set up the appointment.

Eaker talked feverishly from nine in the evening until two o'clock the next morning, machine-gunning arguments at Churchill, who, uncharacteristically, could hardly get in a word of objection.

When it was over, Churchill grasped the lapels of his suitcoat collar, jutted his massive chins toward the general and said, "Young man, you are wrong. . . ."

Eaker began to feel sick.

"I am entirely opposed to your plan," continued Churchill, pausing for dramatic effect, "but, I think you should have the right to try it."

General Ira Eaker and his Eighth Air Force tried it, and, without abnormal losses, devastated strategic industrial areas of Germany: ball-bearing plants, aircraft factories and synthetic-oil-production operations.

As I left Ira's offices, I nodded toward the photo mural of Kathy. I had to agree; she was indeed the sweetheart of the air force.

The time had come for General Ike to turn his attention to another theater of war—England—and another campaign— the most critical of the war. He had been appointed supreme commander for the invasion of France.

Ike informed General Marshall, President Roosevelt, Prime Minister Churchill and the Joint Chiefs of Staff that he needed Major General Sir Kenneth Strong to direct Intelligence operations in London and later on the continent.

General Beetle Smith, Ike's chief of staff, had mentioned casually to me in Algiers that one of the first shortcomings the Boss had discovered in Allied North African activities was in Intelligence operations.

Ike had asked that Strong be sent out to reorganize and

direct Intelligence needed to conclude the campaign and for the invasions of Sicily and Italy.

"The Boss is very high on Ken Strong," Beetle informed me. "He has been from the very beginning. Strong served in Berlin as Britain's military attaché and speaks German fluently. He participated in military maneuvers of German forces before Hitler invaded Poland. He knows intimately how Hitler and his marshals and generals think and work.

"Strong helped negotiate terms of the Italian surrender, and Ike admires not only his work in Intelligence but his skill in handling difficult situations and negotiations."

Near the end of 1943, Ike began to wind up affairs at his Algiers headquarters.

Colonel McChrystal filled me in on some of the last happenings there:

> One morning I received a phone call from Patton's staff officer. "Colonel McChrystal, General Patton has been called upon to make several speeches. What would you advise him to do?"
>
> "I will be much happier if you will tell the general to confine his remarks to 'Forward March' to his troops," I replied.
>
> That's not exactly the right approach to dealing with Georgie Patton, so I expected an uproar any minute. Two hours went by, and suddenly, a phone call came from Patton.
>
> I thought, "Now I'm going to have to tangle with *him!*"
>
> "McChrystal, what you said is the funniest thing I ever heard in my life!"

Now Eisenhower called his final staff meeting in North Africa. McChrystal told me:

> The Ike, as we referred to our commanding general, wanted any minor or major suggestions that might help him in his new assignment. When it was my turn, I mentioned having been stationed in England and that, due to that experience, I had a suggestion. "General, it is my opinion you should not be seen too much in public with your WAC driver, Kay Summersby."
>
> As soon as the words came out, I regretted them. After the conference, Ike thanked us all. A couple of hours later, a driver came to me and said, "the Old Man wants to see you."

I thought, "Why did I have to open my big mouth? I will be put on a slow boat for home."

Entering the Ike's office, I threw him a magnificent salute that made my elbow snap. "Sir!"

"Sit down, McChrystal," he said, wearing a poker face.

"Here it comes," I told myself.

"McChrystal, you probably know that if one doesn't get promoted, people will think he's no good. With that in mind, I have just recommended you to be a brigadier general."

That was the Ike for you. I was sorry he was leaving and that I had to stay behind.

D-Day or Disaster Day?

December had gone the way of all Decembers, and the harsh, wet January of 1944 brought sharp anticipation to England—especially southern England.

Allied troops migrated steadily southward. The civilian population showed a marked restlessness. No one knew for sure—yet everyone knew for sure—that this was the year for invading Hitler's *Festung Europa.*

That was the frame of reference in which I found myself in the London United Press offices. A cablegram on a plateau of newspapers that hid my desk caught my attention. I read it and felt sick.

On the verge of the greatest event of the war, my boss, Hugh Baillie, wanted me in the United States for a speaking tour to stimulate war-bond sales, blood-bank drives, scrap-metal collection and defense efforts. I kicked and screamed via cable, but what seemed inevitable proved to be inevitable.

Possibly I could complete the tour and rush back in time. I made an appointment with General Ike, to tell him my problem and get an approximate idea about when to expect D-Day. His clear-blue eyes twinkled. "Virgil, that's no problem. It's an opportunity."

"That's fine, but I don't want to be away when the balloon goes up."

He thought for a second and appraised me. "I don't see that you could miss the big show if you were back by early April. That's about all I can say."

That was all he had to say.

Back in the United States, I gave 173 talks and radio interviews in 7 weeks, lost 14 pounds and got back to England on a 27-ship convoy (an oceangoing mule train) with more than enough time.

What a change in southern England! This sylvan, peaceful area crawled with artillery, tanks, ammunition, aircraft and uniformed men and women.

A strange contrast greeted me under blooming English elms: ugly, blunt-prowed amphibious LSTs, metal barrels of ammunition, stacks of gigantic reels of steel cable, vehicle wheels and ominous-looking bombs.

In open fields along the coast were P-51 Mustang fighters, swarmed over by crews in fatigue clothing, who cleaned off thick weather-protecting grease. Nearby were gigantic piles of bombs, artillery and mortar shells.

My eyes popped at an incongruous sight; as far as I could see, across green meadows, were new, shiny locomotives and thousands of flat and tank cars that would soon end up somewhere on the continent.

Then Eisenhower asked Prime Minister Churchill to seal off southern England from the rest of the United Kingdom. Soon there would be a showdown between the allied offense and the German defense.

Intelligence reports and photos produced a frightening picture of Nazi defenses: an extravagantly thick concrete wall along the Atlantic (a coastal Maginot Line), concrete-and-steel command posts, blockhouses and firing points.

General Ike was aware of land-and-sea obstacles surpassing any ever built to discourage and destroy invaders. Near the beaches, sharp steel pilings, visible only at low tide, could rip out the bottoms of ships.

More than 500,000 steel piles sprouted up from the beaches, along with hundreds of thousands of wooden stakes, armed with mines and interlocking iron bars—all connected with barbed wire. Beyond that were walls of barbed wire, mine fields and antitank ditches.

Added to these man-made horrors was one that neither men nor Hitler's supermen could ever have conceived: the English Channel, diabolically treacherous water—particularly during storms—with perpetual motion of unpredictable, choppy currents and crosscurrents.

The element of surprise could be an equalizer during invasion. Eisenhower knew that history is studded with examples of surprise helping to turn the tide of battle or bringing victory in ancient and recent wars.

Hannibal's troops and their elephants used a little-known, snow-covered route over the Alps to defeat the Romans. George Washington and his men crossed the Delaware River on a frigid Christmas night in 1776 to seize Trenton and boost sagging Colonial morale. Early in the war against the Axis, General Jimmy Doolittle led United States Army Air Force bombers from "Shangri-la" to blast Tokyo, showing the Nipponese that they were vulnerable and that the Americans could bounce back from Pearl Harbor and Bataan.

General Ike was well aware that one major element of surprise for the Allied invasion of western Europe had long disappeared: the selected month for D-Day. As agreed upon at the 1943 Teheran Conference by President Roosevelt, Prime Minister Churchill and Premier Stalin, D-Day was to be no later than May 1944, to coordinate with a counteroffensive by the Russians and to allow the most possible, good fighting weather. The smoke from Churchill's omnipresent cigar had not cleared before German Intelligence knew the approximate period for the great cross-Channel thrust.

Remaining surprise elements were the precise date, the exact landing area along the 1,800-mile western European coastline and the strength of the invaders.

Millions of tons of weapons and supplies were massed in the south of England, seemingly enough to sink that part of the nation. The Germans were snug in their fortifications, and the Allies hoped for more landing craft and the end of contrary weather, which had whipped, churned and tortured the English Channel into a Nazi ally.

General Dwight D. Eisenhower, of Abilene, Kansas, was about to conduct a symphony—on a magnitude that would make the mind reel—of men, ships and aircraft: 1.5 million American officers and troops, 1 million British and Canadians, and thousands of Norwegians, Danes, French, Belgians, Czechs and Poles.

The invasion armada—nothing this gigantic had ever been imagined, let alone assembled—was composed of more than 900 warships, from PT boats to heavy cruisers and battleships, including 229 LSTs and 3,372 landing craft. Carrying out their rendezvous in the English Channel's nightmare waters, from ports separated by 200 miles, would be an almost-incomprehensible feat. Men and ships were to be aided by 11,000 aircraft from 163 airfields, giving cover and support and dropping airborne troops behind coastal fortifications to intercept German reinforcements.

Success would be impossible without the right combination of moon, tide, sunrise and weather. Darkness was essential to keep the Germans from knowing the strength and specific destination of the invasion prongs. Moonlight was necessary to reveal

bomber targets. Timing of the triphibious attack had to be accurate enough to allow forty minutes of daylight to finish
softening-up bombing and bombardment.

The tide had to be low enough to disclose near-shore and
beach obstacles for hurried removal. But the biggest element,
the most-fickle imponderable, was something that Eisenhower
couldn't control: the weather. Stormy weather would conceal
targets, roil the waters, generate heavy surf and make beach
landings treacherous to impossible.

Operation Overlord could not succeed unless the Allies could
delay the Germans in bringing up reinforcements. Key bridges,
freight yards, rail lines and switching areas throughout western
France and Belgium had to be bombed, Eisenhower insisted.
Prime Minister Churchill, his mobile chins massed into pugnac-
ity, disagreed. "It will cost 80,000 lives," he said.

"You know we intend to warn the French and Belgians,"
replied Eisenhower. "Losses will be only a fraction of that." He
refused to yield; the bombings were carried out and the objectives were leveled with a small fraction of the losses predicted
by Churchill.

Throughout most of May, the weather had been ideal for
invasion, but the landing-craft situation hadn't been. When that
condition was corrected, early June brought perversely foul
weather. One low-pressure area after another chased over the
English Channel—sullen gray clouds, driving winds, and frequent rain.

An officer at SHAEF headquarters reminded General
Eisenhower that the weather is always neutral.

"Nonsense," Ike snapped. "Bad weather is obviously the
enemy of the side that seeks to launch projects requiring good
weather."[1]

No one could convince Eisenhower that the weather wasn't
wearing a German uniform. All through May, he had met daily
with meteorologists of the SHAEF staff, headed by Group Captain J. M. Stagg, a tall, dour and laconic Scotsman and weather
wizard.

The right combination of moon, tides and sunrise would

come together on June 5, 6, and 7. After two weeks, some of the conditions would be right again, but the moon would be wrong. Furthermore, delay would shorten the summer fighting season.

The plan's first phase, air attack, had already been realized, blasting the Luftwaffe out of the skies and bombing rail systems, bridges, roundhouses and vital points in the highway system to isolate the sixty-mile Normandy coastal area. The air mission for D-Day was to clobber specific coastal defenses, giving air cover to troops and offering fighter-bomber support as troops moved inland.

The naval D-Day plan had even more missions: bombarding coastal defenses, sweeping mines, escorting troopships and supply ships, offering gunfire support, and protecting the armada from surface and submarine attack.

Ground troops, tank corps, artillerymen and supplies were to be disgorged along Normandy beaches. British and Canadian forces were to attack on the left, near the mouth of the Orne river. At the extreme right, American troops, under Major General J. Lawton Collins, were to assail what was designated Utah Beach, on the Cherbourg Peninsula, and capture the port of Cherbourg within ten to thirty days.

Fighter-bombers were to coordinate with infantry men in taking land that would permit effective tank strength, followed by artillery. Strategy called for Montgomery's British Second Army to seize the flat ground south of Caen. Between this thrust and that on Utah Beach, American troops were designated to move inland from Omaha Beach, to the right of Caen and parallel with the British.

Also, Lord Louis Mountbatten's plan to supply high-test fuel for tanks and other military vehicles was to be carried out: the laying of a four-inch pipe, flexible enough to be wound and unwound like rubber hose, under the English Channel. Eventually, the Pluto Line grew to twenty lines, pumping a million gallons of gasoline a day to French cities hundreds of miles away.

Always foremost in General Eisenhower's mind was how to take military objectives with the smallest possible loss of men; in sharp contrast with Russian officers, who on occasion activated mined areas with advance-guard infantrymen so that tanks and other troops could pass safely.

On the eve of D-Day, Ike had to make a decision that brought furrows to his brow and a grim set to his jaw. Should he permit an airborne attack on the Cotentin Peninsula? This sector was vital to success of the initial landings and to the rapid capture of Cherbourg, whose harbor would be desperately needed for unloading follow-up troops and materiel.

Despite the best planning of strategists, the only part of the Cotentin Peninsula's east coast on which troops could land was Utah Beach. "Suicide Beach" might have been a better name for it. Beyond the flat, sandy area was a broad lagoon. The only ways into the peninsula's interior were nine narrow necks of land two miles long. General Eisenhower often tossed in bed, imagining the consequences to American boys if Germans held the exits with withering machine-gun fire.

To prevent such carnage, two American paratroop divisions were to be dropped inland, to hold the exits to the causeways. Yet this territory (called bocage country), with many thick and strong hedgerows, seemed designed by nature to discourage airborne invasion.

Added to the hostile bocage country were many antiaircraft installations to blast slow-moving troop transport aircraft and gliders. Despite these hazards, Eisenhower felt he had no choice. He decided in favor of the operation.

The strategy was set; or so General Eisenhower thought until he received a letter on May 30 from Air Chief Marshal Leigh-Mallory. This hit him with the impact of a baseball bat. Leigh-Mallory opposed the Cotentin airborne landings. Due to unsuitable landing conditions and concentration of antiaircraft guns and mobile ground units, two fine American airborne divisions would be slaughtered. He estimated a loss of 50 percent of the paratroopers and 70 percent of the glider pilots.

What if he happened to be right? Eisenhower asked himself. If Cotentin was impossible, then Utah Beach was hopeless, and the whole invasion structure suddenly seemed far too risky—

maybe even foolhardy. But, on the other hand, cancellation of Utah Beach would permit defenders to mass more men against invasion at other points, lowering the chances of success.

For hours, Eisenhower thought and rethought the situation. Then an idea occurred to him: Leigh-Mallory's prediction was based on an *estimate!* No Allied invasions of Sicily or Italy had offered such disheartening statistics. He snuffed out a half-smoked cigarette and phoned Leigh-Mallory.

"Leigh, I've thought it through carefully. We're going to carry out the airborne attack as planned. I'll give you immediate confirmation in writing. This will get you off the hook."

England's south coast, like the Portsmouth headquarters of General Ike at Supreme Headquarters Allied Expeditionary Forces (SHAEF) and those of General Montgomery, seemed electric with the nearness of D-Day. Monty had been placed in tactical command of the invasion until a beachhead was established.

Approximately six miles from the city, in a wooded area, General Eisenhower lived in a caravan that was convenient to his large office tent but seemingly too unpretentious and barren to be the heart of a military campaign unprecedented in magnitude and complexity. Yet the day-and-night activity, the ceaseless comings and goings of Allied officers, rapid-fire meetings and bubbling of coffee pots revealed that little time remained.

All phases of the invasion were ready: all but the weather. Even the many mountains of supplies appeared poised for instant action. Vessels crowded every available port. Southern England was sealed off from the rest of the island. No one but authorized military or government personnel could move in or out.

Briefed on their D-Day roles, combat troops for the first assault waves remained high-strung and restless, behind confining barbed-wire fences that preserved secrecy. In hundreds of camps, barracks and vehicle areas, all units seemed tense and overconscious of the clock. The schedule called for them to arrive at embarkation points precisely when transport ships were ready for them.

Twice daily—9:30 P.M. and 4:00 A.M.—starting on June 1, a United States armed-forces command car stenciled with white stars, stopped at General Ike's office tent or caravan. He was driven to a place a mile away, where many important conferences were held: Southwick House, a three-story country mansion whose exterior paint showed some neglect due to wartime shortages.

The general and key commanders felt the pressure of readiness and the deep frustration of unrelenting bad weather.

On June 2, RAF Group Captain J. M. Stagg, head of the meteorological committee made up of British and American experts, stood before weather charts stacked on a tripod. He could not hide his pessimism about a succession of low-pressure areas—"a typical December depression"—bringing in gusty winds, choppy seas and a low cloud cover.

All the letter *R*s spoken by Stagg came out with the most mellow Scottish burr that General Ike had ever heard.

Despite the prediction, General Eisenhower clung to the agreed-upon D-Day of June 5 and ordered ships harbored in Irish seaports to set sail on the next morning. This was the only way he could assure that they would reach rendezvous points on time.

On the evening of Saturday, June 3, Stagg again addressed General Eisenhower and his commanders of the Allied naval and air force, the United States Air Force in Europe, the British Admiralty and the British Air Ministry. Another low-pressure area would bring stormy weather for at least forty-eight hours. "There's little likelihood that a benevolent high will move in for twenty-four hours beyond that."

Gloom settled over the group. Harsh weather would apparently kill off the prime invasion dates. "We'll hold off the final decision for postponement until the four A.M. meeting on June fourth," announced General Eisenhower.

Again, at that time, the report was dismal: low clouds, high winds and formidable wave action would make handling small boats difficult, landings hazardous, naval bombardment inaccurate, and air support hopeless.

General Eisenhower turned questioningly to British Admiral Sir Bertram H. Ramsay, who replied: "We can handle the mechanics of landing, but adjusting gunfire would be difficult. I am neither for nor against going."

Eisenhower glanced at General Montgomery. "I favor going. Otherwise, we risk the loss of security and the high morale of the troops."

None of the other commanders agreed with Montgomery, especially Tedder and Leigh-Mallory. "Air dominance has always been essential to success of the overall plan," Tedder said sharply. "Under the circumstances, there could be no air support at all on June fifth."

General Ike said, without hesitation, "We'll postpone for twenty-four hours."

Immediately, orders were issued to ships and troops at sea to find ports. Heavy bombardier vessels from Clyde and Belfast, and even mine sweepers already in the Channel, weathered the wind, rain and heavy seas to land and faced the hectic job of being readied for action the next day.

"No break in the weather," was the report at that evening's 9:30 meeting. Prime Minister Churchill and Foreign Minister Anthony Eden had no constructive suggestions. Like everyone else, they understood the dire consequences of more delay. The meeting was adjourned. A final decision would be made at 4:00 A.M on June 5.

Many years later, Anthony Eden, British foreign minister, told me that when he and Churchill returned to London by special train, the prime minister shook his head, his considerable jowls trembling. "I wouldn't want to be in Ike's shoes tonight, because he's going to have to make this decision by himself. I pray that God gives him excessive wisdom and strength."

That night, General Ike slept fitfully, wakening at 3:15 in the black of morning. Unwelcome thoughts jostled one another for attention. He—no one else—was responsible for the life or death of hundreds of thousands and the success or failure of the mission.

Winds of near-hurricane force screamed through the trees, rocked his "circus wagon" and hurled horizontal sheets of rain against the caravan.

A wry idea brought the hint of a smile to his broad mouth as he finished shaving. What sane person would even go outside in such weather, let alone launch an invasion in it?

He dressed for rain, considered the warmth and brightness of his circus wagon for an instant and opened the door into the cold and darkness.

Streaks of wind-propelled rain splashed his face as he felt his way down the aluminum steps. At the end of the soggily crunching gravel walk, he could make out the shadowy configuration of his car, waiting with lights out.

Through muddy, pooled roads, the car sloshed to naval headquarters in the dark Southwick House.

Each time General Eisenhower entered, the mansion's interior brightness came as a slight shock. The emptiness of the library's dark, floor-to-ceiling wood bookcases on three walls always seemed surprising. Most of the commanders were already there, some standing near a large table draped with a green baize covering, others seated on a pair of sofas or in easy chairs. As the wind whistled and hurled rain against tall windows, the thick blackout curtains moved almost imperceptibly. Eisenhower sensed the high tension. Usually his meetings were relaxed. British commanders had grown to like the informal atmosphere and exchange of ideas. Not this morning!

General Eisenhower turned the conference over to Group Captain Stagg. The foul weather predicted by the meteorological committee for the Normandy coast had materialized. If the Allies had made June 5 D-Day, a major disaster would have occurred. The general trembled. Then came an astonishing announcement: ". . . some rapid and unexpected developments. . . ."

Almost as one, General Eisenhower and the commanders leaned toward Stagg.

Off the coast of Spain, a stationary high-pressure area was moving in a northwesterly direction. "This should result in gradually clearing skies and moderation of winds, over both the Channel and assault areas, for probably thirty-six hours." Stagg added that a partly cloudy condition should prevail on the morning of June 6, leading to cloudiness by noon and more wind and rain by June 7.

General Eisenhower slowly paced the library, hands clasped behind his back, his brow furrowed and a subtle suggestion of perspiration on his face.

There was reason for some cheer, but what if the first waves landed successfully, and rough weather prevented a buildup? Troops cut off from reinforcement would be driven back into the ocean.

Everyone wanted more reassuring details. Stagg said there was no guarantee. "What we have supplied is only a summary of probabilities—not of certainties," he explained. It would be impossible to say with certainty what kind of Channel weather would develop within thirty hours—just as it would have been to have forecast the break in the weather that was about to occur.

Suddenly all the commanders started talking: nervous, tension-packed questions, answers, comments, opinions. Admiral Ramsay gained the floor. The American naval task force destined for Omaha and Utah Beaches had to sail in a half hour, to arrive at destination by H-Hour on June 6. A postponement would mean a delay of forty-eight hours, because the ships would have to be refueled.

General Eisenhower turned to his commanders for their votes.

"It's a gamble, but I'm in favor of June sixth," replied General Beetle Smith.

Again, General Montgomery cast his vote to go.

The cloud-cover that was forecast for the afternoon of the sixth would probably deprive pilots of visibility to support ground forces. "It's chancy, at best," commented Leigh-Mallory.

Listening, thinking, pacing, General Eisenhower glanced at

the clock. Delay would demoralize the men. Waves of troops were already moving southward to staging areas, to replace those at point of embarkation. Bringing men back from ships would result in the greatest chaos since the Tower of Babel. Security could easily be breached. The Russians were impatient about the Allied invasion promised for May.

Intelligence reports from Major General Sir Kenneth Strong gave chilling details of horror missiles so devastating that they could flatten Britain's major cities and harbors, turning the tide of war. The Nazis were producing hundreds of V-2s and rapidly building launching sites for them.

Too fresh in Eisenhower's mind was the security violation of an American general, who, while drinking at a pub, announced that D-Day would come before June 15. The fact that he had been shorn of his stars and shipped back home could not recapture what he had said.

Two other security blunders had Ike on edge. A Top Secret Overlord brief had been accidentally addressed and sent to a young woman in Chicago, and an Associated Press teletype operator in London, thinking her machine was disconnected, had sent a practice message to New York, saying that General Eisenhower had announced Allied landings in France.

Every hour that passed gave the Germans more opportunity to learn about British Lieutenant General Sir Frederick Morgan's brilliant invasion plans, Overlord and Operation Bodyguard.

The latter program had been ingeniously designed to encourage the German fixation that the Allies needed a major port immediately, for landing of troops and materiel, and that they would invade Pas-de-Calais, across the narrow western part of the English Channel.

Bodyguard outlined the strategy for assault on Pas-de-Calais from Dover, designating units to be deployed and support data. Detailed documentation about logistics and tactics made it totally convincing. This eventually fell into the hands of German Intelligence.

Making the Bodyguard plan seem authentic were simulated landing craft of wood, sheet iron and canvas; creations that could have served admirably on a Hollywood set. These were anchored in the Thames River estuary and other waterways and harbors opposite Calais, as were the real things in all southern England ports. Also, facsimile concrete aprons, to make possible landing on beaches, were constructed at and around Dover, just as the real things appeared in all English southern coast harbors. Near Dover, phony staging areas for housing of imaginary invasion troops also looked authentic in German aerial photographs.

Eisenhower recalled that people, as well as objects, were key parts of Operation Bodyguard. Sleight of hand had been performed with top American generals and their army groups, to manipulate German military defensive thinking.

Intelligence agents of the Germans kept close track of Allied military brass and were well aware that General Omar Bradley was in command of the First United States Army Group. Then—as far as the Germans were concerned—the First United States Army Group disappeared, and the Twelfth United States Army Group was created, under Bradley's command.

All at once, colorful General George Patton, not commanding any specific army group, began appearing in many parts of Britain, getting heavy press coverage. German agents began to suspect that Patton had taken over the First United States Army Group, formerly under Bradley.

The Germans respected and feared Patton's military ability and concluded that the Allies would put Patton in charge of the major invasion thrust at Pas-de-Calais. Anything else would be a diversion to cover the major thrust.

As these thoughts whirled through his mind, General Eisenhower glanced at the clock again: 4:15 A.M. Only he could make the D-Day decision for June 6. He sat down, lost in thought, as his commanders watched and waited. Then he spoke softly, as if to himself, "The question is, how long can you hang this operation on the end of a limb and let it hang there?" [2]

As if suddenly realizing he had revealed his innermost thinking, he stood before his commanders, the muscles of his face taut, a ceiling light reflecting from his nearly bald head. "I am quite positive we must give the order. I don't like it, but there it is. I don't see how we can do anything else." Then, turning to his commanders, he said loudly and decisively, "Okay, we'll go!"

Modern Miracle

As General Ike stepped into the blackness toward his car, wind-whipped rain lashed at him. There was something important he still had to do.

Within the bright circus wagon, he removed his dripping raincoat, toweled beads of moisture from his face and sat down at a small desk. If things went wrong, he wanted no one else blamed for his decision.

On a scrap of notebook paper, he hastily scribbled:

> Our landings in the Cherbourg-Havre area have failed to gain a satisfactory foothold, and I have withdrawn the troops. My decision to attack at this time and place was based upon the best information available. The troops, the air, and the navy did all that bravery and devotion to duty could do. If any blame or fault is attached to the attempt, it is mine alone.

In nervous concern, he mistakenly dated the note July 5, instead of June 5, and slipped it into his wallet.

Wind screamed through the trees, shuddered the caravan and dashed a sheet of rain against it. He could not get the weather out of his mind. The Mark Twain witticism that had been worn into a cliché came to him: "Everybody talks about the weather, but nobody does anything about it."

Nobody? An idea lit up his mind, as he told me many years later. Why hadn't he thought of it earlier? There was *Somebody* who could do something about the weather! General Eisenhower fell to his knees, closed his eyes, and clasped his hands in prayer: "God, Creator of the world and all things, grant us good weather and protection of Allied troops."

He hesitated for an instant. "God, I've done the best I can. You are my Commander in Chief. I now turn the command over to You!"

Two weeks before the invasion, I was told to be ready at any hour of day or night and to know at all times where all United Press correspondents could be reached. Several of them would be assigned, with others, to invasion forces, and their dispatches pooled for all news services, newspapers and radio stations.

Between 125 and 150 full-time war correspondents in the United Kingdom experienced the gamut of events—day-and-night bombings of London, the buzz bombs, and now the V-2s. Some had gone on bombing missions over the continent. Others had joined convoys enroute to the Mediterranean or to frigid Murmansk, near the top of the world, close to the borders of Finland.

Those consistently on the job suffered greater casualties than any other units connected with the armed forces, because they followed the action, to report the scenes and sounds and smells of war.

Frequently, when I or one of our United Press correspondents, Walter Cronkite, asked to go on an air raid, the pilot would invariably say, "Why any fool would go on a mission over Germany unless he has to, mystifies me. You must be an idiot."

Invasion rumors were flying thicker than hail and traveling as fast as the speed of sound. Unanswered questions flooded our minds. Exactly when would it take place? Where? Norway? No, that's too far from the heart of action. Southern France?

Ridiculous! The buildup would probably be in North Africa, if that were the target. Pas-de-Calais? That's nearest England, but wouldn't that be too obvious to the Germans? Why were some correspondents equipped with winter gear: thermal underwear, warm coats and high boots? Could it be Norway *and* another invasion point?

So much confusion entered our minds that the most likely military course seemed the least likely. As events unfolded, we could only conclude that Kenneth Strong's Intelligence had done an admirable job—even to using us as an additional factor to fool the Germans. Only twenty-eight of the correspondents accredited to supreme headquarters were chosen to cover the opening D-Day assault phases. Correspondents were assigned to be with the infantry, several with the navy and others at air force headquarters, to cover airborne troop jumps and activities at General Eisenhower's headquarters.

Shortly before D-Day, several correspondents were phoned early in the morning by Colonel Jack Redding, of the Public Relations Office. "I'd like you to be in my office in an hour. You'd better pack a musette bag. You may be going out of town."

There had been so many previous false alarms that even this call struck some as phony. Upon arrival at Redding's office, they were given specially treated clothing as protection against possible gas attacks, blankets, a shovel for digging a foxhole, seasickness pills, *K* rations and a medical kit. After several shivery nights in tents air conditioned by harsh winds and humidified by heavy rain, some correspondents were escorted to the office of Major General Clarence Huebner, commander of the Big Red division, who welcomed them in his unique and hearty way:

> Men, I want you to regard yourselves as members of this unit. You will have complete freedom of movement, and I want you to get all the information you can. We are ready to help you in every possible way. The people at home won't know what is happening, unless you are given the information.
>
> You know how to take care of yourselves, but if, unluckily, a

shell should get you, we'll do all we can. If you're wounded, we'll take care of you. If you're killed, we'll bury you. So you have nothing to worry about.

Several correspondents grinned at the general's social-security program.

One of my greatest disappointments was having to remain behind to supervise the United Press London office, write the lead story for the day and night services, and coordinate sending the invasion news stories that would soon pour out of the continent.

All night long, and during the invasion, waves of bombers roared over western France like leaders of a thunderstorm, blasting coastal and inland targets with 10,000 tons of bombs, making orange explosions. Nothing in the history of warfare could have come close to the savagery of this attack. It topped anything in Dante's *Inferno*. Around midnight, airborne troops dropped behind the Cotentin Peninsula.

Earlier, the Allied armada—2,700 ships of all sizes, dimensions and functions, including warships, transports, landing ships and smaller craft—had rendezvoused south of the Isle of Wight in a great five-mile radius called Piccadilly Circus.

Ragged white and gray clouds, scudding before the brisk wind, occasionally let moonlight shine on the English Channel's four-to-six-foot waves. Everywhere, the water bobbed with vessels, as if all the ships in the world were there waiting.

These vessels maneuvered into fifty-nine mighty convoys and five task forces twenty miles in breadth (one for each of the beaches: Juno, Sword, Gold, Omaha, Utah), heading into ten lanes marked with twinkling buoys left by minesweepers that had made the lanes safe. Fast ships sliced off into the lanes designated for them. Slower ships took other lanes.

Many ships towed gray barrage balloons, not unlike those that kept German aircraft from flying too low over London. Explosives and small bombs were wired to the balloons' steel cables. Landing troops sat crowded on decks, hugging their equipment.

Now battleships, cruisers and destroyers fired deafening

shells at coastal defenses. Even troops with cotton earplugs recoiled from the continuous firing. As transports neared shore, they disgorged troops down yawing, netlike rope ladders, into snub-nosed landing craft shaped like king-sized coffins, dancing crazily in the choppy waters.

Some of the first correspondents to land on French soil followed the initial wave of the 116th Regiment. A veteran correspondent told me that he looked around and everyone else appeared to be trembling violently. "I knew everybody was scared, but not *that* scared. And then I realized the appearance of trembling was caused by the concussion from the giant navy guns. The air simply vibrated from sound."

The 116th Regiment ran into hard luck in the opening minutes. Thirty-two amphibious tanks, which were designed to give fire power to troops that had already landed, were put into the pitching waters some 6,000 yards from shore. Wild wave action and winds ripped huge, inflated canvas life preservers from thirty tanks, which gurgled and plunged to the bottom, some with their crews. Only two of these tanks made shore.

Long lines of barriers, constructed under the direction of Field Marshal Rommel, and thousands of flat mines attached to wooden posts and steel spikes, caused explosions, injuries, deaths and indeterminable delays and confusion. Correspondents reported the beach as "one mass of moving chaos."

From SHAEF came this D-Day announcement: "Under the command of General Eisenhower, Allied naval forces, supported by strong air forces, began landing Allied armies this morning on the coast of France."

Next, General Eisenhower broadened his order of the day to soldiers, sailors and airmen of the Allied Expeditionary Force:

> You are about to embark on a great crusade. . . . In company with our brave Allies and brothers in arms on other fronts, you will bring about the destruction of the German war machine, elimination of Nazi tyranny over the oppressed people of Europe, and security for ourselves in a free world. . . . We will accept

nothing less than full victory. Good luck, and let us all beseech the blessing of Almighty God upon this great and noble undertaking.

During the day and into the night, the skies were gray with Allied aircraft—wave after wave—towing troop-carrying gliders with taut steel cables. As Allied forces scored spectacular success on Gold, Juno, Sword, and Utah beaches, they met with unexpected resistance at Omaha and, only after remarkable heroics, gained a tenuous foothold toward early evening.

What the Germans next observed by telescope from their fortifications was almost as much of a surprise as the D-Day attack itself. Numerous tugboats headed for the beaches, towing huge concrete boxes. Like blockhouses on steel, these watertight boxes had been anchored in English river mouths for months—a riddle to the Germans.

In their wake was a line of ancient, derelict boats. Some could hardly negotiate the unruly, swamping waters. They appeared to have come out of Queen Victoria's times, resurrected from maritime mortuaries.

Once the cement blockhouses were maneuvered into two long rows, from far out to near shore, their seacocks and caissons were opened, and water flooded in, causing them to sink, forming an artificial harbor. Mulberry harbors, conceived by Winston Churchill and designed and developed under Lord Louis Mountbatten, enabled the invaders to bring in men and mountains of materiel.

To quiet the unruly, restless Channel even more, the old ships, anchored in a semicircle outside the Mulberries, were sunk to make up a breakwater, code named Gooseberry.

Taking advantage of these harbors, Allied engineering experts bolted together giant steel structures as bridges to shore. After a few days' use, the American port, Mulberry A, was totally destroyed by a violent storm. The British port, Mulberry B, held together and served day and night, long after Cherbourg was taken and reconstructed after Nazi sabotage.

General Eisenhower, at naval headquarters, listened intently for reports from Omaha Beach and another landing site that, from the outset, seemed a problem: Utah Beach and the Cotentin Peninsula, which Leigh-Mallory had predicted would bring enormous losses.

Late on the previous evening, General Ike had made a surprise visit to the camps of the United States 82nd and 101st Airborne divisions, outfits that would drop behind Cotentin Peninsula.

The paratroopers, faces blackened with paint and dressed in bulky combat uniforms, broke into a cheer when they saw that their supreme commander had come to see them off. Eisenhower stayed until the last man was in the air. Despite a number of negative factors that befell the American airborne divisions—missed parachute drops, the crashing of numerous gliders in the bocage country and some landings in a swamp that no one knew was there—they captured land as far in from the coastline as seven miles with casualties of 20 percent, much lower than that predicted by Leigh-Mallory.

Their landings so surprised, confused and diverted the Germans that parts of the United States Fourth Division Infantry waded ashore without enemy fire. By late afternoon, airborne troops had captured the causeway inlets and joined infantry troops.

General Ike was cheered by the news. All D-Day objectives had been reached. The first to phone to congratulate him on the success at Cotentin was Leigh-Mallory, who apologized for having given Eisenhower additional concern.

Taking nothing from Allied surprises, ingenuity, gallantry, logistics, efficiency and persistency, the D-Day victory came about, in no small measure, due to the weather and problems of the defending Germans. Although hazardous Channel conditions caused many Allied landing accidents and losses of men and equipment, the weather in reality turned out to favor Overlord.

The wind velocity, cloud cover and churning waters on June fifth had convinced Field Marshal Erwin Rommel, commander of the Channel-area German forces, that invasion was highly improbable. So he traveled to Ulm to celebrate his wife's birthday, and then planned to visit Berchtesgaden, to convince Hitler that he needed more panzer divisions. News of the invasion kept him from seeing Hitler.

Severe weather conditions had made other important commanders feel it was safe to leave. The commanding officer of a reserve panzer group had left for Belgium. A second commander was away for the night. A third key commander had traveled to Brittany, to direct a military exercise.

But the stormy weather was not limited to the English Channel and Normandy. It had long prevailed in relations between Rommel and his commander in chief, Field Marshal Karl Gerd von Rundstedt, and between Hitler and von Rundstedt. Rommel made a practice of going around von Rundstedt, communicating directly with Hitler. Von Rundstedt believed that the invasion would come across the narrowest part of the Channel: Dover to Dieppe, Rommel did, too, at first.

Adolf Hitler, who often acted on intuition, concluded that the Allies would land in Normandy, but his hunch was based on some facts, according to General Warlimont, a member of Hitler's staff. Intelligence reports had shown that most American troops were in southwest England. If the invasion were to be from Dover, wouldn't the Americans have shifted to the southeast? Hitler theorized that a major port, such as Cherbourg, would be one of the first Allied objectives.

Many times, between March and May, Hitler said that the Allies might land between Caen and Cherbourg. Von Rundstedt insisted that Pas-de-Calais would be the prime target, for practical, logistical reasons. By failing to plan on Hitler's intuition, Rundstedt lost stature. Rommel agreed with Hitler and made Normandy defenses even more dense. Time and lack of resources kept the Germans from making the Atlantic Wall in that area as strong as the defenses at the Seine River.

Another storm center of the Germans was sharp disagreement between von Rundstedt and Rommel on the best defense strategy. Von Rundstedt believed that fixed installations, such as the Great Wall of China and the Maginot Line, were vulnerable. He also knew that the "unassailable" Atlantic Wall was made not only of concrete, but also of propaganda. Nothing could stop the Allies from landing and penetrating inland to a degree. Therefore, he favored a mighty counteroffensive, to cut down the Allies after landing.

"No," contradicted Rommel. The best tactics would be to direct withering fire on the Allies before they could land or dig in. Allied air power, as well as naval and artillery fire, could prevent (or at least delay) the bringing up of reserves.

Hitler came around to Rommel's view. He drove a final wedge between the two field marshals, creating a paradoxical situation, making Rommel, the inferior officer, superior to von Rundstedt.

Another factor not known by the Allies was that Hitler had decided to direct the battle strategy and use of reserves from distant Berchtesgaden: a frustration to both Rommel and von Rundstedt.

A schizophrenic defense policy, the weather, absence of key commanders from Normandy, and Hitler's insistence on being commander in chief by remote control led to eventual defeat.

Long after the Normandy invasion, when the whole picture of German conduct just before and during D-Day was pieced together from Intelligence data, General Ike realized that not only his prayers had been answered. The Allies had actually experienced a modern miracle.

The weather that he feared would defeat the Allied invasion had, in reality, helped to defeat the Germans.

General Ike Versus the Prime Minister

Now it can be told!

General Ike had the greatest respect and affection for Prime Minister Winston Spencer Churchill, but he often became exasperated when Churchill interfered in his military planning.

The prime minister fought Ike on the Normandy invasion. He predicted that the beaches would be choked with American and British youth and the tides would be "running red with their blood."

General Ike thought estimates of 90 percent casualties was far off, outrageous and calculated to discourage Allied invasion.

After checking the final plans, Churchill glanced up at Ike. "If by winter you have a bridgehead from the mouth of the Seine to Cherbourg and the Brittany Peninsula, and if you have thirty-six divisions ashore, I'll consider it a victory; and if you have Le Havre as well, I'll regard it as decisive."

"By Christmas, I shall be on the Rhine," said Ike.

He was.

"I would usually give in to the prime minister on political

matters, but not on military affairs," General Ike informed me during retirement. "Often I was taxed to exhaustion finding diplomatic ways to turn down his abundant military ideas."

Sometime after D-Day, in late July, Churchill visited Eisenhower at Portsmouth, to sell him on sending troops to Pas-de-Calais to knock out launching sites for buzz bombs and the devastating V-2 missiles.

Allied bombers were already plastering the area, while avoiding damage to the harbor. "We simply don't have enough landing craft to invade Pas-de-Calais while sustaining our advance in Normandy. Besides, this port is too well fortified and manned."

"Well, General, if you won't do that, why don't you seal off the Germans in the ports of Antwerp and Dieppe? Let them sit there and rot as we go on."

"Mr. Prime Minister, if we divide our forces, we won't be able to push the Normandy invasion as planned."

Churchill reflected for an instant. "Well, why don't we then strike Germany through the soft underbelly of Europe, the Balkan States?" This was a revival of Churchill's old World War I campaign, which had failed. "Entry through the Balkans would fan the flame of those who hate Hitler to open revolt," continued the prime minister.

"Such a campaign would take men and supplies away from our major thrust: invasion of Germany and destruction of her fighting potential," replied Ike.

The prime minister was not easily discouraged. "The Balkan campaign would cost fewer Allied lives than an assault on the south of France," he insisted, the omnipresent, brown, Havana cigar clamped between his teeth.

"But we need more port facilities, to drive the Germans from the occupied countries and destroy them in their own land," countered Ike. "We need Marseilles."

"Ah, my dear General. That is where you are in error. Troops and supplies from America could enter through ports in Brittany."

Ike shrugged his shoulders. "Cherbourg is the only Brittany

port available now, and it is hardly adequate to support the troops presently in the field, let alone reinforcements and their supplies. We must have Marseilles. General Devers can come up through Marseilles and sweep France clean of Germans and protect the right flanks of our armies in northern France. We can then approach Germany on a broad front: Switzerland to the North Sea."

"General, the lines of communication from Marseilles to Germany are longer than those from the Normandy ports."

"Not at all," contradicted Ike. He drew upon his Battle Monuments Commission experience in France. "Mr. Prime Minister, I must take exception to your knowledge of geography. The distance from the Normandy port of Brest to Metz is greater than that from Marseilles to Metz. Don't forget also that the Germans will defend the Normandy ports savagely. When we overcome the enemy there, we will find that he has destroyed the harbors."

Churchill removed the Havana from his mouth and gestured with it toward General Ike. "The Germans can also destroy Marseilles harbor."

"Not as easily, Mr. Prime Minister. We can surprise them. They will not have the time. We need Marseilles and Antwerp to speed the inflow of materiel and men to end the war as soon as possible."

"It would be disastrous to enter France in the south," Churchill replied. With an overdramatic, thespian sweep of his arm, he said, "The earth will run red with Allied blood. Reducing coastal defenses could take weeks. Troops will not reach as far north as Lyons in three months."

"Again, I must differ with you, Mr. Prime Minister. Our intelligence reports fail to show such a potential for resistance. We need to drive northward through France, not only to liberate all of France, but also to equip and supply French forces there. They can help us destroy the German military potential."

Churchill was not finished yet. "Allied troops could be far better used in Italy than in southern France," countered the Prime Minister.

"Southern France makes the best sense to me," replied Ike. "We have great Allied naval strength in the Mediterranean. We hold Italy up to the Rapido River and have excellent air cover available from Corsica, Sardinia and Italy.

"Most of the Axis troops in southern France are poor quality—belly troops—the old, ill and wounded, pressed back into service," explained General Ike. "If we invade the south of France, Hitler will have three choices. He can bring down strategic reserves, especially mechanized and paratroop divisions from the Pas-de-Calais area, and our air forces will have at them by night and day and rip them to shreds.

"The Germans can stand and fight and be decimated, or they can drop back gradually toward the frontiers of Switzerland and Germany. Here again, our overwhelming and crushing air power will wipe out most of their troops and equipment."

No matter how convincingly Eisenhower presented his case, Churchill came back with new heated arguments for his own plans. He presented three in all.

This verbal Ping-Pong had been going on for seven hours, through lunch, when Churchill had more brandy and cigars, into early evening. Finally, in exasperation, the prime minister stood up, dramatically grasped the lapels of his suit coat and pugnaciously shoved his face close to the general's.

"Ike, if you insist on this absurd, stupid program to land in the south of France, I shall be forced to go to His Majesty and offer the robes of the great office I wear."

General Ike stared right back into Churchill's eyes. "I'm very sorry, Mr. Prime Minister, but in that case, perhaps you'd better go to His Majesty and offer the robes of the great office you wear!"

Even when the contest seemed to be over, it continued, to a humorous surprise twist. Ike felt sorry for his friend and leaned toward him. "Mr. Prime Minister. Would you do me and the Allied cause a great favor?"

Now curiosity replaced the hurt look on Churchill's cherubic face. "What's that?"

"When we land in the south of France, I'd like you to be there."

"You want me to go ashore with the troops?"

General Ike shook his head. "No, I can't quite agree to that. But you can be on a cruiser lying off Grasse or Nice, and when you're back at base in Corsica, you can send a signal to let me know what we're doing right or wrong. I want you to be my eyes and ears, because I'm charged with the responsibility of this invasion, too."

Now Churchill's eyes rounded with childlike pleasure. "I could really be on a cruiser when we shell the coast of France?"

"Certainly."

Churchill did go aboard a cruiser on the eve of the invasion, and when he got back to base that night, he sent the following signal to General Ike:

> The invasion of southern France is an accomplished fact. Historians will consider and describe it as a great military movement, but I must tell you, my dear general, it was the fourth-best possibility.
>
> Yours ever,
> Winston Spencer Churchill

Monty's Foes–Germany and General Ike

Sometimes the correspondents who knew about Montgomery's differences with Eisenhower would ask, "Is Monty fighting the Germans or Ike?"

My answer was "Both."

General Mark W. Clark, told me that the first Monty-Ike clash took place shortly after he and Eisenhower arrived in England. They visited the Midlands, to watch British troops train and hear Montgomery lecture on modern warfare.

They sat in the back of the packed room. Ike, then a chain-smoker, lit up. Monty immediately saw who it was and decided to make an example of the American general. "I don't permit anyone to smoke in my presence," he called out. "Whoever is smoking should leave!"

Every head turned. Embarrassed, Eisenhower arose and snuffed out his cigarette. "General, I'm sorry that I am the culprit. I didn't know you had such a rule."

Ike did his best to cultivate friendly relations with Monty, but it wasn't easy. He had to contend not only with Monty, but also with his heredity and upbringing.

Psychiatrist Alfred Adler would have regarded Bernard L. Montgomery—the man and the general—as a classical example of overcompensation for inferiority. Montgomery was not unlike other small-of-stature military men who proved themselves superior: Alexander the Great, Caesar, Lord Nelson and the "Little Corporal," Napoleon Bonaparte.

Short, slight and poor, Montgomery was ridiculed, scorned or shunned by schoolmates and could never do anything that pleased his perfectionistic, stern and rigid mother. He would show them!

Somebody once committed the sin of oversimplification in saying, "We are the product of our wounds." As with us all, Monty was the product of his wounds and everything else that interacted significantly with him—especially his later triumphs.

Soon the hurts no longer hurt. Slurs and slights ricocheted off his elephantine hide. At his tactful best, he was tactless. Often his remarks cut sharply, deeply, unforgettably.

Every military achievement supercharged his cocky self-confidence, superiority and authoritarianism.

Blatant glory grabbing for himself and his Eighth Army chafed and alienated many fellow commanders, particularly Air Marshal Sir Arthur Coningham, whose desert air force had magnificently supported Monty at El Alamein. Monty attracted all the headlines for himself and the Eighth Army. From his accounts, the press would not even have known that Coningham and his flyers had even been there. El Alamein was Monty's victory.

Many of his wartime associates felt that his reputation far exceeded his ability. Even his most shining moment—El Alamein—was a time of failure. He had not pursued the fleeing Germans fast enough to capture tens of thousands of prisoners. Speed and determination could have shortened the war in North Africa.

Monty's slow and cautious fighting in Sicily had almost as much to do with Patton beating him to Messina as Patton himself had.

Before D-Day, when Monty briefed the Allied command at Saint Paul's School in London, he promised a rapid break-through of his armored forces near Caen after invasion of Normandy. He failed. After the long-delayed breakthrough toward Caen, he again stalled, later explaining his caution as something ingrained in him in Africa before El Alamein. In-heriting a broken, demoralized Eighth Army, he vowed that no army under him would ever be defeated.

"I was conservative at Caen to nurse Britain's limited re-sources of men and materiel," he once told me.

Shortly after Allied forces broke out of the Normandy bridgehead, I lunched with Carl "Tooey" Spaatz in his camou-flaged caravan. Spaatz was commanding general of the United States air forces in Europe. In one corner of a surprisingly large dining room, Tooey's brown guitar leaned against the wall. His shirt collar open, Tooey munched a bit noisily on Southern-fried chicken.

I made the innocent mistake of complimenting Montgom-ery. "Wasn't it great the way Monty and the Twenty-first Army Group crossed the Saint Lô River and started toward the Seine and Belgium?"

Spaatz gave me a look that could have withered stainless steel and explained that if Monty wanted an area bombed on a front of 5,000 meters and a depth of 2,000 meters, he would advance only as far as the carpet of bombs was laid. "If the bombs we, the RAF and the Royal Canadian Air Force laid on the east bank of the Saint Lô had not been dropped, Monty would still be sitting in Normandy. In fact, the bombs sucked him across the river."

All the ill feeling toward Montgomery was not subjective. Many of his critics correctly observed that he rarely executed military plans up to his predictions.

Ever since El Alamein, Monty felt that he deserved to be supreme commander. A taste of this role on D-Day made him want to continue. When Eisenhower assumed command, as had been agreed, Monty resented him. It was not in Monty's nature to quit. He never stopped trying to get the job back.

Like Montgomery, Lord Alanbrooke, chief of the Imperial Staff, felt strongly that he should receive the appointment. They wanted Ike kicked upstairs, to a meaningless supertitle.

Their fantasies were derailed by the facts: The United States was furnishing most of the troops and materiels and would not tolerate anybody but an American as supreme commander.

Although Allied armies were moving eastward toward Germany on a broad front, Montgomery, farthest north, insisted on a pencil thrust into Germany, rather than capturing the desperately needed port of Antwerp, as Eisenhower had ordered. Eisenhower needed this port to help replenish dwindling supplies and keep all thrusts moving.

When, finally, Monty's troops entered Antwerp and seized the docks intact, they made no effort to capture the key bridges over the Albert Canal. Two days later, before Monty's oversight could be corrected, the Germans blew up the bridges.

Eisenhower, Bradley and Patton were constantly frustrated at Montgomery's slow advances and lengthy halts. Ike once told Prime Minister Churchill that he was fed up with Monty always stopping to "draw up his administrative tail." He asked Churchill to light a fire under him.

While General Patton's mobile forces to the south were on a lightning drive across France, Monty told Eisenhower he needed more gasoline, ammunition and supplies, to permit him to drive toward Berlin. He wanted them from Patton. Although Eisenhower knew that Monty was preoccupied with his own goals and had funnel vision as far as needs of other commanders were concerned, he shared some of Patton's fuel and supplies with Monty, while Patton fumed when his tank engines coughed to a halt.

One of General Ike's greatest difficulties with Monty was insubordination. Not only did Monty ignore and disobey orders, he never showed Eisenhower the courtesy of coming to meetings set by the supreme commander. His chief of staff, Major General Francis "Freddie" de Guingand, substituted for him. In order to see Monty, Ike had to travel to wherever Monty was in the field.

Why did Ike let this happen? Five of us set up a special impromptu conference with Ike in a forward area, to find out. Alan Moorehead, outstanding Australian journalist for the Beaverbrook newspapers, headed our group, which also included the brilliant Drew Middleton, of the *New York Times*, and Bill Stoneman, of the Chicago *Daily News*.

Alan asked a pointed question: "General Eisenhower, why is it that whenever you and Field Marshal Montgomery meet, it is at his headquarters, some neutral point, or—as yesterday—in a cow pasture? If Monty was the supreme commander and you were his deputy, you would always meet at the time and place of his choosing. He would not countenance your absence at his high-level meetings."

Eisenhower broke into a broad grin. "Alan, my assignment from the President and the Prime Minister and the Combined Chiefs of Staff is to win the war in the shortest possible time with the least cost of life.

"The British have seen fit to name Montgomery as their commander in the field. If meeting him at his headquarters, some neutral point, or even in a cow pasture, as you put it, would shorten that assignment by a single hour or save a single Allied life, I would gladly do so. . . ."

A crisis situation which began before daylight on December 16, 1944, made Eisenhower and Montgomery forget their differences. This was the Battle of the Bulge.

For months, Adolf Hitler had been preparing a major offensive to turn the tide of the war. As the Allies had advanced toward Germany, they were short of manpower and supplies, which were spread thin in certain areas, particularly the Ardennes Forest.

There Hitler had secretly assembled twenty-four divisions—two panzer armies—for a surprise thrust. The German objective was the port of Antwerp, where they hoped to annihilate the British Twenty-first Army Group and the United States First and Ninth Armies north of the Ardennes. They desperately needed American gasoline supplies along the way and those at Antwerp.

Due to prolonged, devastating Allied bombing, the Germans

had only enough fuel to advance beyond Bastogne, near a strategic network of roads over which their offensive could fan out. American gasoline at the Meuse River could carry them to the Atlantic Ocean.

This attack was also a psychological weapon. The Allies had had things pretty much their way, and the end of the war seemed in sight. A successful offensive could change this outlook and lower Allied morale.

Before their surprise counterattack, the Germans had used every sort of trick to keep the Allies from being suspicious. Noise devices accustomed American troops to the sound of tanks, trucks, and marching men. German use of the area for training recruits and re-forming divisions conditioned Americans to incoming and outgoing troops. Many more soldiers moved in than out.

Once the offensive started, English-speaking Germans in American uniforms, many driving captured American Jeeps, headed into the Allied lines, spreading false information and panic along the battle line. Supposedly, a group was out to assassinate Eisenhower. Orders went out to American military policemen to stop all vehicles and ask special questions to reveal whether the occupants were Americans or Germans: "Who was Mickey Mouse's wife? Who is Betty Grable's husband? Who won the last World Series?" Even General Omar Bradley was stopped by an MP and asked, "What is the capital of Illinois?"

"Springfield," answered Bradley, and the MP, who mistakenly thought it was Chicago, arrested him. Eventually, a hot-headed general was released from the cooler.

At first, territorial gains of the Germans were phenomenal. Then Americans, although outnumbered and inexperienced, fought well. They refused to budge from the Monschau area, blocking roads needed by the Nazis for broader penetration. At another critical point, Saint Vith, United States troops held up the Germans for eight days. But the most-magnificent American stand was at Bastogne, at the hub of vitally needed roads.

The weather was bitter cold and damp. A ghostly fog shrouded the Ardennes Forest, and the United States Air Force and the RAF were helpless to bomb or strafe the Nazi armies. It looked as if the Germans would take Bastogne.

Already the Tenth and Eleventh Armored Units in beleaguered Bastogne were short of food, ammunition, medical supplies and medical personnel. General Ike rushed the 101st Airborne Division there by trucks. The 101st stopped the Nazi advance. Finally, the Germans decided to go around the city.

Eisenhower called a conference of key commanders: Bradley, Patton, Devers, and other American and British seniors. General Freddie de Guingand, as usual, substituted for Montgomery. Morale was low. Eisenhower looked at the circle of morticians' faces and announced, "That's enough glumness. There will only be cheerful faces at this conference table. This situation is not a disaster. It is an opportunity."

Eisenhower set the tone for the meeting. He asked Patton how long it would take him to change the direction of his Third Army and reinforce Bastogne. "Forty-eight hours," responded Patton.

British officers laughed. That was a little faster than *any* general could move masses of men, armament, munitions and supplies—any general but George Patton.

Eisenhower, through de Guingand, ordered Monty to sweep in from the north, to pinch off the Germans. He ordered General Anthony McAuliffe, of the 101st Airborne Division, to hold Bastogne at all costs.

At noon on December 22, a German carrying a white flag entered Bastogne with an ultimatum. "The city of Bastogne is encircled. This is your last chance to surrender."

McAuliffe sent one word back to the Germans: "Nuts."

Meanwhile, Patton's Third Army—tanks, trucks and foot soldiers—moved over rocky ground, through brush and trees, and over icy or puddled roads. Shoes of some infantrymen were cut to shreds. They marched in bare feet or torn socks, leaving bloody footprints in the snow.

Later, Patton said that a Jeep drove alongside the Sherman tank in which he was standing, and a soldier told him that Tony

McAuliffe had said "nuts" to the Nazi demand for surrender of Bastogne.

"Any man who uses the King's English that brilliantly should be relieved and his troops saved."

Despite the long, fatiguing march over rough terrain and under miserable conditions, Patton, through his loudspeaker, ordered all forces to move even faster. "Run, if you can! Don't let anything block your forward progress. If you encounter obstacles, blow them out of existence."

Arrival of the Third Army enabled Patton, McAuliffe and their men to halt the Nazi drive.

Then the fog lifted. Allied bombers blasted German troops and supplies, while low-flying fighters strafed columns.

The German thrust had cut off Bradley's communications with two of his armies. Eisenhower decided, based on circumstances, that these armies—the United States First and Ninth—should be temporarily assigned to Montgomery.

Monty had always felt a rivalry with Bradley. Now he interpreted this change as a sign that Bradley had failed and that he was the appointed heir to bail out the Americans. A chagrined Bradley objected, but Eisenhower held his ground.

Meanwhile, Montgomery failed to attack. He again was insubordinate to Eisenhower, sitting on his haunches, waiting for the enemy to dissipate himself before attacking.

Patton insisted that Ike fire Monty. Prime Minister Churchill considered doing the same thing. Finally, on January 3, pressured by General Ike, Monty attacked.

Powerful offensives by Patton, Bradley and Montgomery smashed the Germans. The Ardennes was safe.

Shortly after the Battle of the Bulge, General Ike, whose football knee had swollen to twice its normal size, asked Montgomery to his headquarters. The marshal replied that he was too busy fighting a war. "Why don't you come to my headquarters?" Monty suggested. "We could discuss the war and future plans."

General Ike flew to a landing field near where Monty's caravan was parked. One of the British officers there told me that

Monty would not see Eisenhower immediately. He was having tea.

When they met in the trailer, Monty picked up a large stack of signals from Eisenhower. Derisively, he read one out loud. "Anyone who has ever commanded troops in the field under fire couldn't possibly have sent such a message," he commented, tearing the signal in half and throwing it into the wastebasket.

He read the next signal and said scornfully, "Absurd! The thinking of an amateur." He continued through the stack.

With each insult, the red rose higher up General Ike's neck, and the blood vessel over his right eye expanded to pencil thickness. He controlled his temper.

When Monty discarded the last signal, General Ike leaned forward and said firmly, "Monty, I'm glad you got that off your chest. But let me remind you of something that may have escaped you. I am your boss. You are my deputy. You work for me, not the other way around."

Monty got the message. Suddenly, he realized he had gone too far and said hastily, "Perhaps I did state my case too strongly."

As he did after El Alamein, Monty held a press conference to describe his Ardennes victory. In an offhanded way, he told correspondents that the British had again saved the day for the Americans, and he implied that British troops under him had won the battle.

English newspapers circulated to Allied troops featured the story. American soldiers who had fought well were angered by the story. Eisenhower and Bradley were infuriated.

General Ike was concerned about his soldiers and Bradley's image. After all, Brad's men, serving Monty, had helped make the victory possible.

The German propaganda ministry broadcast Montgomery's claims on the BBC wavelength, imitating a British announcer and exaggerating Monty's statements.

The rumble of American protests was clearly heard at 10 Downing Street. A final insult was a letter from Monty to General Ike, accusing Bradley of making a mess of the Ardennes campaign. Monty claimed that unless he were made field commander of all Allied armies, the next offensive would fail.

General Ike became red in the face and had trouble controlling his temper. Bradley blew a fuse. If he had to serve under Montgomery, he wanted to be relieved and sent back to the United States. Patton sided with Bradley. If Brad was going back, so was he.

Eisenhower, who had been promoted to a General of the Army during the Battle of the Bulge, told Bradley he had applied for his promotion to full general. Even this did not placate Bradley. No, Ike had had enough. He and Beetle Smith drafted a signal intended for Marshall, recommending that Monty be fired. Churchill was beginning to have doubts about Monty too.

Freddie de Guingand learned about the signal and asked Beetle Smith to hold it up for twenty-four hours. He wanted to talk to Monty. Smith agreed.

At first Monty was shaken up by the news. Then he recovered and told Freddie that Ike couldn't get him fired. Churchill would never stand for it.

"Don't bet your life on it," Freddie replied. "Churchill is one hundred percent behind Ike."

Now Monty was frightened and backed down. "What can we do?" he asked.

Freddie drafted a signal for his approval. It appears in the *Memoirs of Field Marshal Montgomery*:

> Dear Ike, I have seen Freddie and understand you are greatly worried by many considerations in these very difficult days. I have given you my frank views because I felt you liked this. I am sure there are many factors which have a bearing quite beyond anything I realize. Whatever your decision may be, you can rely on me one hundred percent to make it work, and I know Brad will do the same. I am very distressed that my letter may have upset you, and I would ask you to tear it up.
>
> Your very devoted subordinate,
> Monty[1]

Rather than create an international incident and give aid and comfort to the enemy, Eisenhower accepted the apology.

Although he admitted that Monty had done a fine job in reorganizing the armies and in flanking the Germans in the Ardennes, Ike would not and could not concede that Monty's generalship was superior to Bradley's. He continued to feel that Bradley outclassed Montgomery in every way and let Bradley know his feelings. Brad was reassigned his armies.

General Ike is often given sole credit for averting crises with Montgomery. Freddie de Guingand deserved plaudits, too. Not only did he get the letter of apology from Monty, he also called a meeting with newspaper correspondents, headed by Alan Moorehead, and explained the problems caused by Montgomery, asking them not to fan the fires of nationalism and disrupt Allied harmony.

Toward the end of the war, when Churchill and Field Marshal Alanbrooke stood with General Ike in a tower overlooking the Rhine, they congratulated him. "Thank God, Ike, you stuck by your plan. . . . The German is now licked. It is merely a question of when he chooses to quit. . . ."

Field Marshal Alanbrooke also sent a wire to General Ike, who shared his satisfaction in a cable to General Marshall:

> . . . This morning I received a very nice telegram from Field Marshal Alanbrooke on Army Day. In it he took occasion to make most-flattering references to my leadership throughout this campaign. This was especially pleasing because of the past arguments we have had and to my mind shows that there is a bigness about him that I have found lacking in a few people I have run into on this side of the water. . . .

"Blood and Guts" Patton— Pearl-handled Problem

Much of the colorful "Blood and Guts" Patton story has never before been told. Few individuals know the endless, rasping problems that General Patton caused Eisenhower, his supreme commander.

Indiscreet remarks to the press, the slapping incidents, back stabbing, arbitrary, unauthorized actions, accusing the supreme commander of being pro-British, boasts and other ego trips (or odysseys) were merely red-flag symptoms of something that kept General Ike concerned and in suspense.

Would Patton have an emotional or mental breakdown? Where, or when?

Eisenhower shuddered at the thought. Loss of Patton could set the Allied war effort back by months. That is why he insisted on handling Patton's problems personally and ignored Patton's references to him as the "messenger boy," "chairman of the board," "international cheerleader" or "Limey Ike" (for being more British than American). Georgie's slurs were less embarrassing to Eisenhower than his tearful, blubbering apologies.

General Ike once told me he couldn't understand why Georgie kept popping off about England, his British counterparts and other subjects that strained relations and caused problems for responsible officials in Washington and London. "He's his own worst enemy. But despite his braggadocio, his excessive statements and acts and his exalted opinion of himself, I loved the big mutt like a brother."

However, affection never kept General Ike from correcting Patton when his conduct was detrimental to the army or the Allied cause.

"Blood and Guts" once banned *Stars and Stripes,* the service newspaper, from the Third Army area. An upset Eisenhower ordered Patton to his Paris headquarters at once.

During the only exclusive interview he granted during the war, General Ike told me what happened next.

He curtly offered Patton a chair opposite his desk. "Why did you ban *Stars and Stripes?*"

"It destroys the morale of the Third Army troops."

"How?"

Patton fidgeted a bit. "It carries that Mail Bag that's filled with complaints from GIs who think they are attending a Sunday picnic with pink lemonade, instead of a fight to kill as many Germans as possible. And those cartoons by Bill Mauldin make soldiers look sloppy, indifferent and lacking any sense of discipline. They break down morale."

Eisenhower's face became florid. "Look. I want *Stars and Stripes* reinstated throughout the Third Army, and I want this effective tomorrow!"

"Can't we at least keep that Mail Bag out of the paper and get rid of Mauldin's cartoons?"

Quietly, with words sharp as an edge of blue steel, the supreme commander replied, "The Mail Bag and the cartoons stay in *Stars and Stripes!*"

General Ike fought to be calm and patient. "Georgie, some of the things we're fighting for in this war are freedom of the press and freedom of speech and, hopefully, restoring them to those nations which have been overrun, conquered and occupied by the Nazis, who have removed these elementary human rights."

Although Eisenhower respected Patton as a military man and

friend, he regarded him as an emotional infant who needed frequent monitoring. I was amazed how effectively General Ike dealt with the complexities and emotional civil wars of the neurotic Patton and kept him functioning at full capacity.

Before war's end, I visited SHAEF headquarters at Reims with Harry Butcher.

"General, Virgil and I are going down to see the closing of the circle around the Ruhr," Butch said.

I had heard what a great job General "Lightning Joe" Collins and his troops were doing and looked forward to seeing the action.

"Fine," responded General Ike.

"Then we're going to Frankfurt," continued Butch. This city had just been liberated by Patton and the Third Army.

"And after that?" asked Ike.

"Then we'll spend some time with Georgie Patton at Bad Homburg." This was the general's temporary headquarters after his rush across southern France to the German frontier.

We were just going out the door when General Ike called out, "Butch, when you've spent some time with Georgie, give me a phone call and let me know the barometer reading. I hear it's rising, and possibly he may break loose again with one of his statements that could get us into trouble."

It was hardly an uneventful trip. Our driver got us temporarily lost behind the German lines, and 88s were firing head-on at us as we rolled into the outskirts of Frankfurt. There we saw a strange sight. As a blonde fraulein heatedly objected in German, an extremely tall and thin soldier stomped out the rear-wheel spokes of her bicycle with heavy GI brogans.

"Driver, stop!" Butch yelled. As he got out of the staff car, the soldier saw all Butch's gold braid and snapped smartly to attention.

"What's going on here, son?"

"Sir," replied the soldier, who was from the back hills of Tennessee, "this fraulein is going to get herself killed. This is the third time I have thrown her off this road marked for military traffic only."

Butch smiled. "Did you speak to her in German or English?"

"In English, of course," the soldier responded.

"How do you know she understands you?"

"Sir, I found out a long time ago if you speak hard-like to them, they understand you."

We arrived in Bad Homburg shortly before dinner. Georgie Patton gave us an effusive, affectionate welcome, which he usually did to those he knew well.

Patton was the smartest-dressed officer I have ever seen. He designed his own uniforms (the privilege of a general) and favored impeccably tailored British riding breeches. One could have shaved or combed his hair in the mirrorlike reflections in his boots. Two pearl-handled revolvers, inserted backwards in holsters, were as much his trademark as Monty's black beret, but, unlike Monty, there was nothing backward about Patton's battle techniques.

Georgie Patton unbuckled his gun belt with a sigh of relief. It was as if the star had completed his performance. He set the gun belt on an overstuffed chair and invited Butch and me to cocktails and a rare-roast-beef dinner.

Over the savory meal, Patton, in his high-pitched, fluty voice, reprised highlights of his North African and Sicilian campaigns—standard procedure whenever we met.

Finally, I interrupted the monologue, "General, I want to write a series of three articles dealing with top military strategy. Do you have the time to go into the subject?"

"Not tonight, Virgil, but I can tell you everything you need to know over breakfast here at 0600 hours."

Next morning, when I was admitted, Patton's famous white English bull terrier, Willie, was half-asleep on the floor and didn't even open his eyes completely.

Before his first sip of coffee, Patton nodded toward Willie apologetically, "I hate to admit this—don't tell anyone—but Willie was named after William the Conqueror, and he's a coward. Can you imagine me having a dog who is a coward?

"Not long ago, when I spoke to a group of women in the Midlands of England about the glories of war, there was a lady in a large coat with a Pekinese dog hidden underneath. This tiny dog, with its nose and face pushed in, poked her head out and barked furiously at Willie. Willie crawled away with his tail between his legs.

"I dislike describing Willie as a coward. The only reason I think the Peke frightened him was because the little dog might have been a female, and, of course, Willie is always a gentleman."

We both laughed. Then the general became serious.

"You asked about strategy. It's difficult for me to discuss strategy, because I am the greatest soldier who ever lived. Few nonmilitary people understand strategy. Ike is a wonderful country boy and a great international cheerleader. Omar [Bradley] is an excellent commander of troops in the field, but he knows little about strategy.

"I am a good fencer. Not the greatest fencer who ever lived, but I am the greatest soldier who ever lived. I competed in fencing in the pentathlon during the 1912 Olympic games in Stockholm. I did not win the championship, finishing fifth, but I learned that when you are fencing, there comes a precise moment when your adversary's nerve centers are all frozen, as he shifts from offense to defense or vice versa. I simply watch, and when this happens, I reach forward and touch him.

"That is my military strategy: Hit them when they're most vulnerable, on my terms. I never let the Huns or the Ities get set. The whole strategy of offensive warfare is to move so fast and so daringly that the enemy doesn't know from which direction the next blow is coming. He can't set up adequate defenses.

"The greatest defense on earth is a slashing, smashing offense, but few generals understand this, because they are not the great soldier I am.

"I may take a few losses during the first hours of a battle, but after that, they are minimal. I never let the Hun get set to build fortifications or plant mine fields. I simply knock him, rock him and sock him back on his heels. This is because I am the greatest soldier who ever lived.

"Most people don't realize that I adapted the classic Stonewall Jackson cavalry maneuvers in the Civil War to modern tank operations and added my own twists and wrinkles, varied to the enemy, terrain and other circumstances.

"You probably don't know that when I was called on to stop Rommel's advance after the Kasserine Pass setback in North Africa, it was simple.

"I had read Rommel's book on tank warfare. I knew exactly what he was going to do. Every move he made telegraphed his next maneuver. I was ready for him. A man is a stupid fool when he outlines how he is going to fight battles, because some upstart is smart enough to read his book or articles and, if they meet his needs, use them to defeat him.

"When we crossed the Moselle River, do you know how many casualties we had?"

"No."

"Our total casualties consisted of two GIs bitten in the arm by a jackass.

"I said to the commanding general, 'Why aren't you on the right side of the river?'

" 'I am on the side of the river I was ordered to take.'

" 'Why, you silly so-and-so,' I replied. 'Unless you are on both sides of the river, you are not on the correct side.'

" 'Well, I don't know how deep the river is or where we might find a satisfactory ford.'

" 'There's one way to find out,' I said. 'Come on, let's go!'

"We waded across the river, and I never even got wet up to my armpits."

Patton frowned at me, "It is utterly impossible for me to discuss strategy, because no one knows enough about the subject to be really intelligent."

My ego got little fortification.

"I have an international goal rating in polo of eight," Patton continued. "This is due to the wonderful string of polo ponies Mrs. Patton—God bless her—has always provided me. I am not the top polo player of all time, but I am the greatest soldier who ever lived."

Patton believed in reincarnation. He once took me to several places in North Africa and pointed out spots where he claimed to have advised or directed the Carthaginians.

"I told the Carthaginians how to defeat the Romans and direct their movements on the left flank of their adversaries. I advised Napoleon strongly not to march to Moscow and have his troops trapped in the deep freeze of winter weather and snow. He didn't take my advice, and you know what happened."

Near the end of our meeting, he said, "Perhaps I can best sum it up this way. If Julius Caesar was an officer in the Third Army, he would be a one-star general. When I trained the _____ enough, he might advance to a two-star general, but that's as high as he ever could have gotten in the Third Army."

When I saw Butch a little later, he asked, "How is Georgie?"

"Based on what he has been telling me about being the greatest soldier who ever lived, I think you should talk to him and judge for yourself."

Within a half hour, Butch came out and said, "Let's go over to the radio shack. I want to talk to the Boss." When he got General Ike on the line, he said urgently, "The barometer is rising, Boss. There could be an explosion."

That afternoon, Eisenhower flew down to Bad Homburg in a Flying Fortress to see Patton. They got into the rear seat of a Jeep, inspected the troops and toured up and down the line.

When they returned, Eisenhower said to Butch, "I've talked to him like a Dutch uncle for three hours. I think he's back on the reservation. But please make a note to check on this situation in two weeks and let me know the outlook."

Just before leaving, I thanked General Patton for the time and information. He said, "Ike is mad at me. What have I done to upset him?"

"Well, what did you say to him?" I asked.

"Only that if I hadn't been robbed of my gas and oil to give to that no-good Montgomery, I could have gone all the way to Berlin on a number of occasions. Ike tried to hush me, but I told him every time I start to make a big sweep, Montgomery yells for more gasoline, shells, artillery, tanks, soldiers, planes, and I have to halt in my tracks.

"Virgil, it isn't fair to say that Montgomery is a poor general. It's inaccurate to describe him as a second-rate general, even in tactical maneuvers. That no-good _____ is the worst general who ever lived—even in prehistoric times."

26

Tribute From a Friend

Hearing words like *masterful* and *ingenious* used to describe his broad-front strategy to defeat Germany only embarrassed Ike. "Forget the high-powered adjectives," he said. "The only important thing is that we won."

Allied armies driving across northern France, Belgium and the lower Netherlands, and others thrusting into central Germany, joined forces that had invaded southern France.

The central armies captured the Saar, Germany's second-most-important industrial section. Forces from the north encircled the major industrial area, the Ruhr, while armies from the south also encircled it, for a double envelopment.

There was no high drama in the formal surrender at Reims, which took place on May 7, 1945, in the pale-blue, map-covered war room of Eisenhower's headquarters. (I decided to stay at the Scribe Hotel in Paris and direct filings of messages, sending Boyd Lewis in my place.)

Quietly, Field Marshal Jodl and Admiral Friedeburg, ramrod stiff, signed the necessary documents as a transcription recorder turned, camera shutters clicked, flashbulbs exploded and newsreel cameras ground. The Germans were arrogant to the last.

The war was over, and the lights went on again all over Great

Britain. It was a time for peace and celebrating for peace. The mobs of hysterically happy GIs outside Rainbow Corners USO were singing, "Don't Fence Me In," "Deep In the Heart of Texas," and " 'Til We Meet Again."

In a little more than a month, June 12 would be here—an important date in General Eisenhower's life. On that day thirty years before, he had been graduated from West Point. Now, on June 12, 1945, he would be made a Freeman of the City of London, an honor extended to few individuals.

Prime Minister Churchill told him he would be presented the jewel-encrusted Wellington Sword at historic Guildhall and be required to make a speech.

For many nights, Eisenhower agonized over his speech, penciling notes on a yellow tablet. On the morning of June 12, he decided to be alone and go over his address. He stepped outside the Dorchester Hotel, into Park Lane. It was only then that he began to realize he was a new Ike Eisenhower.

A cab driver thrust his head outside his parked vehicle and spotted Ike. "Blimey, it's Ike," he shouted. "Good old Ike."

He asked for an autograph. General Ike gave it to him, and soon hundreds of people crowded in with writing pads, ten-shilling and one-pound notes for his signature. A fleet of Bobbies finally rescued him in time for his appointment.

Ike's preoccupation with his heavy wartime responsibilities, his crowded schedule, his loneliness for Mamie, home and the United States had prevented him from realizing that he had become a celebrity. The Park Lane scene had come as a surprise.

Within historic, bomb-pitted Guildhall, Eisenhower was received by a uniformed and bewigged sexton and the Lord Mayor of London. Ike felt nervous as he glanced out over the packed hall. Ceremony and formality always bothered him. He was relieved when the ritual of the Wellington Sword and the flattering introduction were over, and the audience of well-bred dignitaries, hushed for his address.

> The high sense of distinction I feel in receiving this great honor from the City of London is inescapably mingled with feelings of profound sadness. All of us must always regret that your great

country and mine were ever faced with the tragic situation that compelled the appointment of an Allied Commander-in-Chief, the capacity in which I have just been so extravagantly commended.

Humility must always be the portion of any man who receives acclaim earned in blood of his followers and sacrifices of his friends.

Conceivably a commander may have . . . . given everything of his heart and mind to meet the spiritual and physical needs of his comrades. He may have written a chapter that will glow forever in the pages of military history.

Still, even such a man—if he existed—would sadly face the facts that his honors cannot hide in his memories the crosses marking the resting places of the dead. They cannot soothe the anguish of the widow or the orphan whose husband or father will not return. . . .

. . . In the superficial aspects by which we ordinarily recognize family relationships, the town where I was born and the one where I was reared are far separated from this great city. Abilene, Kansas, and Denison, Texas, would together equal in size, possibly one five-hundredth of a part of great London.

By your standards those towns are young, without your aged traditions that carry the roots of London back into the uncertainties of unrecorded history. To those people I am proud to belong.

But I find myself today five thousand miles from that countryside. . . .

Yet kinship among nations is not determined in such measurements as proximity, size, and age. Rather we should turn to those inner things . . . those intangibles that are the real treasures free men possess.

To preserve his freedom of worship, his equality before the law, his liberty to speak and act as he sees fit, subject only to the provision that he trespass not upon similar rights of others—a Londoner will fight. So will a citizen of Abilene.

When we consider these things, then the valley of the Thames draws closer to the farms of Kansas and the plains of Texas.

. . . So even as I proclaim my undying Americanism, I am bold enough and exceedingly proud to claim the basis of kinship with you of London. . . .

In London my associates and I planned two great

expeditions—that to invade the Mediterranean and later that to cross the Channel. . . .

They were composed of chosen representatives of two proud and independent peoples. . . . Many feared that those representatives could never combine together. . . to solve the complex problems presented by modern war.

I hope you believe we proved the doubters wrong. . . .

No man alone could have brought about this result. Had I possessed the military skill of a Marlborough, the wisdom of Solomon, the understanding of Lincoln, I still would have been helpless without the loyalty, vision, and generosity of thousands upon thousands of British and Americans. . . .

. . . a fact important for both of us to remember—neither London nor Abilene, sisters under the skin, will sell her birthright for physical safety, her liberty for mere existence.

No petty differences in the world of trade, traditions, or national pride should ever blind us to our identities in priceless values.

If we keep our eyes on this guidepost, then no difficulties along our path of mutual cooperation can ever be insurmountable. Moreover, when this truth has permeated to the remotest hamlet and heart of all peoples, then indeed may we beat our swords into plowshares and all nations can enjoy the fruitfulness of the earth. . . .

Then it was over. Hardly anyone in the audience moved. The few individuals who clapped because they thought it was the thing to do stopped self-consciously. Tears shone in Winston Churchill's eyes. Everywhere Ike looked across the audience, white handkerchiefs appeared.

I recall the large headline and subhead in Lord Beaverbrook's *London Daily Express:*

GENERAL EISENHOWER SPEAKS IN IMMORTAL WORDS
OF HIS MEN AND THE MEANING OF THEIR WORK
THE HUMILITY OF A GREAT SOLDIER

In the midst of the printed text was a box containing Lincoln's Gettysburg Address. Other newspapers, editorial writers and commentators called the speech a masterpiece and likened its simplicity, grandeur and power to that of Lincoln's.

A month later, another generous tribute was paid to General Ike—this by Prime Minister Churchill at a private meeting. He was not even aware of it until many years later, when I related the verbatim account I had received from Sir Anthony Eden and Sir Desmond Morton.

On the eve of a general election in July 1945, Winston Churchill and Foreign Minister Anthony Eden attended a dinner for forty members of the Conservative Party. When the business was over, a question was directed at Churchill: "Mr. Prime Minister, you have often referred to General Eisenhower as the chairman of the board. What do you really think of Ike? How would you evaluate him?"

The old boy sat there for about a half minute, pushed his chair back, took out a fresh cigar, and poured another snifter of brandy:

> I have described General Ike as the perfect chairman of the board, which, indeed, he is. He's master of what he calls logistics. In His Majesty's service, we call it Quartermaster Supply. No one ever lived who understood logistics to the degree that General Ike does.
>
> You will remember that I once made a speech in Commons in which I said I had not been elected first minister of His Majesty's government to preside over the dismembering of the British Empire. Remember that well!
>
> Now, to answer your question. When the military historians one hundred years from now have all the facts before them and they can write about this war, they will say that Eisenhower's plan to cross the Rhine on a broad front exposed the rumps of Germans so that they could be destroyed in the field, so that the Saar and Ruhr could be encircled—the areas from which the Germans got ninety percent of their war materials. They will agree that this was the greatest enveloping movement ever conceived and carried out. It was Ike's, so he is a great strategist.
>
> If you really want to know what I think of General Ike, remembering what I said before about how I feel about Britain and the Empire, let me say that if Great Britain or the British Empire ever is involved in any dispute, I would gladly submit that dispute to General Ike and abide by his decision. That is what I think of General Ike.

The Dove Is a Hawk

"I almost blew a mental gasket when I learned for sure that the Allies planned to divide Germany into zones to be occupied by the Russians, British and Americans," General Ike confided to me several years after the Yalta Conference.

He knew he could trust me to keep off-the-record information off the record. During our many discussions after he left the White House, he rarely put restrictions on what I might write.

"Somehow the heads of western Allied nations lacked confidence that we at SHAEF could rapidly defeat the enemy," he revealed. "If they had had more confidence, they would not have made so many concessions at Yalta. Certainly they would have made the Elbe River imperative as the dividing line of the eastern and western areas of occupation.

"Early in 1944, I secretly flew to Washington to see President Roosevelt," he told me. "I was ushered into his bedroom, where he was sitting up, propped against two pillows and smoking a cigarette in his famous, long holder. He had influenza.

"I was appalled by his appearance and deterioration since the last time I had seen him. He was gaunt, haggard, and his skin sallow.

"With his cigarette, he gestured me to the chair nearest him, ashes falling on the bedspread. He briefed me on postwar plans for occupying Germany, explaining that he favored the northwest section for the United States.

" 'Mr. President, I must speak frankly. Dividing Germany into national sectors will lead to serious problems. A system more likely to succeed would be to have the Allied powers occupy all of Germany in a setup similar to SHAEF. It is the only practicable solution. The Russians make even the most simple relationships difficult. They will probably be even more difficult at war's end—from Stalin on down.'

"Roosevelt smiled, with the slightest hint of condescension.

" 'Don't worry about Joe Stalin,' he reassured me. 'I can handle him. I can lead the Russian people in any way I desire."

Eisenhower felt a sinking feeling in the pit of his stomach. The president really didn't understand Stalin and his cohorts, and he was seriously ill.

Hardly had the western Allies had a chance to catch their breath from the Normandy invasion when there was a clamor to reach Berlin before the Russians. This issue kept clouding the agreed-upon, most-important mission: destroying German troops.

Churchill was all for driving on Berlin, General Ike once told me, but he was not confident that American troops were ready. Then he negotiated an agreement with the Russians on the so-called Linz-Eisenach-Stettin Line—what he thought was a great concession.

"It was a shame he did," Ike said to me. "That agreement kept American troops from penetrating a hundred and fifty miles more into Germany. We could have done this easily."

In war and the pursuit of peace, not only the British but the Americans sometimes failed to appreciate Eisenhower fully and draw upon his expertise. During the Potsdam Conference, President Truman failed to ask General Ike to take part in any way, but he did make him a surprising offer as they were riding down Unter den Linden. "General, there is nothing that you may want that I won't try to help you get. That definitely includes the presidency in 1948." [1]

Ike was stunned. The *presidency!* All he could do was laugh it off. "Mr. President, I don't know who will be your opponent for the presidency, but it will not be I." [2]

Truman then changed the subject. "One of our major objectives in Potsdam is to bring the Russians into the Japanese war."

Eisenhower got a sickening feeling. "Mr. President, the Japanese are already beaten. We don't need the Russians. Furthermore, they are most eager to get into the fight with the Japanese. They don't need incentives. The only thing that could stop them is a quick victory," said General Ike.

Something else at Potsdam troubled Ike. Secretary of War Stimson confided that he was about to warn the Japanese that unless they surrendered unconditionally, they would be atom-bombed.

"I am sorry that our nation is going to be the first to employ this horrible weapon," Eisenhower told me he replied. "I think that Japan is much closer to defeat than most people realize and that it will not require atomic bombs to finish the job. Japan is nothing but a hollow shell.

"Mr. Secretary, it was obvious from three to six months before the Nazis capitulated that Germany had been badly beaten. The same applies to Japan at present."

General Ike's advice went unheeded.

When the Potsdam Conference was over, the president commented, "We have achieved our objectives."

"Mr. President," said General Ike, "I hope you did not make concessions to bring them into the war in the Far East."

Truman smiled noncommittally.

Eisenhower felt pessimistic, but there was more to concern him than the Far East. The Russian allies were beginning to look like anything but allies.

Of course they had allowed American B-17 and B-24 bombers taking off from Italy to overfly Germany, bomb military targets there and then fly on to Russia for refueling and fresh loads of bombs. American airmen had to stay within barbed-wire enclosures and were watched every moment of the day and night. After two such missions, the Russians canceled the arrangement.

"Stalin and the top Russian marshals didn't want their troops exposed to Americans and American ideas," General Ira Eaker told me.

Many knowledgeable American military officers felt that, in time, there would be an open clash with the Soviets—particularly General Patton. "We now have the strongest army and air force in the world," he told me at his Czechoslovakia headquarters. "No one packs our firepower, armor and ability to move. We are the most highly mechanized force in the world today. What we should do is go into the Ukraine and capture this area, which would rob the Russians of their breadbasket and much of their oil.

"If we don't do this now, when it could be accomplished relatively cheaply and easily in terms of casualties, we will be forced to do the job fifty years from now, and the expense will be a lot more."

Shortly after the VE-Day honeymoon with the Russians, Eisenhower saw signs of an uneasy future. Berlin was in the Russian zone of occupation, with one narrow access corridor, controlled by the Soviet Union. Already their officials were getting touchy to belligerent about giving access permissions.

When General Ike and his wartime commanders met, they did not talk about the wartime past, but about the uneasy future. "Even then we seemed to sense that the future problems of peace would overshadow even the great difficulties we had to surmount during hostilities," Eisenhower said.[3]

Clearly, the dove of peace was a hawk.

Yet neither Eisenhower the general, nor Eisenhower the president could accept war against the Russians as anything but retaliatory. To him, war was a last resort. The feelings of Southern Civil War General Robert E. Lee on this subject were like his own. "It is well that war should be so terrible; if it were not, we might become too fond of it." [4]

Ike himself once said, "I hate war as only a soldier who has lived it can, as only one who has seen its brutality, its futility and stupidity." [5]

The more obvious the frictions with the Russians became, the more Eisenhower was berated for not having taken Berlin before them. Shortly after Normandy, when Churchill backed Monty for a drive toward Berlin, Eisenhower showed that Russian troops were already on the Oder River, thirty miles from Berlin. The Americans and British were almost three-hundred miles away, with serious supply shortages and no bridgeheads over the Elbe.

Before VE-Day, the cement that held the Allies together was the common cause of defeating Nazi Germany. After the war, the cement began to crumble. Objectives differed.

Britain wanted to preserve her empire. FDR frowned upon empires and colonialism. His prime goal was a stable Europe, built around the hub of a strong industrial Germany purified of Naziism.

Roosevelt's goal was a horror story to the Russians, French and British, who had experienced German aggression. They wanted no part of rebuilding Germany's industry and encouraging a third world war.

The Russians also wished to export communism throughout the continent (as well as the rest of the world), much to the fear of the Americans and British.

FDR hoped that the United Nations, then in embryo form, would hold the Allies together. Above all, he wanted harmony with the Soviet Union. Otherwise, how could world peace be assured?

Winston Churchill placed little reliance on the United Nations as a restraint to the Russians. He felt that a strong Central Europe had to be developed to blunt Russian aggression.

Would the Allies have gained tangible benefits by beating the Russians to Berlin? Could they have?

Historian Stephen Ambrose writes that Franklin D. Roosevelt was against a race for Berlin.[6] He felt that the Russians, who had sacrificed the most men in the war, should have the honor of taking Berlin. Churchill wanted the western Allies there first. That would make negotiations with the Russians much easier.

Eisenhower decided not to try for Berlin.

Some historians consider this to be the greatest blunder of his career. They claim that an opposite decision could have prevented Communist control of the access to Berlin and the takeover of East Germany.

Others differ. Soviet Union armies had already occupied much German territory, while the British and Americans were still trying to cross the Rhine. Could the western Allies, with less than half the troops of the Soviet Union, have driven them out of eastern Germany? Very likely not. Furthermore, Germany had already been carved up into occupation zones by the Big Three at Yalta.

Berlin, too, had already been partitioned. If the western Allies had been able to take Berlin first, would they have ignored the Yalta accord and tried to keep the Russians out?

Robert Murphy, who represented President Roosevelt and was General Ike's adviser, told me in a personal interview that the Berlin decision and others in the war's final months fell to Eisenhower, because neither Roosevelt nor the secretary of state would accept the responsibility and assert the required authority.

"A supreme commander should never have been called upon to make a decision of such international consequence," Bob Murphy once told me. In a letter of February 20, 1970, he elaborated:

> General Marshall had left the Berlin decision entirely to General Eisenhower. President Roosevelt was ill. This was, in addition to the military aspects, distinctly a political decision, which should have been decided by President Roosevelt.
>
> General Eisenhower, I thought and still think, erred, but for reasons he expressed and believed valid. Berlin, he said, was no longer an important military objective. Its political fate had been decided at Yalta. If the United States captured it first, we would have been obliged by the Yalta decision to vacate it, except for our own occupational sector.
>
> Eisenhower had before him several Intelligence reports estimating the casualties necessary to capture Berlin [10,000 to 100,000—General Omar Bradley estimated losses to be at least 100,000] . . . I heard Eisenhower say that he would have difficulty justifying to an American mother even one casualty if that concerned her son . . . .

As political adviser, I had no guidance from Washington, and my opinion was not asked.

In a letter of April 24, 1970, Murphy gave me more facts:

> . . . as supreme commander, General Eisenhower was justified to decide the case on its military merits, having special consideration to the question of casualties.
>
> What Eisenhower had a right to expect was an order from the commander in chief in Washington, as this was also a political problem of major importance. President Roosevelt was a sick man at the time; otherwise I feel sure he would have intervened, would have made this particular decision.

Was Eisenhower's decision good or bad?

However it will be judged, this question will go back and forth as long as historians are able to unearth new fragments of information.

In any event, the militant Russian conduct in Berlin set the tone for strained international relations for coming decades.

General Ike served as military governor of Germany for a time, found it not to his liking and was soon ordered back to the United States, to serve as chief of staff of the army when General Marshall retired. General Lucius Clay (one of Ike's blackbook candidates) was made military governor. When Ike found himself bored with the demobilization, he asked to be relieved. His close friend, General Omar Bradley, recommended by Eisenhower, accepted the position.

It seemed General Ike could retire, do some golfing, fishing, cooking and revive his interest in painting, at which he had dabbled with Churchill. Maybe he would work with young people as dean of men or president of some small college.

His plan took an unexpected turn.

Five Stars Over Columbia

Scathing detractors of Dwight D. Eisenhower as president of Columbia University say his greatest accomplishment there was publishing his unique personal recipe for vegetable soup. More moderate appraisers claim that, while the vegetable soup was very good, his record of accomplishment wasn't bad, either.

After accepting the position, he revealed, in a letter of July 3, 1947, to Beetle Smith, the battle he had had in making up his mind.

> With regard to the Columbia post, you can well imagine that it was a difficult decision for me. . . . In this one, I had to struggle against every instinct I have.
>
> Moreover, I encountered the conviction of many friends that acceptance was a duty. As you know, I loathe the prospect of living in New York—possibly a throwback to my rural boyhood. Next, I wanted to lead, after leaving this post, a semi-leisurely existence with enough to keep me occupied but without any feeling of tremendous compulsion driving me to long hours and to continuous work weeks.
>
> I think my real dream was to get a small college of an undergraduate character somewhere in Virginia or the Pennsylvania area or possibly even in the northwest, and to live quietly with

Mamie in that kind of atmosphere. Under those conditions, I felt that I could write or not, just as I chose. . . .

He admitted knowing nothing about the workings of a great university and was "certainly far from being an 'educator.' "

"You've selected the wrong Eisenhower," he told IBM's Thomas Watson, Sr., chairman of Columbia's committee of the Board of Trustees. "You should have my brother Milton."

While saluting Milton, with his depth in government, economics and academics (he was former president of Kansas State University), Watson hadn't got his Eisenhowers mixed. He wanted General Ike.

His reasons were quite obvious. Ike had decades of experience in dealing with human beings and their problems. He knew, from personal exposure, about many regions of the world and their people. He had always been interested in young people and their education, from training and coaching in the service. And, after all, he wanted to be in university administration.

"Above all, I saw in Columbia, because of its standing among American educational institutions and its influence on the educational process, opportunities as large and rewarding as the environment might be strange and difficult," he wrote. "If the faculty could stand me, I decided, I could stand the job." [1]

These were moderately happy years for the general, as he occasionally mentioned to me. Yet there always seemed to be a gulf between him and much of the faculty. Communications with students seemed much better and warmer. He heard subsurface criticism of his "absentee presidency," since he was shuttling to and from Washington as senior military adviser to Secretary of Defense James Forrestal, counseling him on many problems, mainly about unifying the armed forces.

Despite the carping, General Eisenhower worked for twelve-to-fifteen hours daily at no salary, making speeches on behalf of the university, improving communication between students and administrators, helping to cure Columbia's deficit by economies and fund raising, launching a new engineering center, a scientific nutrition center, an Institute for the Study of

War and Peace, activities for education in citizenship and one of the most-unique contributions to education: the American Assembly.

General Eisenhower created the American Assembly as a center where national leaders, in every phase of industry, business, government and the professions, could meet, insulated from telephones and demands of the daily world, define and examine larger problems and attempt solutions. He worked out the concept with Dean Philip Young, of the Graduate School of Business.

Eisenhower persuaded W. Averell Harriman to donate Arden House, on his family's wooded estate not far from New York City, as headquarters for the American Assembly. Eisenhower also raised $500,000 for start-up expenses and another $250,000 to fund assemblies on a wide range of subjects.

He made many speeches on many subjects: more social and economic opportunities for blacks; organized labor versus rugged individualism and initiative; bureaucratic government eroding human individualism and independence; materialism and the decline of morality; and, among other subjects, government and veterans' education.

Two of his acts drew mild-to-sharp criticism. Some members of the faculty were surprised when the general decided to present an honorary doctorate to Ralph Bunche, black undersecretary general of the United Nations, who had helped bring peace to the Middle East.

They were even more taken aback when he invited Dr. Bunche and his wife as his dinner guests. One of the professors asked, "You are not going to have a black man seated beside you, are you?"

Ike replied, "Yes, he will be seated on my right hand, and Mrs. Bunche on my left. I trust that you and others invited will come to dinner, but if not, I will proceed with the Bunches as my distinguished guests."

The flak was even more plentiful when he introduced Russian-language courses. Was he encouraging communism? Was he trying to make young minds receptive to communism?

What naive criticism, he thought. The more young Americans learn the language and how the Soviet Union functions, the better prepared they are, to protect American freedom and liberties.

"If intelligent young men and women really know the facts about competitive free enterprise and communism, there would be no question in which direction they would go," he once informed me. He went even another step forward. "If our relations with the Red Chinese ever improve sufficiently, I would like to see thousands of young Americans learn to read and speak the most-used Chinese language. This would help them to interpret the Chinese mind and what the people might do under various circumstances."

His concerns were not limited to training minds. One concern was physical. A doctor giving him his annual medical exam shook his head soberly.

"General, I'm going to give it to you straight."

An alarm went off inside Ike.

"I'm not going to lecture you, but if you continue smoking four packs or more of cigarettes each day, I would guess you might, with luck, live for three years. If you stop smoking, you might live for fifteen to twenty years. It is entirely up to you. Do you place cigarettes ahead of your family, your obligations and the opportunity to render further service to your country?"

Without a second's hesitation, Eisenhower pulled a package of cigarettes from his shirt pocket, put it on the mantel above the fireplace next to the clock and said, "I have had my last cigarette."

He kept his word and lived for twenty-one years more. If the doctor were right, Ike figured he had enjoyed eighteen more years of life by quitting.

Columbia meant not only the end of something, but also the beginning. General Ike became artist Ike. Several books, including his own, say that he launched his art career at the university. This is true, but he actually tried painting several times before. Once was during World War II, while at the prime minister's residence Chequers, as Mr. Churchill later related to me.

"I told him painting was an ideal way to become absorbed in something outside one's self and problems—of relaxing from the pressures and tempo of daily activities. He used my brushes, a palette and canvasses. He was remarkably good for a first-timer."

After the war, when the Labour Party won the general election and Churchill lost his office to Clement Attlee, he requested that Ike host him in the south of France for one of his first vacations in years. Ike did, and again dabbled in painting. Sir Winston coached him on painting eyes and mouths, which Ike found difficult. They also discussed colors, lighting and shades.

As far as can be determined, there was no surviving work from the pre-Columbian period.

New York artist Thomas E. Stephens revived Ike's interest while painting a portrait of Mamie. While Stephens and Mamie toured the large house at Columbia University to find a proper setting for the painting, Ike could not resist trying his hand with the leftover paint on Stephens's palette. He improvised a canvas of clean white dust cloth over the bottom of a wooden box, and copied Stephens's portrait. Less than an hour later, Stephens and Mamie reappeared.

General Ike's copy was not good enough to hang in an art museum, but it was good enough for a laugh. Eisenhower never quite understood why Stephens encouraged him to continue trying, or why he asked for the painting as a keepsake.

Several days later, a surprise package arrived for General Ike. Stephens had gifted him with paints, canvasses and brushes—everything he needed "except ability," wryly remarked Eisenhower.

Between the time the general committed himself to Columbia and officially assumed his position, he ran into a serious situation. The university's fine football coach, Lou Little, had been offered a generous contract to coach Yale.

Prominent alumni sent an SOS to Eisenhower. He had known Little when Lou was coach of Georgetown University's football team, which, more than twenty years before, had defeated an Eisenhower-coached team by one point.

Ike renewed the acquaintance with his old friend. He had no pat arguments to change the coach's mind. He said, "Lou, you cannot do this to me. You're one of the reasons I'm going to Columbia."

Lou stayed on.

Now Western Europe was threatened by the aggressive Soviet Union. No single nation could stop the juggernaut; but wasn't there a chance if various nations forgot their past wars with one another, their grievances and jealousies and formed a fighting team for common defense?

President Truman asked General Ike to go to Paris and try to put together the North Atlantic Treaty Organization (NATO).

General Ike took a leave of absence from Columbia.

As he looked back on his time at the university, Ike felt as if he left the place in better shape than he had found it. He laughingly confided to me that he liked to think he had contributed more to Columbia than his recipe for vegetable soup and talking Lou Little out of defecting to Yale.

The General Who Wouldn't Run

From the very beginning, Ike had not sought the presidency. The presidency had sought him. He had dismissed with laughter my frequent 1942 predictions in North Africa that one

day he would run for the presidency. He had received specific
offers of help from the nation's most prominent and influential
men, beginning with President Harry S Truman, when Truman was in Germany after VE-Day for the Potsdam Conference.

William E. Robinson, publisher of the New York *Herald
Tribune,* had quietly started an Ike-for-President movement
among key business leaders and publishers in 1945. His premise was: Republicans had taken a beating in four consecutive
elections. Why not go with a winner like Eisenhower—a non-
politician, a person of unquestionable integrity?

When President Truman had asked him to serve as Army
Chief of Staff, Ike had accepted out of a sense of duty, defer-
ring retirement. Washington reporters and columnists never
ceased shooting questions at him about his political ambitions.
They tried to trip and trap him in every conceivable way. It was
like being a target on a firing range. No matter how forcefully
he denied political ambitions, they suspected the opposite.

When publisher Leonard Finder, of the Manchester *Evening
Herald,* urged that Ike allow his name to be entered on the New
Hampshire Republican slate, he wrote a reply that he hoped
would answer America once and for all.

> I have hitherto refrained from making the bald statement that I
> would not accept nomination, although this has been my intention
> since the subject was first mentioned to me. . . . This omission
> seems to have been a mistake, since it has inadvertently misled
> sincere and interested Americans. . . . In any case, my decision
> to remove myself completely from the political scene is definite
> and positive.

The finality of his statement seemed to turn influential
people on, rather than off.

Radio commentator Walter Winchell asked his listeners to
write Eisenhower at Columbia, requesting that he seek a presidential nomination. A flash flood of correspondence—twenty
thousand cards, letters and wires the first week and more
later—inundated his office, leaving no high ground, but he still
refused. Consequently, Governor Thomas E. Dewey, of New

York, became the Republican nominee and was defeated by Harry Truman.

Convinced that the Republicans could never depose the Democrats unless they had a dynamic candidate with a record of accomplishment, integrity, warmth and magnetism, Dewey kept in frequent touch with Eisenhower.

His two-hour visit to Columbia is laid bare in the general's hand-scrawled, hard-to-read desk diary entry of July 7, 1949:

> . . . The Governor says that I am a public possession—that such standing as I have in the affections or respect of the citizenry is likewise public property. All of this, therefore, must be carefully guarded to use in the service of the people. . . .
>
> Although I'm merely repeating someone else's opinion, the mere writing of such things almost makes me dive under the table. . . .

Thomas Dewey strongly recommended that Eisenhower start a political career by 1950. Otherwise it would be too late for Ike to serve as governor of New York State or as a senator from there.

"I shall *never* want to enter politics," Ike's diary continued. "I shall never willingly seek a vote. I shall always try to do my duty to the United States, but I *do not* believe that anything can ever convince me that I have a *duty* to seek political office. . . ."

Dewey told him that New York State is vital to any Republican aspirant to the presidency and that he assumed Eisenhower was a Republican and would like to be president. He offered to help Ike become governor or senator from New York State. It would be more advisable to be governor than a Washington-based senator, said Dewey, offering candid counsel on political fence-sitting: "Get elected governor, and New York State is yours without the necessity of taking unequivocal stands on national issues. This will not be true in Washington."

Near the end of 1950, Eisenhower took a leave from Columbia and, with Mamie, went to Paris to head the North Atlantic Treaty Organization.

"NATO needed an officer with whom various member nations were familiar—someone associated with victory in World

War II—who could weld together West Germany, France, Italy, Belgium, the Netherlands, Luxembourg and the United States into a force to deter Russian aggression," he told me. "They wanted someone they could trust implicitly, follow and know he would always be fair to all. President Truman said these nations wanted me for the job. So did he."

General Ike's major challenge was dissolving rivalries, so that the nations would unite for defense, contribute funds and also provide service men and women to wear a common uniform for NATO.

After eighteen months, he mentioned NATO progress in a letter of June 21, 1951, to his friend Swede Hazlett:

> . . . Anyone acquainted with Europe would . . . sense a tremendous increase in morale, courage and determination. . . . Each country must provide the heart and soul of its own defense. If the heart is right, other nations can help. If not, that particular nation is doomed. Morale cannot be imported. . . . Europe must . . . provide in the long run for its own defense. The United States can . . . help to produce arms, units and the confidence that will allow Europe to solve its problem. . . . In the long run, it is not possible—and most certainly not desirable—that Europe should be an occupied territory defended by legions from abroad, somewhat in the fashion that Rome's territories vainly sought security many hundred years ago.

One of the things that surprised me on a visit to NATO was that Field Marshal Lord Bernard Montgomery, General Ike's wartime nemesis, had been appointed deputy supreme commander with Eisenhower's approval.

"Why?" I asked General Ike.

"There's no mystery about it, Virgil. Monty's an outstanding military man—an important requirement for his new office. He is well-known and respected by NATO nations and can speak and act with authority. What is past is past. As you know, I never hold grudges. Our relationship is most cordial."

Eisenhower was stonewalled when he returned to the United States to get Congress to help strengthen NATO by deploying United States troops there. Truman said he had the constitutional right to deploy troops according to his best judgment.

Senators Robert A. Taft and Kenneth Wherry were seemingly more interested in cutting Truman down to size than in containing the Russians. Taft's isolationism frightened General Ike, because the Ohio senator was already being mentioned as the Republican candidate for the presidency in 1952.

Eisenhower felt that there was enough water between him and the United States to discourage those trying to influence him to run, but the Atlantic Ocean proved too narrow.

Despite his reluctance, seventy-eight resolute persuaders streamed into SHAPE headquarters during the autumn of 1951: friends, political leaders, governors, senators, house members.

He devoted at least a small amount of time to each one, explaining his NATO activities and listening courteously, if not overpatiently, to each entreaty.

He was thankful for brilliant, loyal and indispensable General Alfred M. Gruenther, head of the allied staff, to keep NATO work moving ahead. Ike considered him "one of the most able all-around officers I have encountered in my entire army career."

The New York *Herald Tribune* came out for Ike's candidacy on the Republican ticket. (The *Herald Tribune* wasn't the first to declare itself for him. The Los Angeles *Mirror-News,* of which I was founding editor and publisher, frequently editorialized in 1947 and 1948 that Dwight D. Eisenhower should go to the White House.)

Governor Thomas E. Dewey called for Ike to be a presidential candidate in 1952. A small group of Republican house members pledged their support, and Senator Henry Cabot Lodge visited Eisenhower in France again, on September 4, 1951.

Throughout General Ike's history of refusing to consider candidacy, he had never declared his party preference. "I don't intend to run, so my preference is academic," he often said.

And it was academic, until events of late summer and early fall. Lodge told him that many large groups wanted to place his name before the 1952 Republican National Convention. A friend since World War II, Lodge talked so convincingly that the general listened with more than simple courtesy.

Five Republican presidential defeats in a row showed the

need for a strong candidate, Lodge maintained. If the trend were not reversed, the two-party system could be destroyed, along with the democracy. There were other perils: uninterrupted accumulation of power in Washington, growing paternalism of the federal government toward citizens, dangerously mounting deficit spending, and continuous debasement of currency. The nation was speeding toward disaster. Military strength was weak and growing weaker. Lodge said that a victory by the Democrats would only accelerate the condition.

The death-wish Republicans would probably nominate Senator Taft, who would undoubtedly lose and contribute to the extinction of the Republican party—and maybe the nation. Only one man could unite the different elements of the party and win: Dwight D. Eisenhower.

After talking with Lodge and William E. Robinson, a guest at the Eisenhower's Villa Saint Pierre home during the Christmas holiday, the general finally said with reluctance that he would not mind the public knowing he had voted Republican in the 1948 and 1950 New York State elections. That was all that Lodge needed to call a press conference in Washington, D.C., to announce this fact and enter Eisenhower's name in the New Hampshire primary.

Now the general's party affiliation had been established for New Hampshire and all other states where voters had to swear to party affiliation before being allowed to vote.

Amateur Strategists, Professional Results

Eisenhower couldn't believe it. All he had done was admit to having voted Republican. The announcement of his party affiliation and placing him on the New Hampshire ballot was Senator Henry Cabot Lodge's idea.

Despite heavy pressures on him, the general still wouldn't commit himself to run. Meanwhile, his supporters refused to permit him not to run. Citizens-for-Eisenhower groups stepped-up efforts and became one of the most powerful political forces the nation had ever experienced. They worked under the leadership of General Lucius Clay, Paul Hoffman, Walter Williams, Mary Lord, Sigurd Larmon and Bradshaw Mintener. W. Allen Jones, Clifford Roberts, Sidney Wainberg, John Hay Whitney and Ellis D. Slater raised funds.

Working in a Hoboken, New Jersey loft, two young men, Charles Willis and Stanley Rumbaugh, organized an Ike Club in the summer of 1951, spreading the pattern for the organization to like-minded individuals nationwide, until eight-hundred clubs were campaigning by early 1952.

The prestigious *New York Times* joined the New York *Herald Tribune,* the Kansas City *Star,* the Los Angeles *Mirror-News* and other influential newspapers in supporting an Eisenhower nomination. Political experts gave the movement direction: Governors Thomas Dewey (New York), Sherman Adams (New Hampshire), Arthur Langley (Washington) and Dan Thornton (Colorado) and Senators Henry Cabot Lodge (Massachusetts), James Duff (Pennsylvania) and Frank Carlson (Kansas).

No one person could have convinced Eisenhower that he had enough support to be a candidate, but something that happened in New York City did convince him.

Amateur Eisenhower partisans planned a February 8 mass meeting at Madison Square Garden, to show the need for the general to declare himself. "It will be a disaster," predicted party professionals. "Why not wait for a better time?"

On the surface, they seemed right. The only time the partisans could schedule the Garden was after the fight card—around midnight.

"Who's going to attend a rally at midnight?" the pros asked.

But the amateurs went ahead. As if they didn't have enough problems, that particular night was rainy and blustery.

Neither the late hour nor the rain discouraged anybody. Some 15,000 cheering, optimistic Ike fans turned out. Motion pictures were taken. Record-holding aviatrix Jacqueline Cochran went sleepless for thirty-five hours to monitor the film's processing and fly it to France for showing to the Eisenhowers in the Villa Saint Pierre's living room.

General Ike was deeply touched by Jackie Cochran's dedication and by what the motion picture conveyed. "It was a moving experience to witness the obvious unanimity of such a huge crowd—to realize everyone present was enthusiastically supporting me for the highest office in the land," stated the general.

"As the film went on, Mamie and I were profoundly affected. The incident impressed me more than had all the arguments presented by the individuals who had been plaguing me with political questions for many months . . . I think we both suspected, although we did not say so, that our lives were to be once more uprooted." [1]

On February 16, Eisenhower met to discuss his future with General Lucius Clay and two of his best friends from the United States (George Allen and Sid Richardson).

The result was that Eisenhower agreed to return to the United States as soon as he could satisfactorily finish his duties in Europe. Yet he still had reservations. He would not actively seek the nomination, but, if nominated, he would campaign for the presidency.

"I won't take part in preconvention activities under any circumstances," he said. "I will heed a call to political service only from the standpoint of duty, under the condition that the call is unmistakable."

Over and over, friends and well-wishers had said, "Ike, all you have to do is announce that you're available, and you'll be nominated."

With the March primary in New Hampshire only weeks away, Governor Sherman Adams and a few co-workers began a vigorous Eisenhower campaign. Senator Robert A. Taft had had his high-precision political machine covering New Hampshire for months.

"These last-minute efforts will be a debacle," the pros predicted. "It would be better not even to enter the contest. Taft's got it locked up," they said gloomily.

If so, Sherman Adams was determined to unlock it. During one of the snowiest winters in history, he crisscrossed New Hampshire—by car, Jeep, and bus, over icy, rutted roads, frequently on snowshoes—to spread the Eisenhower message. Then came the big test.

Totaled votes showed Eisenhower with 46,661 and Taft with 35,838.

"Would you believe it?" asked a surprised General Ike. More voters wanted him than he had imagined!

Now the next hurdle: Minnesota. It was too late to get on the ballot, so amateur party organizers made him a write-in candidate. The professionals frowned on that. Eisenhower's easy-to-misspell name would have to be written in by voters. Further, how could a write-in candidate make any sort of showing against Harold Stassen, Minnesota's popular young governor? Negative results would tarnish the New Hampshire win.

Bradshaw Mintener, chairman of Minnesotans for Eisenhower, and his organization, frantically covered most of the snow-laden Gopher State, asking personally and through the media for voters to work a miracle at the ballot box.

Mintener was soon singing "I Believe in Miracles," for that is exactly what he got: more than 100,000 write-in Eisenhower votes.

Amazed, Ike knew he could not stay in the military with such strong forces working.

Primary results had influenced Roy Roberts to editorialize in the Kansas City *Star* that he felt General Eisenhower would respond to an Ike-for-President movement only from a sense of duty and that a bona fide draft was underway.

He airmailed the editorial and a letter to Eisenhower, stating, "I have felt all along that you would never even look at the presidency for yourself but only out of duty." [2]

An almost-wistful quality emerges from General Ike's March 28 reply: "I cannot tell you how grateful I am for your letter. It means all the more to me because of its insistence upon a factor that all too many people seem to be able to brush off or explain away, just simple self-respect and personal honor." [3]

In April, Eisenhower had written President Truman that he wanted to resign on June 1 and be retired without pay. This was okayed by the president in a letter of April 11.

General Matthew Ridgway was appointed to Eisenhower's post, with General Gruenther continuing as NATO chief of staff. Eisenhower was pleased with the timing of his resignation, for by June, organization, training, and national recruiting systems were well underway. A second major hurdle was negotiated in Paris on May 27, when foreign ministers of West Germany, France, Italy, Belgium, the Netherlands and Luxembourg signed a history-making document bringing into fact the European Defense Community.

Leaving France brought mixed feelings to the Eisenhowers. Both Ike and Mamie had grown to love the charm of their white-trimmed home. Mamie had enjoyed her backyard garden, where she had planted Indian corn seeds from the United States, because Ike liked eating Indian corn.

Now the military nomads braced themselves for another move. Often, in his foreign service, the novelty and enchantment of distant lands and challenging assignments had neutralized his nostalgia, but now they had lost their power.

Oh, how tired it made him, even to consider the span of years since he had a permanent home. He had left Abilene in June, 1911, to enter West Point. Then, after some thirty-six rootless years in government-provided housing, he and Mamie had bought the Gettysburg farm.

In a letter to Swede Hazlett, Ike revealed his feelings:

"I assure you that we are not enjoying Paris in the sense that we would prefer to be here instead of in the United States. I think that, if ever two people have had enough of foreign service, we are they. *We look forward to coming home. . . .*"

On June 1, Eisenhower and Mamie returned to Washington, where the general resigned. It was the honorable thing to do, he felt—honorable but painful.

Immediately, political life crowded in: advisers, friends, new faces, new places, bewildering, exhausting, mentally numbing meetings and strategy sessions. He often heard that Taft's machine was close to capturing enough delegates to the Republican National Convention to win, claiming nearly 500 of the 604 necessary.

And now he and his party were in Abilene, Kansas.

Disillusionment in the rain might have been an appropriate way to describe the innermost feelings of Ike Eisenhower in the downpour on the gloomy afternoon of June 4, 1952.

It was an inspired electrical storm—lightning in eye-dazzling intensity and Wagnerian thunder. Around noon, the rains came—and kept coming until easing to a sprinkle around four-thirty.

Ike regretted that the city park, where he was to present a nationally televised and broadcast homecoming political address at five o'clock, was now an ankle-deep bog of water.

Events of the morning had gone happily. Ike and Mamie had attended the dedication of his boyhood home, bought by Abilene's foremost citizens as a historical monument. His mind had made a happy trip to times past, as the cornerstone of the Eisenhower Museum was laid in the garden plot where he had grown sweet corn, tomatoes and green beans.

Then came a long lunch and reunions with friends. Then, suddenly, it was time for him and his party to drive to the park. Mud and pools of water stood between the parking area and the platform. Raincoat tightly secured and gray felt hat protecting his head, Ike bent down, rolled his trousers to knee level and picked his way carefully along, his overshoes making sucking sounds as they pulled out of the muck.

It was then that he felt disillusionment. The mere announcement that he was available wasn't going to get him the Republican party nomination! Tonight was only the start of a sustained and strenuous effort.

He, Ike Eisenhower, had been had; and the only person to blame was himself. Somehow, in the hurried confusion of events, he had suspended the reflective part of his mind.

How simple he had been! No, how *naive!* If it were not happening to him, he could never believe it.

Here he was, about to launch a campaign for the presidential nomination, about to do exactly what he had said he would never do. He sagged, as if all the energy had gone out of him. He felt sick of soul. As he tried to move vigorously up the platform steps, the harsh glare of television lights briefly dimmed his vision. Then TV cameras and thousands of glistening, wet and empty seats appeared.

A cheer went up from the small, hearty scatter of rain-clad spectators. He did his best to smile—something that had always been spontaneous to him. He thrust his open right hand skyward in greeting. Those in the audience who knew him sensed something was wrong. The smile was *from* Ike Eisenhower, but it was not *of* him. The power and the magic were missing, as if his internal batteries were nearly dead.

He wiped beads of rain from his oval, metal-rimmed eye glasses. There was no time to take up the pieces of his shattered illusions and rearrange them into a factual picture that he could live with.

A brief introduction, and he was on camera.

Rain spattered on the giant, triple-spaced typewriter script of his speech. Somehow, he managed to get the leaden words off paper and into the microphones.

Haltingly, mechanically he spoke of international and national problems: the need for firmness toward the ambitions of world communism; the futility of a policy of isolation; the requirement for less centralization of government and greater vigilance for "dishonesty and corruption at any level"; the need for guarding the nation's finances as much as its physical frontiers, and for America, with others, to carry the burdens of world leadership. . . .

Reporters wrote that Eisenhower looked "tired and old." TV and next-day's newspaper photographs bore them out. His speech was equally tired and old.

A gray gloom weighed down the spirits of Eisenhower's advisers. How could the campaign have gotten off to a worse start?

Then came the general's painful blunder. A Nebraska delegate to the Republican convention, Arthur J. Weaver, also a member of the vitally important convention Credentials Committee, called on Eisenhower in his corner room at the Sunflower Hotel, for advice on anticipated problems. The general knew that contests for seating rival delegations could end in the Taft group getting more seats and therefore more votes, but he refused to influence him. "Why don't you follow your conscience? These matters are your responsibility, not mine. I have no counsel other than I have just given you." [4]

A look of horror crossed the faces of Bill Robinson and other advisers. Had the general slipped a few mental cogs?

Then something strange happened: Weaver wasn't upset. He admired Eisenhower's directness and honesty. Because the general didn't try to manipulate him, Weaver became a strong supporter.

Despite a steady stream of convention delegates and delegates-to-be, Eisenhower advisers couldn't shake their low spirits. The next morning's nationally covered press conference at a local theater went somewhat better. The General was adjusting to the idea of campaigning for nomination and discarded a prepared speech, to discuss his views off the cuff. He talked of his opinion of Truman's foreign policy, his relationship with two Democratic administrations, farm price supports, conservation, and an estimate of his delegate strength at the forthcoming Republican National Convention.

One question irritated Eisenhower, and another amused him. A reporter mentioned the general's reference to the tragic loss of China and asked, "Who's to blame for that?"

For an instant, the general hesitated. "I am not going . . . to indulge in personalities. . . . I believe in certain principles, certain procedures and methods that I will discuss with anybody at any time. I am not going to talk personalities." [5]

The next question made him smile: "Did you ever dream when you left Abilene that you would come back, running for the presidency of the United States?"

"As a young boy, I had difficulty in determining whether I wanted to be a railroad conductor, a cowboy in Argentina, or another Honus Wagner," he replied.

Everybody laughed. Reactions of the media were somewhat better, but his broad-gauge platitudes in answer to narrow-gauge questions troubled reporters searching vainly for a lead for their stories.

On one thing, most agreed: Eisenhower radiated something of great value for the nation—honesty and moral goodness.

Why did he speak in generalities?

There were good reasons, beyond the facetious one that a five-star general could be permitted some five-star generalities.

He was not fully prepared. His feet had hardly gained traction on United States soil before he was expected to be an expert on every issue. On international affairs, few could equal him. On domestic matters, after stating his basic philosophies, he was thin.

He also knew little about campaigning. A rookie in political boot camp, he received an unforgettable cram course for the next five weeks. Still, his campaign was ineffective. Scripps-Howard newspapers, which supported him, editorialized that he was running like a dry creek.

Thou Shalt Not Steal Delegates!

When Ike stopped making artificial, manufactured speeches—somebody else's words—his real personality broke through, and the campaign gained momentum.

Committed to battle for the nomination, Ike became the general who had directed the liberation of North Africa and Western Europe. He was out to win.

He realized that Taft was going to be tough to beat. Ike Eisenhower knew a stacked deck when he saw one. Taft's organization controlled the Republican National Committee's most important committees, had selected the keynote speaker (General Douglas MacArthur) the temporary chairman (Walter Hallanan) and the permanent chairman (House of Representatives member Joseph W. Martin).

Senator Taft had done careful planning and organizing for several years to assure his nomination. As a matter of fact, he had plotted a course toward the presidency for much of his life.

Eisenhower set out to narrow Taft's lead, with nine speeches to enthusiastic crowds in midwestern cities, hammering hardest on three subjects: The dangerous centralization of authority in Washington during twenty Democratic years; the need to sustain individual liberty, competition and freedom of opportunity by enlisting more young people to the Republican party, and apparent irregularities in the naming of pro-Taft delegations from Texas, Georgia and Louisiana.

General Ike had solid evidence that Taft forces had not followed accepted ground rules in naming pro-Taft delegates from these states, particularly Texas.

During the May 3 Texas voting at precinct conventions, Eisenhower partisans defeated Taft's in most precincts. In nearly every instance where Taft supporters lost, they rejected the majority vote, walked out and elected their own slate.

The Texas Republican State Convention, under control of pro-Taft Henry Zweifel, gave the bulk of the national convention seats to delegates for Taft. Locked out, the pro-Eisenhower group elected its own delegates to attend the national convention in Chicago.

Traveling to Dallas on June 21, General Ike objected, on public record, to Zweifel's arrogant overriding of the majority vote and disenfranchising legally elected pro-Eisenhower delegates. He charged that "the rustlers stole the Texas birthright instead of Texas steers."

Regardless of credentials, both groups of delegates were sent to the Republican National Committee for making up a temporary roll of delegates.

Both delegations converged upon Chicago. Obviously a showdown was in the making.

A non-Texan from Massachusetts, Senator Henry Cabot Lodge, foresaw how Taftites were planning to dry-gulch Eisenhower delegates. Rules of the 1948 Republican National Convention permitted members of the temporary roll, including some contested delegates, to vote on the seating of other contested delegates—but not on themselves. Lodge was going to fight against temporarily seated Taftites from Texas voting permanent seats for Taftites from other contested states and vice versa.

Lodge wanted to break Taft's hold on the Credentials Committee. He prevailed upon the press to urge that the dispute on contested delegates be voted upon by the entire convention, rather than by the pro-Taft Credentials Committee.

Senator Lodge hired a truck with an open-throated bullhorn to circle the Hilton, continuously bellowing, "Thou shalt not steal."

Assorted liberal newspapers and *Life* magazine made the same point in less obvious wording, but did not go as far back as Mount Sinai for their historical references. They cited Texas and the political wrangle of 1912, when Senator Taft's father, President William Howard Taft, had been favored by the Republican National Convention's Credentials Committee on the contested seating of his delegates over those of Theodore Roosevelt.

Teddy Roosevelt and the press on his side had characterized this process as *steamrolling,* which led to Roosevelt's forming the Bull Moose party, running under its banner, splitting the Republican vote and making possible the victory of Woodrow Wilson. In its June 23, 1952, issue, *Life* ran an article titled "The 1912 Overture to 1952" and a cartoon of Senator Robert A. Taft, on the seat of a steamroller, flattening delegates.

A close friend of General Eisenhower, Freeman Gosden, and others rented a large steamroller with a shrill whistle and a calliope. As it traveled around the Hilton Hotel, Taft's headquarters, a loudspeaker blasted out the message: "Don't let the Taft forces steamroller this convention!"

On Sunday night, July 6, General Eisenhower and his aides learned that Taft had a possible total of 530 pledged delegates—458 uncontested and 72 contested and temporarily seated—out of a required 604 for victory. As far as they could determine, Eisenhower had 427 pledged delegates—406 uncontested and temporarily seated and 21 contested.

The general remained undismayed. "It's a challenge," he said. Yet, it was clear that the contested states—Georgia, Louisiana and Texas—could play a decisive role.

Similarly, populous Pennsylvania and Michigan remained critical. If these two states could be persuaded to throw their support to the general before the nomination, they could start a trend for uncommitted delegations.

Senator Lodge and Herbert Brownell had long exerted friendly persuasion on heads of these delegations, Governor Fine (Pennsylvania) and Arthur Summerfield (Michigan). They could see little progress, and were well aware that Taft forces were also at work on these men.

Much jockeying went on to convert delegations pledged to favorite sons: California, with eighty-one votes bound to Governor Earl Warren, and Minnesota, with nineteen votes pledged to Governor Harold Stassen.

That's the point where I came in. One morning at 7:15, I received a phone call from Paul Hoffman, at General Eisenhower's headquarters: "Virgil, how well do you know Dick Nixon?"

"Quite well." As editor and publisher of the Los Angeles *Mirror-News* and an ABC-radio commentator, I had often interviewed him. I had met him and his wife, Patricia, socially on a few occasions.

"Good! Can you come to General Eisenhower's suite right away?"

"Sure." I suspected the reason, but to find out for sure, I hurriedly dressed and rushed over.

Paul introduced me around. I already knew many of the advisers—Governor Adams, Senator Lodge and Sig Larmon, president of Young and Rubicam, one of the nation's largest advertising agencies.

"Virgil, we need a favor," said Hoffman.

"Name it."

"Will you go over to the California Hotel and ask Nixon if he will consent to have his name added to the list of potential vice-presidential candidates, in the event that General Ike wins the nomination?"

"Yes."

"Don't give him a definite commitment. All we want is an expression of availability. Please make sure he knows that others are under consideration, too."

Senator Nixon was responsive to my phone call.

He and Pat invited me to join them for coffee and orange juice. Soon Pat excused herself, and I gave him the message, which did not come as a total surprise. Yet I could sense his controlled elation.

"Yes, Virgil. Tell them that I would be happy to be General Eisenhower's running mate, under certain conditions. If the role of the vice-president were enlarged, if I were to represent the president on missions to foreign countries, and if I were to serve as a liaison between the White House and the Hill, I would find the office stimulating and challenging; but if I were only to preside over the Senate, no. That would drive me up the wall."

We shook hands and parted.

An Unconventional Convention

Those of us covering convention activities heard rumors that the solidarity of the California delegation behind Governor Warren was being undermined by Senator Nixon. Supposedly, Nixon had twenty-three delegates (more than certain states had altogether) who would desert Warren for Eisenhower. Their early defection could influence many, if not all, of the remaining delegates to line up with Eisenhower.

At this point, Taft's trump cards began to show.

General Douglas MacArthur, the keynote speaker, was due to arrive at the International Amphitheater momentarily. Possibly one five-star general would neutralize the other. A hush fell over the crowd.

"He's here!" someone shouted.

And he *was*.

It was a high-voltage moment, because a man above men, a legend and part of American history had burst upon us. Somehow, the welcoming committee moving down the aisle ahead of MacArthur seemed a redundancy. The general himself was enough. Wearing a tasteful blue business suit and an unchanging smile, MacArthur first favored the crowd on the left and then on the right.

Initially, there was almost worshipful silence and then a thunder of applause. Here was the general who, after Pearl Harbor, had turned America's fear and depression into new hope, who had eventually subdued and governed Imperial Japan, then had shocked the world by defying President Truman and—relieved of his command—had stirred the nation with his "old soldiers never die" speech.

He stood, unmoving, on the platform, through deafening handclaps, cheers, whistling and foot stamping, his smile fixed and his hair surprisingly thick and black under TV lights. (It had been said that he constantly wore his military cap to cover semibaldness and gray hair.)

Then, as if a wax model from Madame Tussaud's had come to life, the imposing figure moved, and he began to speak.

It was typical MacArthur: long sentences, sometimes convoluted, often ornate, almost-rococo expressions that made commonplace thoughts seem impressive.

Soon Taft's second trump card became visible: whisperings that the Ohio senator would invite MacArthur to be his running mate. Four months previously, Taft had sounded out the general's aides on this subject. The answer? "Yes, if the position's responsibilities were enlarged to be worthy of the general's stature."

On June 29, a group of us had asked the Ohio senator if he would like MacArthur to run with him. "It would be quite a ticket," he said, without answering the direct question. "It would be entirely up to General MacArthur, and I don't know whether he would accept."

Some of us were aware that MacArthur had expressed his qualified willingness. Was Taft capitalizing on MacArthur's popularity, without serious intentions of having him on the ticket?

On the convention floor, it was apparent that the Taft forces were trying to undermine Eisenhower by making him look like a puppet of New York's Governor Thomas Dewey, one of his strong backers. Dewey's popularity had declined with two consecutive presidential campaign losses. Also, he represented the powerful northeastern Republicans—the so-called "eastern establishment"—disliked by many party members from other parts of the nation.

Eisenhower forces were less concerned with such propaganda than with Taft's efforts to gain disputed delegates through the strongly conservative makeup of the Republican National Committee and through his control of the Credentials Committee.

From the start, Taft had recommended that the national committee settle the Texas dispute by awarding twenty-two delegates to him and sixteen to Eisenhower. Ex-President Herbert Hoover beseeched Senator Henry Cabot Lodge to accept a compromise. A battle on the convention floor, covered by TV and radio could deface the Republican party image.

Lodge was repelled by the idea. One does not compromise on a moral question, he replied. He had no intention of letting Taft make it look as if he (Lodge) would swap delegates.

Now he would not be open to attack when he brought the disputed-delegates issue before the entire convention, as General Eisenhower wished.

When the national committee followed the Ohio senator's recommendation and voted Taft twenty-two delegates and Eisenhower sixteen, Lodge made his move.

Taft forces fought deciding the issue by a vote of all delegates. They wanted the national committee's decision to stand. Lodge countered with a letter to Credentials Committee Chairman Gabrielson (released to the press), outlining his planned action:

> Governor Arthur B. Langlie, who is a delegate from the state of Washington, will offer a "Fair Play" amendment. It will provide that no person on the temporary roll whose right to be seated is being contested shall be entitled to vote in the convention or in any committee until the contest as to such person has been finally decided and such person has been seated.

Furthermore, Lodge let it be known that the whole convention, the nation's media, and voters would be witnesses if Gabrielson tried any hanky-panky.

Following Herbert Brownell's strategy, Senator Lodge and Governor Adams directed the campaign on the convention floor.

Governor Langlie introduced the Fair Play Amendment. After a heated hassle, the amendment was passed, providing that the convention would decide on the disputed delegates from Texas, Georgia and Louisiana and that no contested delegates—except those put on the temporary roll by more than two-thirds of the national committee—could vote on seating any other delegates.

Although the vote took some steam out of the Taft steamroller, the machine continued to roll, for on July 8, the Credentials Committee voted to:

(1) Seat the entire pro-Taft delegation from Georgia

(2) Give Eisenhower eleven delegates from Louisiana

(3) Divide the Texas delegation with twenty-two members for Taft and sixteen for Eisenhower.

Irate Eisenhower advisers immediately brought the matter to the convention floor. On the next day, the Credentials Committee recommendation was reversed by a vote of 607 to 531. The pro-Eisenhower delegates from Georgia, Texas and Louisiana were seated.

Finally, the critical Friday came. It was time for delegates to choose between Taft and Eisenhower. The General, his brothers, and intimate friends gathered around a TV to watch the balloting.

Eisenhower was deeply concerned—but not about the voting. Mamie had developed an infected tooth, complicated by a frightening allergic reaction to antibiotics, and suffered excruciating pain. He spent much time at her bedside.

Stress, fatigue and numbness after long days of political activity had left him in a neutral state.

Then the voting began down the alphabet of states from Alabama toward the Virgin Islands. All eyes watched California

for the unexpected, but saw only the expected. Governor Warren received all eighty-one votes, and pro-Taft delegates
applauded. It was a good sign for them.

Perched anxiously on the edges of our seats, we newsmen
looked for any telltale sign of a trend.

And now it was Michigan's turn. Arthur Summerfield called
out thirty-five for Eisenhower and eleven for Taft.

Taft advisers held their breath for Minnesota. If favorite-son
Governor Stassen captured one-half of the votes or less,
Eisenhower would have a good leg up. Senator Thye rose and
announced nineteen for Stassen and nine for Eisenhower. Taftites roared approval.

Then Georgia, a Taft shoo-in until the Fair Play Amendment, went for Eisenhower, fourteen to two.

The voting moved northward, to New York State. Governor
Dewey stood and quietly announced ninety-two votes for General Eisenhower and four for Taft.

After Ohio's unanimous fifty-six votes for Taft, came
Pennsylvania. Governor Fine cast fifty-three for Eisenhower,
fifteen for Taft.

Texas went for the general, thirty-three to five.

At this point, Eisenhower held a lead but was not likely to
garner enough votes to win on the first ballot.

The count showed Eisenhower nine votes short of victory:

Eisenhower	595
Taft	500
Warren	81
Stassen	19
MacArthur	9

Would another balloting be necessary?

Governor Fine, of Pennsylvania, stood, yelling for recognition, but in the confusion, chairman Joe Martin didn't see him,
or want to see him. Suddenly Senator Thye, of Minnesota,
leaped to his feet, waving arms, and calling for the floor. Martin
noted Thye and gave him recognition. Enthusiastically, Thye
shouted, "Minnesota wishes to change its vote to Eisenhower!"

The general was over the top!

Opposite the hotel TV set, Eisenhower showed restrained excitement. He did three things: share the good news with Mamie, check on her condition, and then phone Taft. The news cheered Mamie, who was feeling better. Ike rejoined his group and told them he was going to see Taft.

"That would violate precedent," objected friends.

"Doing the right thing is worth violating a precedent," Ike responded.

Taft, surprised, agreed to see him.

A noisy, enthusiastic, happy mob jammed every square foot of the Blackstone Hotel's corridors and lobby. The street milled with humanity. It was one of the longest street crossings in Ike Eisenhower's life, taking him twenty minutes, even with an aggressive police escort.

The quiet and heavy gloom in the Hilton—disconsolate expressions, tears and deep fatigue, multiplied by defeat—contrasted sharply with the loud and extravagantly happy New Year's Eve atmosphere at the Blackstone.

After a handshake, Taft, with a forced smile, asked if Eisenhower minded if his sons were present while they talked. Ike didn't mind and said, "This is no time for conversation on matters of any substance; you're tired and so am I. I just want to say that I want to be your friend and hope you will be mine. I hope we can work together." [1]

After posing for a photo with Taft, Eisenhower left the somber setting and soon was back at the Blackstone, in the center of New Year's Eve in July.

With Senator Richard Milhous Nixon as vice-presidential nominee, the Republican ticket was ready to face the nominees of the Democrats—Governor Adlai Stevenson of Illinois, and Senator John Sparkman, of Alabama.

The harmony of Eisenhower and his advisers brought about by victory in Chicago took a severe jolt in Denver, when the general divulged plans to campaign in southern states usually ignored by Republican presidential nominees.

Why squander time, money and effort, when they could be

used profitably in areas where there was a chance of winning, advisers asked. Republicans had made no significant inroads into the Solid South since Reconstruction days. Hoover had carried seven southern states in 1928, but only because he had been opposed by Alfred E. Smith, a Roman Catholic who was antiprohibition and could never carry a predominantly Protestant South.

A flare of temper showed in the excessive ruddiness of Eisenhower's face. "I'm going south if I have to go alone," he responded.

The advisers felt that he wouldn't draw enough people to crowd a telephone booth, but Eisenhower had his reasons. He had lived with southerners for many years, and liked them. If a person expects to occupy the White House and be president of all the people, he should campaign in all parts of the nation and learn of thoughts, attitudes and problems there, he insisted.

So he campaigned in Jacksonville, Miami, Tampa, Birmingham and Little Rock, to huge, noisy and cordial crowds and, later, in other large southern cities.

Although the Eisenhower party traveled far more miles by airplane than by train, they spent considerably more time on tracks than on wings. One frustrating aspect of train travel is being cut off from the world while between principal cities. On one such occasion (September 18), a news story that was about to stun Eisenhower, his team and the nation made headlines in the *New York Post:* SECRET RICH MAN'S TRUST FUND KEEPS NIXON IN STYLE FAR BEYOND HIS SALARY.

The Eisenhower party got its first inkling of the apparent exposé when a newsboy threw a bundle of *Des Moines Register-Tribune*s aboard. Only a brief summary of the New York story appeared. Now they would have to wait until their evening arrival in Nebraska for more details.

On the next day, thousands of newspapers plastered the story on page one. It appeared to be a gift atom bomb to the Democrats, to blast chances of the GOP.

The scandal story was especially explosive because Eisenhower and Nixon, in campaigning, had regularly exposed wrongdoing by Democrats in the Department of Justice, the Reconstruction Finance Corporation and the Bureau of Internal Revenue. One of Senator Nixon's favorite themes had been the administration's "scandal a day."

Eisenhower, snowed under by telegrams and letters at his Denver headquarters, kept reading the same irate advice: "Dump Nixon pronto!" "Get rid of him." "Scuttle the guy!" Messages ran three to one for Ike to shed his California liability.

Almost all of the general's political advisers, and one of his brothers, insisted that he fire Nixon. Senator Nixon himself offered to resign, to help the ticket.

Eisenhower said no. He refused to judge Nixon or to take action without a full investigation.

> Stories written with the purpose of damaging the reputation of a candidate have been a sleazy feature of many political campaigns. I resolved not to let such a story stampede me. Of course, I knew that within a reasonable time a decisive statement was required. But I also knew that should I decide without investigation and reflection, the American people would see me, justifiably, and on sober second thought, as one who was either desperately trying to court popularity through self-righteousness, or who would succumb to every pressure by noisy partisans. Quite apart from the fate of the ticket and the reaction to my conduct was the consideration that a young man's personal reputation and future were at stake.[2]

Lawyers and accountants unearthed and revealed all the facts about the fund. Seventy-six California individuals had contributed $18,235, to be used by the senator for political expenses. A Pasadena attorney, Dana Smith, administered the fund. No political favors were extended to the donors.

Eisenhower and Nixon agreed that Nixon should make a full explanation on national television. In an emotionally charged talk, he stated that the fund "enables me to keep my speaking and mailing schedule without recourse to padding my federal office payroll, free government transportation, misuse of the senatorial franking privilege, or any subterfuge."

He stressed the Republican cloth coat, without even a fur

collar, worn by Pat and insisted that his daughter's little pet dog was the only gift that his family had kept.

(Shortly after that, it was revealed that Governor Adlai Stevenson had a similar special fund, provided by friends. This ran to almost $60,000, three times the amount of Nixon's.)

Now wires and letters again bombarded the Denver headquarters, heavily in favor of retaining Nixon.

Ike's decision had apparently been a solid one.

Even at the height of the Nixon-fund allegations, Eisenhower's quiet confidence in a November victory never wavered. And this was not to disparage his opponent. He respected Governor Stevenson's high intelligence, his legislative achievements in Illinois, and his planned reforms.

While the Nixon-fund story at first appeared a turning point that would assure a Republican defeat, another development proved to be a turning point to assure a Republican victory. General Ike made a decision to visit Korea, to explore how to end the no-victory war there. He credited C. D. Jackson, of Time, Incorporated, a staff adviser, with the idea of announcing his intentions immediately.

On October 24, in Detroit, Eisenhower stated that, if elected, he would fly to Korea before January 1953 to "seek an early and honorable" end to the war.

"If there must be a war in Asia, let it be Asian against Asian," he said, adding that, in the future, Americans "must avoid the kind of bungling that led us into Korea."

On November 4, when the nation went to the polls, Eisenhower received a whopping victory—almost 34 million votes out of an unprecedented 61,250,000 cast—55 percent of the popular vote and an electoral college total of 531 to 89 for Stevenson, including four southern states.

During the campaign, Ike had covered 51,376 miles by air and rail, through 45 states, with stops in 233 towns and cities— quite a bit of mileage for the general who wouldn't run.

Who Knows Exactly How to Be President?

Few presidential candidates swept into office by American voters felt more quietly confident of their capabilities than Dwight David Eisenhower.

Then, too, few felt more aware of, and more humble before, the numberless unknowns that lay ahead in the world's most complex and awesome executive office.

As he contemplated becoming the thirty-fourth occupant of the White House, he found himself thinking how helpful it would be if somebody had written a book called *How to Be President of the United States.*

That was what he told me as we golfed in Palm Desert, long years after his initial reaction to the vastness of his new responsibilities. He did laugh about the somewhat limited market for the book.

Fortunately, he got his wish to a great degree. He had access to a human how-to book named Henry Cabot Lodge, who helped him avoid serious toe stubbings.

On the day after election, November 5, General Ike had

planned several days of rest, relaxation and golf. That meant going to Augusta National Golf Club (Georgia) with Mamie and the family. Then he would consider candidates for cabinet positions.

He and his party had just arrived when a telegram from President Truman put him to work. Truman asked that he immediately appoint a liaison man for the state and defense departments and for the Bureau of Budget, and meet with him soon.

Eisenhower named Senator Henry Cabot Lodge for the first two departments and Joseph M. Dodge, of Detroit, for budget.

The general's decision to run on the Republican ticket and the campaign rhetoric on both sides had produced a chilliness between him and Truman.

Whatever their differences, they agreed on one point: The ten weeks between election and inauguration should be used to the maximum for briefing incoming cabinet members and other key executives.

Eisenhower had a pet idea that he bounced off Lodge for a reaction. He was thinking of appointing a close administrative aide to function like an army chief of staff. Lodge told him by letter that it would be a serious mistake:

> . . . If your Chief of Staff operates so as to exclude you from seeing people, it can get you into serious trouble. If your sincere friends who wish to give you information get the impression that you don't really want it and are shunting them onto somebody else, they will stop coming. This would arouse suspicions of Congress. It would mean that people who see you every day would cut you off from the realities of America. . . .[1]

Eisenhower set aside the idea.

Truman invited Eisenhower to the White House for a November 18 meeting. Senator Lodge urged the general "not to agree to issue any statement of policy before being sworn in as president in January."

President Truman's announced purpose for the meeting was to demonstrate national unity, to maintain respect for the

United States abroad and to block the Kremlin's plan to divide free-world Allies.

General Eisenhower settled down and made cabinet selections, assisted by Herbert Brownell, General Lucius Clay and Governor Sherman Adams:

> John Foster Dulles, Secretary of State
> Charles E. Wilson, Secretary of Defense
> Douglas McKay, Secretary of Interior
> George M. Humphrey, Secretary of the Treasury
> Ezra Taft Benson, Secretary of Agriculture
> Martin Durkin, Secretary of Labor
> Herbert Brownell, Attorney General
> Arthur Summerfield, Postmaster General
> Oveta Culp Hobby, Secretary of Health, Education and Welfare
> Sinclair Weeks, Secretary of Commerce

Senator Lodge was appointed representative to the United Nations and given full cabinet rank. It was a wise and happy choice. Sherman Adams was named assistant to the president, with cabinet rank.

Appointments were not Ike's only concern. He was disturbed by the international situation: the nation's ominous frame of reference.

The Soviet Union was wound up for conquest. Eastern European Communistic regimes had firmed up their positions and made certain of their control with Red Army legions. Despite roadblocks, Soviet Union-sponsored communism ground ahead on its four favorite vehicles: espionage, blackmail, subversion and brutality.

Relations between the United States and the Soviet Union had their ups and down since the 1948 incidents that seemed to be preludes to World War III: the belligerent Russian Berlin blockade (defused by General Lucius Clay's courageous and creative Berlin Airlift) and the Communist invasion of Hungary.

And 1949 had done nothing to enhance the cause of the free world. That was the year of the debacle in Asia, when Mao Tse-tung's Red Chinese forces drove Chiang Kai-shek's Republic of China Army off the mainland, across the Formosa Straits, to the offshore island of Taiwan.

Equally demoralizing that year was the Soviet Union's first atomic explosion. Now the United States no longer had an exclusive on the world's most devastating weapon.

One of the few bright spots was Truman Doctrine aid to Greece and Turkey, to block Communist aggression. This was followed by the Marshall Plan, to fund war-weakened European economies for the same purpose. Estimated to cost American taxpayers $17 billion, this plan, brilliantly directed by Republican Paul Hoffman, was implemented well ahead of schedule for approximately $13.6 billion. One of the most effective programs ever instituted by the United States, it put Western Europe back in business and stiffened its spine against communism.

But it was not only communism that was upsetting established world order. Political and social ferment had destroyed the foundations of colonialism. India, Pakistan and Indonesia had been independent nations for several years. Despite unrest in Indochina and French Africa, the French still managed to control colonies there.

Conditions in other areas had deteriorated, with encouragement from the Reds. The oil reserve of Iran had been nationalized by Premier Mossadegh, as Communist influence mounted.

Closer to home, Guatemala, under the Arbenz administration, had moved closer to communism with a distinct Russian accent. It appeared that the Monroe Doctrine would soon be raped with international visibility.

War in Korea flared in 1950. The United States became involved. By the end of 1952, the battlefront ran near the thirty-eighth parallel—a stalemate. Over nearly two and one-half years of fighting, 21,000 Americans had been killed, 91,000 wounded and 13,000 were missing. Underground enemy positions—many in impregnable rock—made the conflict seem set for a long and inconclusive run.

A war of containment in a distant land that some citizens had trouble finding in an atlas could not be easily understood and backed by Americans who had not quite recovered from the trauma, life dislocations and sacrifices of World War II.

Eager to keep his campaign promise and fly to Korea, Ike was set to announce the rest of his cabinet appointees and be free to leave.

The Secret Service overruled him. That wouldn't do at all. He had better hold back some announcements, as a cover to keep his trip a secret. Intelligence reports indicated a possible assassination attempt in Korea.

"I learned that a chief executive must frequently defer to the Secret Service—not by choice but as a matter of life or death," he said.

While the Secret Service planned its cover for Eisenhower's departure, General Mark W. Clark, Tokyo-based commander of allied forces in Korea, was preparing his security cover for the president-elect's visit.

Eisenhower was to leave New York on November 29. The Secret Service story had it that president-elect Eisenhower, at his 60 Morningside Drive home, was deliberating on the remaining cabinet posts. Staff members and advisers were to visit Eisenhower's offices daily, as if he were conducting business as usual. News releases on remaining cabinet appointees were timed for release during the president-elect's absence.

Now the trip could be made in total secrecy! Or so it seemed, on the New York end. Since November 21, when Clark had first learned Eisenhower's departure date, he had been delighted. Soon he would have a reunion with his close friend.

He had to observe diplomatic courtesy and inform Republic of South Korea President Syngman Rhee of the impending visit, but he did so with regret.

The aging and enthusiastic president beamed. He would give Eisenhower a rousing reception, a state dinner, mass rallies and a parade.

Clark shuddered. Seoul was crawling with Communist agents. A chilling picture flashed into his mind: Eisenhower's shining, sparsely haired head in the sights of a high-powered

Communist rifle. Before Rhee could start preparations, Clark communicated his problem to the Joint Chiefs of Staff in Washington. President Rhee would be deeply hurt if Eisenhower failed to receive his hospitality.

"Too bad," was the quick response. As Clark had expected, Eisenhower's safety took precedence over Rhee's feelings.

"No public demonstrations," Clark told a disappointed Rhee. "Eisenhower's visit is top secret. My government expects your full cooperation to protect his life!"

"Of course," replied Rhee, "but you are exaggerating the danger."

"Not at all," snapped Clark. "Intelligence reports tell us that the Communists already have specially trained agents in Seoul to assassinate him!"

Rhee sighed deeply. "I shall cancel plans for the public welcome. Do not be concerned."

But Clark was concerned. He knew South Korean security.

One of the general's headaches receded, and two others came on. How could he possibly hide the influx of press correspondents? Forty-five media representatives already lived in the Seoul press billets, a multistoried apartment building near the capital. Six more correspondents were to accompany Eisenhower. A horde was due in from Japan, which would swell the media corps to one hundred and thirty newsmen and women, radio and TV representatives, magazine writers and photographers.

The jammed Seoul press billets would need expandable walls! General Clark worried in the midst of a contradiction—protecting Eisenhower by secrecy and hosting the press, which would tell the world about the event.

For security's sake, Clark and his staff requested that the media observe a news blackout until the president-elect's departure. Further, they arranged reportorial, photographic, radio and TV pool coverage, to limit the group accompanying Eisenhower. Clark censored all United States, Republic of Korea and allied communication.

Another serious headache turned out to be the United States

Army's rest and recreation program. On a rotation plan, thousands of GIs were flown to Japan for five days each month, to recover from the rigors of Korea. Eisenhower's aircraft would land at an air base where many soldiers were waiting for their flight. What could stop them from observing this and talking freely in Japan, where Communist spies abounded?

Clark temporarily canceled the R-and-R program and then met with Secret Service men to plan the president-elect's itinerary. Eisenhower would be briefed at Eighth Army headquarters, talk with American, UN and Republic of Korea forward units, inspect a fighter-bomber squadron, observe Medical Corps treatment of the wounded and sick, have lunch with the battalion of the Fifteenth Infantry (once commanded by him as a lieutenant colonel), visit with his son, Major John Eisenhower, assistant division plans and operations officer of the Third Infantry Division, and talk with President Rhee.

Everything was set for Eisenhower's New York departure.

Under cover of early-morning blackness, the president-elect and Secret Service men surreptitiously left 60 Morningside Drive. Other members of the party—chairman of the Joint Chiefs of Staff General Omar Bradley; cabinet designees Charles Wilson and Herbert Brownell; press secretary James Hagerty and General Wilton B. Persons—took roundabout routes to rendezvous at the airplane.

With cloak-and-dagger precaution, General Clark parked his personal aircraft in its usual space at Tokyo's Haneda Airport and took off for Korea by military airplane from a base outside the city, landing at Suwon, twenty miles south of Seoul. He traveled by car to Eighth Army headquarters, where he later met the Eisenhower party.

After an exchange of warm greetings with Clark, General Ike asked, "Where's John?" As part of the cover, John Eisenhower was not scheduled to arrive until the next morning.

Clark never relaxed during Eisenhower's visit. He felt more than the responsibility for protecting a president-to-be; this was his friend from West Point days. "During his visit to Korea, Eisenhower's hope and belief was that an honorable truce *must* be forthcoming—an optimism that I admit I did not share at the time," wrote Clark.

Only when Eisenhower's transport flew out of sight did Clark feel a letdown of tension. It had been good seeing the Boss. It had been better seeing him off safely.

General Ike also felt relief. He had talked himself out and had heard others talk themselves out. He tried to sift out the main points.

President Rhee favored a major drive, to push the Communists up and off the peninsula. But carrying the fighting across the Yalu River against Chinese bases posed a risk. A local war could explode into a global one, because the Soviet Communists stood behind the Red Chinese. Allied governments supplying troops tacitly agreed on a limited and defensive war. Why chance something more?

Yet this kind of thinking accepted a stalemate. Negotiations with the Communists had produced little more than dialogue. Allied field commanders favored an all-out campaign, Yalu boundary or not, to chase the Communists into China should negotiations fail to produce an armistice.

"My conclusion as I left Korea was that we could not stand forever on a static front and continue to accept casualties without any visible results. Small attacks on small hills would not end this war." [2]

Back in New York, the president-elect told a crowding group of reporters: "We face an enemy whom we cannot hope to impress by words, however eloquent, but only by deeds—executed under circumstances of our own choosing." [3]

President Truman characterized the trip as "sheer demagoguery!" Eisenhower felt an internal bruise, but did not comment. He was concentrating on a possible solution for the Korean War.

Faith of the President

During this period, anything but preparations for the presidency made Dwight D. Eisenhower impatient or irritable.

One interruption did not—the exciting news that Major John Eisenhower had arrived at La Guardia Field. His commanding general had ordered him home to attend his father's inauguration. John had mixed feelings. He was overjoyed at the opportunity and distressed that he had been given a special privilege because he was the president-elect's son.

After the luxury of a day off with John, General Ike planned a special luncheon meeting for Vice-President-elect Nixon, the cabinet and key advisers in the large South Room on the ground floor of the Commodore Hotel.

He inspected settings of the large U-shaped table, whose lime green linen cloth was spaced with vases of dramatic gold flowers. Then he put place cards around.

Just before guests began arriving, he stepped back to the entrance and surveyed the scene: the gray walls; the green carpet, with its geometric pattern; the trio of floor-to-ceiling, golden-draped casement windows; and rich, green leather armchairs, which picked up a soft glow from the elaborate chandelier. His painter's eyes were pleased with the blend of gold and green.

The conservative dark business suit covering his trim, five-feet-eleven-inches and one-hundred-seventy-eight pounds could not hide the dignified erectness of the military man.

Energy seemed to radiate from him. As each guest entered and extended his or her hand, the huge hands (with broken knuckles from forgotten baseball games and Belle Springs Dairy injuries) covered them. Alert, warm, blue eyes lit up affectionately, and his ruddy face seemed to split with the spontaneous Eisenhower grin.

Sherman Adams remembers thinking, "How could some segments of the press consider this man too old for the presidency?"

After the lunch, Eisenhower discussed duties and responsibilities of his office, the cabinet and the National Security Council. "I encourage you to take a broad view of your positions and not be limited by departmental borders. I welcome new ideas from every one of you on any federal government subject," he said.

"Any promises formally made in the party platform or campaign will be fulfilled. I do not believe in political promises, made only to be broken."

Then he placed a yellow legal-size writing pad before him and looked at everyone around the huge oval table. "I am going to read to you a rough draft of my inaugural address, and would appreciate your suggestions."

When he finished reading, spontaneous applause rang through the room. As the color rose in his cheeks, the president-elect fidgeted in obvious discomfiture.

"Thank you." His voice showed a hint of impatience. "I read this only for your evaluation and recommendations, not for applause."

The meeting continued into the next day, and the president-elect sternly made the point that no one claiming to be an Eisenhower relative, friend or political supporter should get special treatment, consideration or favors.

Then the talk shifted to Inauguration Day. Eisenhower favored a short parade and the wearing of Homburg hats, instead of the traditional tall hats.

Before Inauguration Day, Mamie Eisenhower received a beautiful embossed invitation to the inaugural ball. "What should we do about this?" she asked Ike.

"Turn it down," he replied with a straight face. "Tell them we've got another engagement."

The hastily handwritten January 16 entry of Eisenhower's desk diary shows deep concern about the writing of and final effects of his inaugural address:

> For some weeks, I have been devoting hurried moments to preparation of my inaugural to be delivered next Tuesday! I want to make it a high-level talk. By this I mean, I want to appeal to the spiritual qualities of free men more than I want to discuss the material aspects of the current world situation. But how to do it without becoming too sermonlike—how to give it specific application and concrete substance—has somewhat defied me.

As Inauguration Day approached, I remembered a preelection conversation with General Ike in Denver's Brown Hotel. I sensed, through what he said about himself, that he regarded presidents Roosevelt and Truman as showmen. "I'm not out to make news. I want strictly to be a constitutional president at *all* times," he said. "Second, I want to see that the executive, legislative and judiciary branches do not try to usurp one another's powers.

"The nation has been put through one emotional binge after another for twenty years. Now it's time for peace and quiet, for a reunification and genuine healing.

"I have many ideas and plans, some of them major, others not so great. But I have no desire to be a showman and to remind people constantly that I am president.

"Graft and corruption must be eliminated. There is need to restore dignity, dedication and service to government, including the White House.

"I am not going to stuff the government with generals and admirals. If anyone with a military background is selected, it must be on the basis of merit and that he is the best-qualified individual for that particular job."

On the evening before Inauguration Day, Dwight David Eisenhower, with Mamie, his brothers and their wives, son John and his wife, Barbara, enjoyed a farewell party for his status as a private citizen.

Early next morning, General Ike, Mamie, the Eisenhower clan, Vice-President Nixon, the cabinet, the White House staff, Inaugural Committee officials and their families (181 individuals) attended a private service at the National Presbyterian Church, which Ike and Mamie joined.

Mamie had been a Presbyterian since Sunday-school days, but Ike had no church affiliation. He had attended services of many denominations in military chapels. For many years, he had wanted to join a church, and during the campaign, advisers had frequently recommended that he do so, to win votes in his chosen denomination and from other churchgoers.

"I just couldn't bring myself to use my faith in God as a political tool," he told me years later at the Indio, California, home of financier Floyd Odlum. He also said he was offended by the publicity the church had made of his joining.

"God has always been with me, but He had been even more strongly in my thoughts since the election. This is why I emphasized spiritual aspects of living in writing my inauguration address. Yet I didn't want it to be preachy.

"From the time I was a boy, there was embedded in me a deep and abiding faith in God and His beneficence. Virgil, I read the Bible from cover to cover before I was nine—my mother gave me a gold watch for this—and have read it often since. Throughout my military life—especially before major battles—I prayed long and hard.

"My lifelong faith had to be a part of my inauguration address. I felt strongly that the nation was becoming far too secular, that God was no longer a part of our daily life."

Reflecting upon the pre-inaugural church service, Eisenhower came up with the idea of offering a prayer before his address. No chief executive had ever done this before. On a yellow scratch pad, he hurriedly penciled his prayer, now a part of the archives of the Eisenhower Memorial Library at Abilene, Kansas. He memorized it on the way to the Capitol for the inauguration.

> Almighty God, as we stand here at this moment, my future associates in the executive branch of government join me in beseeching that Thou will make full and complete our dedication to the service of the people in this throng and their fellow citizens everywhere.
>
> Give us, we pray, the power to discern clearly right from wrong, and allow all our words and actions to be governed thereby, and by the laws of this land. Especially we pray that our concern shall be for all the people, regardless of station, race or calling.
>
> May cooperation be permitted and be the mutual aim of those who, under the concepts of our constitution, hold to differing political faiths, so that all may work for the good of our beloved country and Thy glory. Amen.

A crisp, sunshiny day and Dwight D. Eisenhower brought out a million excited spectators along Pennsylvania Avenue. The atmosphere in the limousine bearing President Truman, his wife, and president-elect Eisenhower and Mamie to the Capitol was as chilly as the winter air.

Campaign statements on both sides and Truman's slap at Eisenhower's trip to Korea had cooled their relationship. General Ike had declined Truman's invitation to lunch and violated historic custom by not entering the White House to pick up the president. They met self-consciously outside the north portico.

Ike ended the embarrassing silence. "I would like to know who ordered my son, John, from the combat area to attend the inauguration."

Truman glanced archly at Eisenhower, a slight smile on his lips. "I did."

"Mr. President, thank you for your thoughtfulness."

On the steps of the Capitol, Chief Justice Fred M. Vinson administered the oath of office to Eisenhower, who swore on the Bible used at George Washington's inauguration and on his West Point Bible.

The former was open to Psalms 127:1: "Except the Lord build the house, they labour in vain that build it: except the Lord keep the city, the watchman waketh but in vain."

His Bible was open to a Scripture suggested by his friend Billy Graham—2 Chronicles 7:14—"If my people, which are called by my name, shall humble themselves, and pray, and seek my face, and turn from their wicked ways; then will I hear from heaven, and will forgive their sin, and will heal their land."

The inaugural parade that followed disappointed the new president. It was not short. For two and one-half hours, it inched down Pennsylvania Avenue: 50 floats, 65 musical organizations, 22,000 servicemen and women, 5,000 nonmilitary participants, 350 horses, 3 elephants (without party affiliation) 1 Alaskan husky team and 1 huge atomic cannon.

The outgoing and incoming presidents said strained goodbyes. As the figure of Harry Truman receded, Eisenhower experienced a twinge of sadness, and then felt a little better. Approximately a week earlier, he had learned of a glaring lack of governmental courtesy to outgoing presidents. They were not given transportation home. "How barbaric and thankless," Eisenhower commented. He promptly arranged for Truman to travel home to Independence, Missouri, in the *Magellan,* the private car Truman had enjoyed during his presidency.

The Baltimore and Ohio's Capitol Limited pulled out of Union Station with the *Magellan,* and memories rode along with Harry S Truman, for many memories had been made here— particularly during the 1948 presidential campaign, when hundreds of off-the-cuff talks from the rear platform had helped him upset Governor Thomas Dewey and embarrass Colonel McCormick, whose bold, black *Chicago Tribune* headlines had prematurely "elected" Dewey.

As Truman's private car carried him westward toward Independence and private life, President Eisenhower, the new resident of 1600 Pennsylvania Avenue, officially entered public life: the first Republican president since Ulysses S. Grant, destined to serve two full terms.

The initial workday started a bit earlier than for most presidents: shortly after 7:00 A.M. Dwight D. Eisenhower strode vigorously into his office, the oval room in the West Wing of the White House.

Many times before, in the Roosevelt and Truman administrations, Eisenhower had stepped into the oval room, but somehow this seemed the first time.

Even his initial crossing of the English Channel to Normandy after D-Day had not been as exhilarating and emotionally moving as the simple crossing of a threshold into awesome new responsibility and history. Precisely at 8:02 A.M., the duties of the day brought Eisenhower down from the heights to desk level.

Eisenhower's reaction to his new position was hastily scrawled in his desk diary for January 21: "My first day at the president's desk. Plenty of worries and difficult problems. . . ."

Problems of the new president were not limited to the oval room. One concerning etiquette arose during the Eisenhowers' initial White House dinner. Robert Keith Gray, presidential assistant, gave me the inside story, as Eisenhower had told it:

> The first night we were in the White House, this happened, and I told the boy, "Look, in my house the ladies are served first."
> The next day and the day after, they sent in a different waiter each time we were served, and I had to give the same instructions again. Finally, I sent for their head man and explained the new procedure for what I thought would be the final time. When the traditional practice continued, it finally dawned on me: These boys are teaching me how to be president!

While thrown for a loss in the White House dining room on the ladies-first issue, he made a gain in the state dining room on another issue.

On the high marble mantel of this dining room, President John Adams, the first chief executive to occupy the White House, had had a prayer inscribed on November 2, 1800:

> I Pray Heaven to Bestow
> The Best of Blessings on
> THIS HOUSE
> and on All that shall hereafter
> Inhabit it. May none but Honest
> and Wise Men ever rule under this Roof.
> President John Adams

In the White House restoration of 1949, the prayer had not been reinstalled. Eisenhower insisted that it be replaced, and it was done. To him, excluding the prayer symbolized a sin of omission in the daily life of the United States—a nation founded on God and biblical principles, which was turning away from the spiritual.

Ever since his cabinet appointments, which accented wealthy industrialists and businessmen, Mrs. Hobby, and Martin Durkin (former head of a plumbers' union), there had been flak from Adlai Stevenson.

The Roosevelt administration had had its New Deal. Now Governor Stevenson said that the new administration might become the "Big Deal." Around Washington, Eisenhower's cabinet was characterized as "eight millionaires and a plumber."

During Eisenhower's first press conference, he was asked to comment on Stevenson's "Big Deal" label. He refused to indulge in discussing personalities. At the second press conference, he was put on the griddle with his feelings about the Yalta and Potsdam agreements. He refused to attribute improper motives to Roosevelt and Truman.

When aides rough-drafted a message for him to present to Congress, he angrily slashed out words and phrases that criticized Congress and the motives of certain members. Then he pulled off his glasses and pointed them at his aides, his eyes giving off blue frost. "I want to make something clear. I can argue all day, and it won't affect our friendship, but the moment I question your motives, you will never forgive me."

Before his daily duties in the oval room, he usually had a moment's silent prayer for God's wisdom and guidance in decision-making. These were not always on-the-knees prayers. Sometimes they were on-the-leather prayers, as he hurried to his office. He would need them.

Inside the White House

The oval room and the presidential methods rapidly took on the character of Dwight D. Eisenhower. Two conversation pieces hung side by side on one wall—portraits of major figures on opposite sides in the Civil War—General Robert E. Lee and President Abraham Lincoln.

A painting in the president's line of sight, of an Alpine hut on a windswept, mountain ridge, evoked his admiration and frustration. He admired the artist's eminent success in creating a luminous mist over the mountaintop, but was frustrated over his own failure to master this effect in paintings of the Colorado Rocky Mountains.

Inherited from his predecessor, Eisenhower's massive desk, with a top somewhat smaller than an aircraft carrier's deck, dominated the office. Visitors saw little paperwork on its surface. Those who subscribed to the "clean desk-efficient executive" theory marveled at his tidiness.

One afternoon, a visiting businessman asked Eisenhower the secret to keeping his desk so neat. The president beckoned him to come closer. Then, with characteristic honesty, he pulled open the center desk drawer, which was almost overflowing with work.

Usually the only object on the surface was a large appointment pad with the names of the ten to thirty daily visitors and the purpose of each visit neatly inked in each time slot between 8:30 A.M. and 3:30 or 4:00 P.M.

On one of his first days in office, Eisenhower received a phone call from his close friend and associate, General Omar Bradley. After hanging up, he commented in surprise to Ann Whitman, his secretary, "Imagine, my old friend Brad just addressed me as 'Mr. President.' "

Early in the presidency, he shared with the cabinet and the office staff a Fox Conner philosophy that had helped him deemphasize himself and emphasize his work: "Remember, *you're* not important, but your job is."

Each week, he held five high-level meetings with the following: congressional leaders, the National Security Council, the cabinet, the chairman of the Joint Chiefs of Staff and the secretary of defense.

Each cabinet member and key presidential assistant could get additional appointments when needed.

Initially, the president's method of conducting meetings with key congressmen was different from what they expected. Senators Taft, Bridges, Saltonstall, Knowland and Millikin, Speaker Joe Martin and representatives Halleck and Arends were accustomed to rambling, hours-long, or daylong committee sessions. Eisenhower insisted on sticking to subjects and to the allotted times.

After seeing the progress that focus and disciplined discussion permitted, they praised the Eisenhower method. "The work gets done, and we're not forever getting bogged down in side issues," said Halleck.

They were pleased that the president championed his own ideas and gave equal interest to hearing theirs.

"You go away with the impression that the president has at least made an honest effort to listen to you, without trying to make you swallow his ideas as gospel," commented Speaker Martin.

On Capitol Hill, it was acknowledged that Eisenhower was

above piecing together and manipulating coalitions to back legislation—the type of practical politics that both honed and showed the genius of Franklin Delano Roosevelt. It was also acknowledged that Eisenhower had a rare understanding of the legislative process.

"Army politics must be a better training ground than most of us had realized," Martin said.

Dim outlines of a new kind of president, with a new approach, became visible to keen Washington observers. A creative idea that brought Ike favorable comment was his forging the National Security Council into a strategic planning group at the highest peak of government. He encouraged NSC members to be creative, to stand up for their ideas, to disagree with his position. He asked for men—thinkers and planners—not rubber stamps.

At NSC meetings, Central Intelligence Agency director Allen Dulles presented a wide-lens picture of the world situation as it applied to the United States, followed by talking over these facts in terms of the State Department (by John Foster Dulles), the Department of Defense (by Charles Wilson) and the Treasury (by George M. Humphrey).

During Truman's administration, the defense budget had been made up by the Department of Defense, then given to the president, who worked out the final amount with the Bureau of Budget.

Eisenhower, instead of bringing the Treasury Department and Bureau of Budget in after the fact, had them take part in the NSC planning discussions. He wanted financial experts to tell the NSC what the nation could afford, before plans became too grandiose, extravagant, fixed and inflationary.

Eisenhower worked in a similar way with the cabinet. He appointed responsible men and gave responsibility and authority. There were no puppet appointees. He enjoyed delegating, allowing great latitude for decision making and action within his defined policies. He didn't relish FDR's take-it-or-leave-it attitude toward his cabinet.

Truman did not treat his cabinet in the FDR manner—as a

monarch handles his court—but he selected few men of strength and stature, and used this body as advisers, rather than as high-echelon executives. Eisenhower choose strong and capable men, to restore the cabinet to eminence. He had followed the same blueprint in the military, giving authority, responsibility and credit for accomplishment to those under his command.

Each cabinet meeting started with a silent prayer, the secretary of the group, Max Rabb, told me.

A glaring omission in White House administrative procedure immediately caught the attention of Eisenhower and Sherman Adams. It was the type of oversight that led to lengthy delays in completing reports and in answering letters—the sort of careless inefficiency that gave the federal bureaucracy a bad name: There was no system of record keeping and controls.

With thousands of pieces of paper going through the system, it was impossible to tell where anything was and in what stage of completion. Paperwork fanned out to the administrative hinterlands could conceivably languish there and never be acted upon. In many instances, no responsible White House executive would ever know the difference.

Eisenhower had a military cure for this civilian ailment. While at SHAPE, General Ike had a man named Carter Burgess (in time the president of Trans World Airlines) install a methodical secretariat system. Any piece of paperwork could then be tracked down at any time.

Eisenhower and Adams put him to work. In a short time, he was able to turn the system over to General Andrew J. Goodpaster, a West Pointer with a master's degree in engineering and a Ph.D. in international relations, who operated the system like a high-precision machine.

The president also started an innovation of another type: a way of creating closer relations between the executive and legislative branches. He launched daily get-acquainted breakfasts and lunches with senators and representatives.

Still another of his creations, occasional stag dinners, proved to be rewarding and successful. Having attended them, I knew the president's objective was to invite approximately sixteen guests at a time from many fields—agriculture, the arts, education, government, the professions—and representatives from the various media.

"It was a two-way communications arrangement," he told me. "I would learn the thoughts and opinions of Americans from every part of the nation, and guests would have access to me and my thoughts pertinent to their interests."

After dinner, the group sat in a circle in the Red Room and talked. At the end of an evening, the president escorted guests to the door singly, to have a few private minutes with each one.

On one particular occasion, Eisenhower was saying good-bye to a no-nonsense industrialist. Tears began to cascade down the manufacturer's face. Eisenhower was surprised.

"Mr. President," said the man. "I just wanted to tell you what it has meant to me, a farm boy from the Midwest, to spend an evening and dine in the White House. . . ." [1]

Eisenhower placed an arm around the man's shoulders. He understood. As a boy in Abilene, Kansas, he had never dreamed *he* would ever visit the White House, let alone live and entertain there.

Even Ike's long-standing friends experienced a special kind of excitement about visiting the White House, as William J. Robinson shows in his diary:

> . . . I felt a little excited at being the first non-family overnight guest at the White House. . . . Mamie had thoughtfully provided my favorite dinner dish: roast lamb, preceded by consomme and followed by cheese, fruit and coffee.
>
> After dinner, we went on to the miniature movie theater in the White House, joining Dr. and Mrs. Milton Eisenhower, Dr. and Mrs. Howard Snyder and Colonel and Dottie Schulz, to see the film *Peter Pan,* which had been sent around from one of the local movie houses. I sat with Ike at the movie and, as he continued the conversation we'd been enjoying at dinner, Mamie began to "shush" him. At this, he good-naturedly threatened to leave or sit in the back row and continue to talk. . . .

One of the subjects that intrigued me as much as White House visitors was another form of visitors—tons of gifts and letters for the president. How did Eisenhower deal with them? I asked Ann Whitman.

"A gift that clearly reflects thought or love or friendship on the part of the donor is given a presidential reply. A potholder made by a ninety-five-year-old woman or a cane carved by an elderly man—that sort of thing. One woman crocheted a replica of the signing of the Constitution of the United States, big as the wall of a room.

"Everything, but everything, has come in. The gifts have varied throughout the years, reflecting the various sports the president likes, his illness (lounger chairs were strong after the heart attack). Spiritual books are a standard item.

"Items sent with a view for publicity (and such things are easy to detect) get no acknowledgements under my signature."

Ann Whitman also found the president amazingly concerned about gifts to be given: "He worries endlessly about family gifts; he thinks of people who are ill and sends them flowers; both he and Mrs. Eisenhower have a loyalty to and consideration for old army friends that is remarkable to me, in view of the many demands of their present lives."

Ike Eisenhower's gifts often had a creative flair, as Mamie told me in a letter of May 22, 1979. "One incident I shall always remember of Ike doing things unusual was when we lived in the White House. It was my birthday, and I was ill. He had bouquets made of pink carnations for my card-playing friends and had them delivered in my name." Then, to top it off, Ike had the growers in Colorado send her a birthday gift that kept coming—fresh carnations every week.

The amount of mail sent to the president had stepped up considerably in the ninety years between Lincoln and Eisenhower. Abraham Lincoln opened and read his average 30 letters daily. Eisenhower could not possibly have done this, with an average 1,400 letters daily. However, the staff processed and answered those meriting replies, passed some on to the president for reading and response and sent all threatening letters on to the FBI.

Robert Gray made a policy of showing the president humorous letters between appointments. They often served as tension breakers. He tells about this in *Eighteen Acres Under Glass:*

> Two with such refreshing honesty that the President particularly enjoyed them were these written by little girls. The first said, "Dear Mr. President, I love you more than any man in the whole world—except, *of course,* for Perry Como." The second, written by a youngster who was planning a surprise birthday party for her mother, informed the President she was inviting only her *closest* and most special friends, the President, Mrs. Eisenhower, the Queen of England—and Lassie!

During Eisenhower's first months in office, Washington correspondents were mildly surprised that the president and his wife seemed to have little social life.

After Eisenhower's workday, which ended anywhere from 4:00 to 6:00 P.M., the president practiced golf on the White House lawn for thirty to sixty minutes and then joined Mamie for dinner. In emergencies, he worked well into the evening. He was available twenty-four hours a day for crisis situations—accessibility beyond that of most twentieth-century presidents.

When Admiral Arthur Radford became chief of staff, he informed me of an order given him by Eisenhower.

"Admiral, I don't care what hour of the day or night it is, or which day of the week; if anything really important develops, call me immediately at the White House.

"I don't want the information passed to the Pentagon, to the secretary of defense and then eventually relayed to me minutes or hours later. It is my constitutional duty to know what's going on pertaining to all defense matters and foreign policy, and it is an obligation I must meet at all times."

Yet most evenings were quiet. While Mamie enjoyed TV, and Ike sometimes watched with her, he usually read history—books on Lincoln, Washington and Robert E. Lee—and/or western magazines and paperbacks when he wanted to relax and fall asleep around 11 P.M. Rarely did he sleep more than six hours a night.

On one of my trips to the capital, I heard the wits saying: "No wonder the Eisenhowers are doing so little entertaining. On his salary, how can they?" Eisenhower's annual salary was no less than Truman's—$100,000 plus a $50,000 expense allowance—but Congress had chopped a sizeable chunk out of his take-home pay by repealing the tax exemption on his expense allowance.

Out of a total salary and expense account of $150,000 for both presidents, Truman paid taxes of $56,000, leaving take-home pay of $94,000, while Eisenhower paid taxes of about $95,000, leaving take-home pay of roughly $55,000; $39,000 less than Truman.

Conjecture had it that Eisenhower would have to draw on book royalties to keep from going in the hole.

Asked during a press conference for comment on his income, Eisenhower merely responded, "It's a great honor to be president." He was not going to discuss money and undermine the prestige of his office.

Occasionally the Eisenhowers entertained a small number of close relatives and friends, but their major entertaining was at state or formal functions, paid for by the government, and featuring artists such as Marian Anderson, Patrice Munsel, Gregor Piatigorsky, Arthur Rubinstein, Rise Stevens, Gladys Swarthout, and the Mormon Tabernacle Choir. Guests frequently requested the orchestras of Lawrence Welk and Fred Waring.

Although Dwight Eisenhower could live with large formal parties of state, he preferred small, informal groups of relatives or friends.

But, at this point, entertainment and affairs of state became submerged in importance, for President Eisenhower found himself faced with a major crisis—a crisis named *McCarthy*.

Guilty Until Proved Innocent

In one respect, Eisenhower couldn't disagree with Joseph R. McCarthy, junior senator from Wisconsin and chairman of the Senate Permanent Subcommittee on Investigations: Times were uneasy. The Soviet Union's brooding threat to the free world and infiltration into strategic United States government positions had made it necessary to investigate employee loyalty to root out enemy agents. Yet Eisenhower wanted the job done with care and responsibility. All citizens should be treated with dignity. Their constitutional rights should be respected.

When he and McCarthy first met, in Milwaukee, the general backed the Republican senator's reelection but dissociated himself strongly from McCarthy's methods. He still hoped, at that point, that the Wisconsin senator could be brought around by the right influences.

It was not a pleasurable meeting. Eisenhower experienced acute nausea. He studied McCarthy, a bulky, beefy man whose overindulgence showed in a belly rounding over his belt line and the start of a double chin and jowls. Even after a shave, his heavy blue beard made him look as if he needed a shave.

The Wisconsin senator had blighted reputations, careers and

lives of federal-government employees by unfairly conducted interrogations and investigations to uncover alleged Communist party affiliations. Even the most innocent employees lived under a pall of apprehension.

His irresponsible charges, smears, fractional truths, accusations of guilt by association, bullying, destroying the dignity of the questioned and abuse of senatorial immunity neatly filled the capsule called *McCarthyism;* a capsule that stuck in Eisenhower's throat.

McCarthy had started making a name for himself in 1950, with Red hunts in government and attacks on the Yalta and Potsdam agreements, on President Truman, Secretary of State Dean Acheson and his successor, General George C. Marshall.

He was feared by Democrats and by his own party.

In Milwaukee, Eisenhower told McCarthy that he didn't appreciate his way of making investigations. "I intend to make clear my opposition to un-American methods in combating communism." He did.

McCarthy never forgot it.

Shortly after Inauguration Day, President Eisenhower realized that McCarthy was going to harass his administration, just as he had Truman's.

"The State Department has loose security," charged McCarthy, and a wave of anxiety swept through the organization, paralyzing all activity. Secretary of State Dulles could "smoke out subversives," if he had a top security officer like Scott McLeod, an administrative assistant to Senator Styles Bridges.

Dulles conceded.

When President Eisenhower appointed Charles E. "Chip" Bohlen ambassador to the Soviet Union and submitted him for Senate confirmation, McCarthy vehemently objected and tried to kill the appointment.

Bohlen, the best-possible appointee, had dedicated long years to becoming proficient in the Russian language and an authority on Russian history. He understood the people. His record in loyal government service was distinguished.

Senator McCarthy branded him as a "Commie" because

Bohlen had been an interpreter at the Yalta Conference, where the United States had been sold out.

"We find that his entire history is one of complete, wholehearted, one hundred percent cooperation with the Acheson-Hiss-Truman regime," McCarthy said.[1]

Eisenhower was very much upset. He needed Bohlen, and right *now.* He wasn't going to violate his principles and attack McCarthy personally, but he would defend Bohlen.

During his press conference of March 25, 1953, he strongly supported Bohlen, calling him "the best-qualified diplomat" he could find for the Moscow post.

He tried an end run around McCarthy, convincing Senate Majority Leader Robert A. Taft to use his influence for Bohlen. Taft knew that Eisenhower was in an awkward position. He would look bad if he failed to secure an appointment so early in his administration. Taft did not want to show a serious division in the Republican ranks. But rumors had it that there was incriminating material in Bohlen's FBI file.

Eisenhower counterpunched with an invitation to Taft and Democratic Senator Sparkman, as impartial witnesses, to check the Bohlen file to their satisfaction.

"There was no suggestion anywhere by anyone reflecting on the loyalty of Mr. Bohlen or any association by him with communism or support of communism or even tolerance of communism," Taft announced to the Senate. Senator Taft muscled the Bohlen appointment through the Senate by a vote of 74 to 13.

Later, Chip Bohlen told me his reaction to the battle: "Initially, I felt that President Eisenhower could probably have taken McCarthy on frontally, but, in retrospect, I know he was correct in handling this difficult matter constitutionally.

"The president stood solidly behind me throughout the McCarthy attacks. Some officials of the State Department wondered if the president's support was worth his incurring the wrath of the GOP's extreme right wing.

"At that time, it was argued that there was need to mollify the extreme right wing, to gain their support in many matters, especially budgetary and fiscal ones. But in President Eisenhower's mind, I was the man he wanted as ambassador in Russia, and he would not give in the slightest. Further, he felt there was no basis for the attacks on me, and he always fought character assassination, regardless of the individual involved. He backed me fully, even when the secretary of state did not."

Before the executive branch could regroup from one assault, McCarthy launched another. He made a noisy pronouncement that "there are still too many Communists in the State Department!"

Even worse, it seemed that the State Department was disseminating Communist propaganda through libraries in its Overseas Information Program—books written by "reds" and "pinks."

Senator McCarthy's twenty-seven-year-old protégés, Roy Cohn, chief counsel of the Permanent Investigations Subcommittee, and G. David Schine, a consultant, were rushed to western Europe on a whirlwind investigation, to determine how many books in the American overseas libraries "hued" to the Communist party colors.

They were seen skimming books in Bonn, Berlin and Frankfurt and, in after-hours laughingly chasing each other over cobblestone streets. McCarthy reported their findings to a large press conference, claiming they showed "appalling infiltration." This led to a State Department directive, ordering overseas libraries to "remove all books and other materials by Communists, fellow travelers, et cetera. . . ."

Librarians understood what Communists and fellow travelers were, but not knowing precisely what an *et cetera* was, they fearfully got rid of books apparently written by *et ceteras*. Some of the authors who fell into this category were Bert Andrews, Washington bureau chief of the strongly Republican New York *Herald Tribune;* Clarence Streit, who spearheaded the federal union of North Atlantic democracies; Walter White, president of the anti-Communist NAACP; Foster Rhea Dulles, cousin of the secretary of state, an avowed anti-Communist, and mystery writer Dashiell Hammett.

Eisenhower was angry. He didn't counterattack McCarthy by name, but he gave an impromptu speech on book burning at Dartmouth on June 14, when awarded an honorary degree.

> Don't join the book burners. Don't think that you are going to conceal faults by concealing evidence that they ever existed . . . . How will we defeat Communism unless we know what it is, and what it teaches, and why does it have such an appeal for men? . . . We have got to fight it with something better, not to try to conceal the thinking of our own people. They are a part of America. And even if they think ideas that are contrary to ours, their right to them, their right to record them, and their right to have them at places where they are accessible to others is unquestioned, or it isn't America.

Joe McCarthy relentlessly sought and found new individuals or government departments to investigate. Newspaper, TV and radio exposure and fan mail inflated his ego and fueled his drive for more power.

Eisenhower was frustrated by circumstances. The McCarthy wave making was stealing precious time. He had promised much-needed legislation. Republicans controlled the House of Representatives and Senate by such narrow margins that the president needed support from right-wingers such as McCarthy, Jenner, Mundt, Bridges, Dirksen and McCarran. Trying to convert them to his programs called for patience beyond patience, to prevent a breach that couldn't be healed.

Meanwhile, to assure federal employees fair investigation with constitutional guarantees, Eisenhower issued Executive Order 10450—protection against McCarthy-type investigations. It proved effective in eventually leading to the discharge of 2,200 security risks.

Every time Joe McCarthy sighted a new government target for investigation, the president heard renewed clamor from advisers to level him. "I'm not going to get down in the gutter with that guy," he replied.

One stern public rebuke could do it, they argued, because McCarthy was extremely vulnerable.

While an attorney in Wisconsin, he had been charged by peers with dubious practices and was censured. Later, as a circuit judge, he had again bent rules of conduct and been censured by fellow judges.

No one who knew the facts was around to censure him after World War II when, reelected a circuit judge, he glamorized and enriched his military background, to make himself an appealing candidate for the United States Senate.

Voters could find excitement in (and identification with) a combat-injured tail gunner, but hardly in a guy named Joe, an unromantic, desk-bound Marine Corps Intelligence officer of Scout Bombing Squadron 235, whose job had been interviewing flyers and writing reports on their missions.

In a flash of inspiration, his military status went through a remarkable transformation, from "chairborne" to airborne. One of the campaign slogans for "Tail-gunner Joe" became "Wisconsin Needs a Tail-gunner in the Senate." Perhaps Wisconsin did. Instead, it got McCarthy.

Soon "Tail-gunner Joe's" wartime record became even more colorful. He elaborated on horrible bombings and shellings that he had experienced in trenches and dugouts "with the boys under my command." Seeing the slain all around him, he had written innumerable letters to parents or wives of the battle dead. In each one, he had vowed to run for the office of United States Senator and clean up the political mess in Washington, to keep faith with his fallen comrades in arms.

During his first campaign, "Tail-gunner Joe" rarely failed to limp off the platform on a leg he had broken in serving his country. He never mentioned that this service-connected injury had taken place during a boisterous bash on a seaplane tender, when he had become too drunk to negotiate a ladder.

Although healing had been perfect, leaving no sign of a break or injury, McCarthy developed a political limp for his campaign—on occasion forgetting which leg had been "combat injured" and favoring the wrong one.

So many instances of irregular ethics and conduct marked the career of "Tail-gunner Joe," before, during and after

World War II, that a 136-page booklet, *The McCarthy Record,* was required by his 1952 primary opponents to include them all.

Some staff members, advisers and friends urged the president to finish off McCarthy. There was plenty of evidence against him to leak to the press—enough ammunition to shoot down "Tail-gunner Joe."

"I knew that his misdeeds—past and current—would eventually cause him to collapse," Eisenhower told me after retirement. "As the Bible so aptly puts it, in Psalms 7:16: 'His mischief shall return upon his own head, and his violent dealing shall come down upon his own pate.'"

Much of the anti-McCarthy media claimed that the president was doing nothing about him. That was not quite true. Eisenhower's program moved more slowly than a glacier, but it moved inexorably and with constitutional correctness.

He encouraged congressmen to exercise their influence to moderate extremist colleagues and kept communications open with extremists through Vice-President Nixon and General Jerry Persons, liaison with the Senate and House. Any senator who took a public stand against McCarthy or McCarthyism was invited to the White House, to pose with the president for pictures to be released to the press.

A classic fiction plot involves the person who lays a trap for another and falls into it himself. Eisenhower felt that a flaw or weakness would someday catch up with Senator McCarthy. McCarthy was superficial in gathering evidence and subjective in deriving conclusions from it. He was the same in hiring people.

That was how McCarthy happened to name J. B. Matthews to direct investigations. A researcher for the first House Un-American Activities Committee and as zealous as McCarthy, Matthews hardly had settled comfortably in his office chair when his article "Reds In Our Churches" appeared in *American Mercury* magazine.

The first sentence of its lead staggered readers: "The largest single group supporting the Communist apparatus in the

United States today is composed of Protestant clergymen."

Angry protests formed a hurricane that ominously whirled toward Washington, D. C. Three Democrats and one Republican of McCarthy's seven-man committee demanded he fire Matthews. When McCarthy refused, they resigned. Meanwhile, Eisenhower, aided by his staff, issued a formal objection, without naming the senator.

After almost every McCarthy defeat, the president's advisers urged him to finish off the senator, but he refused. Why?

Many answers have been offered by historians. These have been gross, subjective, oversimplified or incomplete, because they merely touch upon parts of a complex system. My long discussion with the president at his Eldorado (Palm Desert) home during his last years revealed the full story.

A popular theory is that he knew that Secretary of State Dean Acheson had lived to regret slugging it out with McCarthy. By doing this, he had increased the senator's importance, raising him to his own level. This theory had a grain of truth in it.

Eisenhower held McCarthy in contempt for several reasons: he was degrading the obligations and responsibilities of his office, violating the constitutionally guaranteed separation of governmental functions, depriving citizens of guaranteed human rights and embarrassing his nation before the world.

Fired with the ideals of the founders of the republic, Eisenhower profoundly respected the presidency. "No man has a right to debase that office," he told me. "There was no way in which I, occupying that high office, could fight with a senator."

Eisenhower would not descend to using McCarthy tactics to defeat McCarthy. He believed in living by the constitution and in separation of the executive, legislative and judicial branches of government. Although McCarthy seemed bent on usurping executive powers, Eisenhower could not bring himself to tamper with the legislative branch.

"I found the authority and powers of the presidency awesome—as defined by the constitution and as acquired. I sometimes had to apply the brakes to stay within constitutional limits," he told me. "Over and above this, I didn't attack McCarthy for a practical reason.

"Probably the worst thing that can be done by a president who needs support of the legislature is to fight with one of its members. No matter how just the cause, the president appears to be a bully, because he has chosen to attack someone not in as advantageous a position.

"Historically, a legislative body rallies around any member attacked by the president. It doesn't matter how unpopular the legislator may be. Despite my impatience with him—often anger—I had optimism beyond what circumstances warranted that he might still come around and do some constructive work toward needed legislation.

"Even if he failed to come around, I felt that his whole effort would crumble by its own weight. His house was not built on rock.

"The public exposure that he so zealously sought, I always felt, would—in the end—undo what it had done for him."

It was always Eisenhower's position that the McCarthy problem belonged to the Senate. He once told CBS commentator Walter Cronkite: "I think that the doctrine of restraint on the part of responsible officials of the government is absolutely necessary. It's vital to the real success of a democracy. I think possibly I have told you before one definition of democracy that I like. It is merely the opportunity for self-discipline. It is the opposite of the kind of discipline that's placed upon you by a dictator when you have to live your life according to his dictates."

Never quiet for long, McCarthy made ominous rumblings about a spy ring at the army's Fort Monmouth Signal Corps facility. When Secretary of the Army Robert Stevens investigated and announced that no such evidence existed, McCarthy himself went to Fort Monmouth and interrogated employees behind closed doors. McCarthy, according to some observers, attacked the army for two reasons: he felt his charges were valid and he wanted to draw the president into the center ring.

Then came Washington whisperings that the investigator

might soon be investigated himself—in the G. David Schine case.

Schine had been inducted into the army at Fort Dix, New Jersey. Subcommittee Counsel Roy Cohn did not relish parting with his close associate. While the army was making a public declaration that Private Schine would receive no preferential treatment, Cohn began phoning army brass, to see that he did get preferential treatment: being permanently stationed in Washington, D. C., or New York City, being made a commissioned officer and having special privileges.

Supposedly Schine was getting an inordinate number of evening passes and weekend leaves not normally given recruits and little, if any, guard duty, target practice, and KP. He was said to be creating morale problems by intimating that he was on a special mission to do research on camp morale.

One bit of scuttlebutt held that Cohn had verbally arm-twisted highest Department of the Army officials to arrange special assignments for Schine, such as checking for subversive literature in the West Point Library.

As quickly as the rumors emerged, they submerged. With the Christmas season near and snow fleecing over the Capitol, McCarthy radiated peace on earth and good will toward men. Harmony rang out from the White House, as well. The president met for three days in the executive mansion, with congressional leaders, to discuss legislation for the new session of Congress.

Eisenhower's major thrust was a bill to authorize construction of the Saint Lawrence Seaway with Canada; a 2,472-mile system of canals, dams and locks to permit oceangoing vessels to steam into Great Lakes ports—Buffalo, Cleveland, Toledo, Detroit, Chicago, Milwaukee, Duluth and Toronto, Canada.

This project had been talked about by presidents for fifty years. Eisenhower's enthusiasm helped sell the project to the legislators. The bill passed during the following year.

The president expressed the need for even more dedication and vigilance in rooting out subversives in government. On several occasions, he and McCarthy discussed security problems at length. After the meetings, reporters questioned the senator from Wisconsin about the sessions and the president. "This is the first time I have had an opportunity to watch the president in action over a period of time. I was tremendously impressed with his handling of the conference and his detailed knowledge of every subject or piece of proposed legislation that was discussed."

The McCarthys spent three days as guests of Vice-President and Mrs. Nixon in Miami. The senator mellowed toward the administration and the army. He hinted that the Treasury Department could be his next target. Settlements of tax cases at low figures might change the direction of his investigations from olive drab to money green.

No sooner had Joe McCarthy returned to Washington than his "all's right with the world" smile faded from his face.

A snide comment of a colleague got under his skin: "First you get cozy with the executive function. Then you start taking orders as to what you can investigate."

McCarthy exploded: "No men of little minds and less morals are going to limit me."

Another stab came when he learned that Senator Allen J. Ellender, of Louisiana, and other Democrats, were planning to cut off his subcommittee's $200,000 annual appropriation unless he took back, on their own terms, the Democrats who had walked out on him. Ellender disliked seeing taxpayers' money sustaining professional snoopers who were more interested in glorifying the name and reputation of McCarthy than in helping the nation.

Senator Ellender's efforts made McCarthy mad. Instead of requesting $200,000 for his subcommittee, he would double his staff of 11 investigators and request $300,000. "Let the Democrats dare interfere with my committee in appropriations and political maneuvers and I'll turn the heat on them again as the party of treason, the party that covers up spies and traitors."

McCarthy's spirited threats and bullying turned most Democrats into jelly. The best they could now hope for was to hold his budget to the previous year's figure.

Senator McCarthy's triumph ended abruptly, when he learned that the rumor about an army investigation into G. David Schine was true. He would certainly be involved, although by his own admission, he was glad to be rid of his former aide, who was "becoming a nuisance." He claimed he had wanted no army favors for Schine.

Slowly, surely the innocent-appearing Schine case and the Fort Monmouth investigations were almost on a collision course that would explode into the greatest show in which Joe McCarthy had ever been involved.

Previously, McCarthy had been invulnerable. His vote getting with the Red issue and the Democrats had made him a tolerable, if not totally acceptable, asset to his party. Democrats feared to attack him and be counterattacked as "Commie Coddlers." They rationalized that McCarthy was a Republican problem. "Let the Republicans tear their party apart," said Minority Leader Lyndon Baines Johnson.

Republicans, not wishing to be considered soft on communism, also were timid about standing up to McCarthy. They looked to the president to keep him in line. Eisenhower insisted that, constitutionally, McCarthy was the Senate's problem.

Everybody turned to somebody else for the solution, so the problem that nobody wanted ended up where it started—with everybody.

All of the big ones didn't get away, as President Eisenhower proved in 1958. *Right:* Better than average on the course, Ike loved golf. He and Bobby Jones were credited with doing more to popularize the game than any other people.

Constantly seeking peace, President Eisenhower hosted the USSR's Secretary of the Communist party, Nikita Khrushchev, at Camp David in 1959. *Below:* A general view of the Eisenhower farm in Gettysburg, Pennsylvania. (Wide World Photos.)

Ike and Mamie enjoying the garden at the Gettysburg farm. (Wide World Photos.) *Below:* Ike watches as cadets of the Valley Forge Military Academy at Wayne, PA, pass in review. (Wide World Photos.)

Eisenhower on a 1961 hunting trip. He enjoyed hunting throughout his life. (Wide World Photos.) *Below:* The four Eisenhower brothers hold a reunion before the formal dedication of the Eisenhower Library. From left: Milton, Earl, Edgar and Ike. (Wide World Photos.)

Ike with Senator Everett M. Dirksen and Charles A. Halleck, in 1962. (Wide World Photos.) *Right:* A 1962 picture of Ike and Mamie on their trip to London. (Wide World Photos.)

President Kennedy and Ike meet while both are vacationing in 1962. (Wide World Photos.) *Below:* Former president Eisenhower showing Senator Barry Goldwater points of interest on the Gettysburg farm during a 1964 meeting. (Wide World Photos.)

Under the watchful eye of Arnold Palmer, Ike sinks a fifty-foot putt. This was the first time Ike played before a public gallery. (Wide World Photos.) *Below:* Ike and Mamie posed with their growing grandchildren in 1965. The grandchildren are (from left): Susan, Mary Jean, David and Anne. (Wide World Photos.)

In 1966, Ike and Mamie celebrated their fiftieth wedding anniversary. They were the first presidential couple to celebrate fifty years of marriage since John Quincy Adams and his wife. (Wide World Photos.) The Place of Meditation, the final resting place of General Ike, in Abilene, Kansas. When he left home to attend West Point, he promised to return one day. His first son, Icky, is buried beside him.

The Eisenhower family home in Abilene. Today the home is open to the public and hosts thousands of visitors annually.

Showdown

Several influential Washington writers came to a troubling conclusion about Senator McCarthy, and it spilled out into print. So much time and attention were being squandered on him and his investigations and political battles that crucial national and world problems were being neglected.

Many legislators and the United States Army—particularly Secretary of the Army Robert Stevens—felt the same way. Two Democrat senators, McClellan and Russell, thought that the Schine issue, properly handled, might finish McCarthy and get him out of the way. So did the army, which gave the media a thirty-four page report, complete with requests and threats on behalf of Schine, including dates and times. (This methodical, documented presentation was the president's idea.)

McCarthy cursed. It was "blackmail" to get him to end the Fort Monmouth investigation and turn his attention elsewhere!

Then came other developments. In a nationally televised speech, Adlai Stevenson bitterly denounced Eisenhower for letting McCarthyism destroy the nation. Republican Senator Ralph Flanders, of Vermont, rose in the Senate and derided McCarthy with a mocking speech.

Edward R. Murrow's CBS program "See It Now," through carefully selected film clips, showed the Wisconsin senator at his McCarthyistic worst: belching, yawning without covering his mouth, picking his nose, scratching vital parts of his anatomy. One of the program's most pertinent comments was, ". . . The line between investigation and persecution is a very fine one, and the junior senator has stepped over it repeatedly."

McCarthy called Murrow part of the "extreme left wing, bleeding hearts elements of television and radio."

Murrow replied, "If the senator means that I am somewhat left of his position and of Louis XIV, he is correct." [1]

Now the army formally charged McCarthy in the Schine case. McCarthy countercharged the army with "Commie coddling."

There was one way to settle the army-McCarthy issue: by an in-depth inquiry. The battle lines were drawn. McCarthy against Stevens? Yes, and more than that. It was the senator from Wisconsin versus the man in the White House: the rough-and-tumble fighter and the one who preferred not to fight—an "eye for an eye" versus "turn the other cheek," the Old Testament versus the New Testament.

Most of the media people knew that the president would never get into the ring with the senator, but they were eager to see what would happen between McCarthy and Stevens. The nation waited breathlessly for what promised to be a television spectacular.

On Thursday, April 22, the Senate Permanent Subcommittee on Investigations opened its public investigation, and *public* it was. Within the arena of the Senate caucus room, more than 500 spectators; 130 news-media representatives; 60 still photographers and TV cameramen, directors and technicians mashed in and elbowed one another to see what was billed as the greatest government fight in history. An estimated 30 million settled before their TV sets, with snacks and cold beverages, waiting for the first-round bell.

Behind an imposing, dark mahogany, thirty-six-foot table sat the seven committee members. Senator Mundt, as temporary chairman (McCarthy had stepped down), sat in the middle, with special counsel Ray Jenkins at his immediate right. Farther right were Republican senators Dirksen, Potter and Dworshak (Idaho). Dworshak had been appointed by McCarthy to sit in and prevent a tie vote. Left of Mundt sat Democrat senators McClellan, Symington and Jackson. Even farther away from Mundt than the farthest-out Democrat was Joe McCarthy, the center of attention. Directly opposite Chairman Mundt was the witness chair, beside which stood chunky Joseph N. Welch, attorney of the Boston law firm of Hale & Dorr, who was serving as army counsel for no fee or expenses.

A graduate of Harvard Law School's class of 1917, Welch, fond of conservative vested suits and bow ties, had an exaggeratedly long face, a partially bald pink head, a deceptively sleepy appearance, elegant manners, patrician gentility and the bite of a rattlesnake in his casually spoken words.

Some distance from the caucus room, in the White House, Eisenhower felt too close to the scene. He was almost physically ill at the thought of his beloved army rolling in the mud with McCarthy.

Most of the evidence against McCarthy in the Schine case was already known, through the previously issued thirty-four-page report. He had had ample time to build his rebuttal.

Supposedly, army counsel John Adams had volunteered data on an air-force base harboring homosexuals, in exchange for McCarthy calling off the Fort Monmouth investigation. Adams was also said to have offered to arrange a law partnership for Cohn in New York City.

These charges—called falsehoods and lies by Secretary of the Army Stevens and Adams—had a creative flair reminiscent of "Tail-gunner Joe's" war record.

Throughout the thirty-six-day hearings, McCarthy and McCarthyism—insolence, rudeness, boorish conduct, accusations, name calling, insensitivity, crudeness—entered the nation's living rooms. All the mannerisms and traits presented in brief on Murrow's "See It Now" were replayed at length daily.

A certain McCarthyistic trait became apparent to viewers. The Wisconsin senator insisted that those interrogated by him strictly obey the legal ground rules. However, when cornered, he made his own rules, particularly when Welch quizzed him about information in a letter taken without authorization from an FBI file.

It was ironic that, near the end of the inquiry, McCarthy introduced an issue that was not relevant and had a devastating effect on the hearings and his senatorial stature.

An agreement had been reached by McCarthyites and the army not to touch upon two subjects: The fact that Fred Fisher, a Hale & Dorr attorney, had briefly been a member of a Communist-related organization, and the army career of Roy Cohn. (There was nothing suspect about the latter—only that it should be an area of immunity.)

Then, after Counsel Welch had baited Cohn about not submitting names of 130 known Communists to the FBI and the Department of Defense, McCarthy lost control and angrily interrupted:

> Mr. Chairman, in view of Mr. Welch's request that information be given if we know of anyone who might be performing any work for the Communist party, I think we should tell him that he has in his law firm a young man named Fisher, whom he recommended incidentally to do work on this committee, who has been, for a number of years, a member of an organization which is named, oh, years and years ago, as the legal bulwark of the Communist party, an organization that always swings to the defense of anyone who dares to expose Communists.[2]

A gasp went up from the caucus-room audience. Cohn tried to attract McCarthy's attention. The senator had violated the prehearing agreement. McCarthy continued, in his sing-song, nasal voice:

> I assume that Mr. Welch did not know of this young man at the time he recommended him as the assistant counsel for this committee, but he has such terror and such a great desire to know where anyone is located. You may be serving the Communist party, Mr. Welch, and I thought we should just call to your attention the fact that your Mr. Fisher, who is still in your law firm today, whom you asked to have down here looking over the secret

and classified material, is a member of an organization, not
named by me but named by various committees, named by the
Attorney General, as I recall.

He belonged to it after it had been exposed as the legal arm of
the Communist party. Knowing that, Mr. Welch, I just felt that I
had a duty to respond here to your urgent request that *before
sundown* that if we know of anyone serving the Communist cause
we let the agency know.

We're now letting you know your man did belong to this organization for either three or four years. Belonged to it long after
he was out of law school. And I have hesitated bringing that up,
but I have been rather bored with your phony requests to Mr.
Cohn here, that he personally get every Communist out of government *before sundown* . . . .

Whether you knew that he was a member of that Communist
organization or not, I don't know. I assume you did not, Mr.
Welch, because I get the impression that while you are quite an
actor, you play for a laugh, I don't think you have any conception
of the danger of the Communist party. I don't think you yourself
would ever knowingly aid the Communist cause. I think you're
unknowingly siding with it when you try to burlesque this hearing
in which we're attempting to bring out the facts.[3]

McCarthy hurriedly thumbed through a mass of papers, and,
on a point of personal privilege, Welch took the microphone:
"Senator McCarthy, may I have your attention?" The senator
continued riffling. "I can listen with one ear."

"Now this time, sir, I want you to listen with both," replied
Welch, with uncharacteristic sternness.

Senator McCarthy, I think until this moment—you won't need
anything in the record when I finish telling you this—until this
moment, senator, I think I never really gauged your cruelty or
your recklessness.

Fred Fisher is a young man who went to Harvard Law School
and came into my firm and is starting what looks to be a brilliant
career with us. When I decided to work for this committee, I
asked Jim St. Clair, who sits on my right, to be my first assistant. I
said to Jim, "Pick somebody in the firm to work under you that

you would like." He chose Fred Fisher and they came down on the afternoon plane.

That night, when we had taken a little stab at what this case was about, Fred Fisher and Jim St. Clair and I went to dinner together. I then said to these two men, "Boys, I don't know anything about you, except that I've always liked you, but if there is anything funny in the life of either of you that would hurt anybody in this case, then speak up quick."

And Fred Fisher said, "Mr. Welch, when I was in law school, and for a period of months after that, I belonged to the Lawyers Guild," as you have suggested, senator. . . . And I said, "Fred, I just don't think I'm going to ask you to work on this case. If I do, one of these days that will come out, and go over national television, and it will just hurt like the dickens."

And so, senator, I asked him to go back to Boston. Little did I dream that you could be so cruel and reckless as to do an injury to that lad. It is true, he is still with Hale & Dorr. It is true that he will continue to be with Hale & Dorr. It is, I regret to say, equally true that I fear he shall always bear a scar needlessly inflicted by you.

If it were in my power to forgive you for your reckless cruelty, I would do so. I like to think I'm a gentle man, but your forgiveness will have to come from someone other than me.[4]

Tears filled Welch's eyes. Sobbing, overcome with emotion, he walked from the room. Applause thundered after him.

McCarthy knew he had lost the round. As the chair called a recess, he sat motionless, staring at the table. Everything after that was an anticlimax for him. There were flurries of the old McCarthy, but they were just flurries. McCarthyism, which had made McCarthy, had unmade him. The trapper had trapped himself.

Eisenhower rated McCarthy in this way:

Measured against all the mental anguish unfairly inflicted upon people and all the bitterness occasioned by baseless charges against them, the benefits flowing from the McCarthy "investigations" do not loom large. . . . those discovered by the subcommittee to be, on reliable information, disloyal or unreliable were few. . . .

. . . Un-American activity cannot be prevented or rooted out by employing un-American methods; to preserve freedom we must use the tools that freedom provides.[6]

Between January and August, Gallup polls showed a dive in McCarthy's popularity from 50 percent who approved of him to 36 percent. An even more devastating blow came in the latter phase of the hearings.

Senator Flanders introduced a resolution in the Senate to censure him: "Resolved, that the conduct of the junior Senator from Wisconsin is unbecoming a member of the United States Senate, is contrary to Senatorial traditions, and tends to bring the Senate into disrepute, and such conduct is hereby condemned."

A special Senate committee chaired by Arthur V. Watkins, of Utah, heard the charge. In December, those who, for fear or politics, had never before openly opposed McCarthy came together. The word *censure* was changed to *condemn* at the recommendation of Vice-President Nixon. McCarthy was condemned by a vote of 67 to 22.

One writer likened his collapse to that of the dirigible Hindenburg, destroyed by fire in minutes. It was actually slower than that. Always a person who had dissipated his physical resources, he began drinking heavily, steadily deteriorating.

Many senators who had dreaded him, those who had catered to him and others who had merely tolerated him, now ignored him. Overnight, one of the most feared and powerful men who ever lived had become a nonentity. Although he was present, he wasn't there. If he was there, it was only a part of him, because one-third of Joe McCarthy—his spirit—was gone. His mind and body might just as well have gone along, too. Approximately three years after condemnation, in 1957, they did go. And with them went a dark and unsettling era of American history.

Did Dulles Run Eisenhower?

Critics of President Eisenhower often referred to him as a ventriloquist's dummy to Secretary of State John Foster Dulles. How well does this label adhere to Eisenhower?

A valid answer can't be given without a careful look at the complex world situation, the individuals involved and their unique ways of adjusting to one another. The international state of affairs inherited by the Eisenhower administration was unlike any in history. World War II had unleashed giant opposing forces in fierce competition for survival. Safety through geography had vanished. Both powers had the A-bomb.

No nation, including the United States, could finance defense of the entire globe against communism. Yet, the USA, staggering under a $272 billion federal debt, was mortgaging the future of its great-great-grandchildren to try: funneling billions into a stalemated, unpopular war in Korea and into the French defense of Indochina, while financially resuscitating West Germany, Japan and other countries.

Eisenhower, with help from Dulles, designed a program to build military muscles in individual free nations and groups of them. Economic and military pledges were made to sixty countries, with a total population of more than 1 billion. Already in the planning stage was aid to seven nations allied for security, the South-East Asia Treaty Organization (SEATO), patterned after NATO.

The military economics learned by Eisenhower in the Philippines, World War II and NATO showed that it costs a fraction as much to arm and train troops of a given nation than to sustain American service personnel there.

Skilled American diplomacy and a clenched military fist seemed necessary to keep the Soviet Union from a surprise nuclear attack on the United States.

Three hundred and fifty military bases were established by the United States around the world, and atomic-bomb-carrying B-52 aircraft stayed aloft at all times, within range of the Soviet Union, to deter recklessness and overambition.

This was the climate in which President Eisenhower hoped to keep the peace and, at the same time, reduce the national budget (eventually balancing it) and the crushing annual interest payments on the federal debt. His fiscal goals created many Washington cloakroom laughs.

With trouble spots flaring up on many continents, Dulles became the most-traveled secretary of state to that date, eventually covering one-half million miles and forty-five nations.

Whatever problems resulted from two sets of hands on the tiller did not surprise Eisenhower. Even before the Chicago convention, he knew that Dulles had personal power to match his bearish bulk, a deep knowledge of Soviet aspirations and a mind with Samson's strength. (The only surprise was Dulles's ill-concealed fear of McCarthy.)

"The major reason I selected Foster as secretary of state was because, after myself, he knew more about international affairs than anyone else," Eisenhower told me after the presidency. "Prior to the 1952 elections, both parties had talked about him for that position."

Dulles stood for a more aggressive and simpler Soviet Union foreign policy than the Truman administration. Costly countermeasures to a succession of brushfire wars in faraway places could bleed the nation's manpower and funds. Instead, the threat of devastating atomic bombing (massive retaliation) on Moscow and Peking would deter the Russians and Red Chinese.

The first priority was Korea. Following the Truman thesis accepting a divided Korea along existing battle lines (the thirty-eighth parallel), Eisenhower and Dulles assigned Robert Murphy to work with General Mark W. Clark to secure a truce.

The president's known desire for peace encouraged the Communists to increase their attacks in Korea, to strengthen their position at the bargaining table, where they were surly and truculent.

Four months of negotiations led only to frustration. At this point, General James A. Van Fleet, commander of UN forces in Korea, attempted to capture a hill position in front of the main battle line. Despite his estimate that the objective could be captured with about two hundred UN casualties, some 6,000 were killed or wounded and the effort failed.

Eisenhower was jolted. If atomic artillery had been used, the objective would have been taken with few losses. Now he would play his trump card. He asked Dulles to get the word to Peking, through Prime Minister Nehru, that the United States, tired of futile peace efforts, was about to finish the war with small atomic weapons. Immediately, the Red Chinese came to the peace table with more serious intentions.

"They were insolent to the last," Bob Murphy told me. "Clark, knowing that a blow-up would destroy negotiations, gritted his teeth and endured the assignment with remarkable restraint and intelligence."

On July 27, 1953, the armistice was signed. It was hoped that this was the first step toward an honorable peace settlement.

Although relieved about Korea, Eisenhower and Dulles were troubled by another part of Asia: French Indochina. Communist Vietnamese in the north, with help from the Red Chinese, were fighting to rid themselves of French colonialism.

The French were already weary of fighting in steamy swamps

and mosquito-infested jungles. Toward the year's end, Dulles strongly favored United States involvement, to stop the tide of communism from flooding all of French Indochina, Burma, Thailand and Malaya. From there, communism would sweep toward Indonesia and beyond. Dulles and Eisenhower could visualize the loss of strategic raw materials such as rubber, tin and tungsten. Australia and New Zealand would be the next objectives.

As grave as the situation was, Eisenhower, on February 10, 1954, told a press conference that he "could scarcely imagine a tragedy greater than American intervention in Indochina."

Before and right after the president's statement, Dulles began briefings for media people, statesmen and congressional leaders on the nation's stake in Indochina. These soon became campaigns to sell the idea that the United States could not survive if Communists took Indochina.

Surprisingly, Senate response to Dulles's hawkish talk was favorable. Already this futile war in a hopeless place was draining the French treasury, even with heavy United States financial aid.

Many factors made President Eisenhower leery about Indochina: his desire for peace, the heavy cost, logistics and the recent death of Soviet Union Premier Josef Stalin. First, he felt that the nation needed peace to heal from two wars. Second, he didn't want increased military expenditures to cause more deficit spending and defeat his effort to balance the budget and stop inflation. Third, Indochina's great distance from the United States would cause logistical problems. Fourth, he wanted time to get clear indications as to whether or not the new Soviet Union regime would relax the Stalin hard-line stance toward the United States.

Even talk of intervention could be harmful to relations with the new Russian leaders and prevent a possible thaw in the Cold War.

Dulles wanted a strong United States posture in Asia. He favored giving the Red Chinese "a licking."

When Eisenhower heard this, his temperature shot up. "If

Mr. Dulles and all his sophisticated advisers really mean that, they cannot talk peace seriously. Then I am in the wrong pew. For if it is war we should be talking about, I know the people to give me advice on that, and they are not in the State Department. Now we can cut out all this fooling around and make a serious bid for peace, or we can forget the whole thing."

On more than one occasion, he shook his sparsely covered head and commented on Indochina (Vietnam): "It's the wrong war in the wrong place at the wrong time."

Eisenhower's eagerness to talk peace with the Soviet Union troubled Dulles. What could be gained?

Over Dulles's counsel, Eisenhower gave a speech titled "The Chance for Peace" before a meeting of the American Society of Newspaper Editors. It turned out to be rich in uncommon common sense, and a diplomatic coup:

> Every gun that is made, every warship launched, every rocket fired signifies, in the final sense, a theft from those who hunger and are not fed, those who are cold and are not clothed. The world in arms is not spending money alone. It is spending the sweat of its laborers, the genius of its scientists, the hopes of its children. The cost of one modern heavy bomber is this: a modern brick school in more than thirty cities. It is two electric-power plants, each serving a town of sixty-thousand population. It is two fine, fully equipped hospitals. It is some fifty miles of concrete highway.
>
> What is the Soviet Union ready to do? . . . A world that begins to witness the rebirth of trust among nations can find its way to a peace that is neither partial nor punitive. . . . The first great step along this way must be the conclusion of an honorable peace in Korea. . . . We seek throughout Asia, as throughout the world, a peace that is true and total. . . . This government is ready to ask its people to join with all nations in devoting a substantial percentage of the savings achieved by disarmament to a fund for world aid and reconstruction. . . . What is the Soviet Union ready to do?

Newspapers called this one of Eisenhower's best speeches. The president was surprised when the USSR's official newspapers, *Pravda* and *Izvestia*, printed the full text, one of the first times this was ever done.

Another of his speeches applied a cold pack to the swelling fears of all free nations after the reverberations from the Soviet Union's first hydrogen-bomb explosion. Such a devastating weapon, along with the Soviet Union's naked ambition for world conquest, horrified thinking people. They foresaw what they hoped never to see: titanic powers reducing each other's cities to rubble, decimating populations and contaminating every living thing.

Where on earth could anyone hide?

This impending, overshadowing, man-made doomsday brought epidemic nervousness, tension, hopelessness and expectancy of the worst.

Eisenhower wanted to reassure the United States and the free world that its own vast atomic arsenal would help deter irresponsible or capricious acts by the Soviet Union. He asked aide C. D. Jackson to write a speech spotlighting the unimaginable, annihilating power of the nation's stockpiled nuclear weapons. This negative assignment fissioned into a positive program, a constructive contribution to world peace, improved diplomatic relations and peace of mind.

Eisenhower struck upon the idea of creating an international pool of uranium for have-not nations to use for peaceful purposes. Perhaps the Russians could be induced to contribute to the pool with the United States.

It was a revolutionary plan from a conservative mind. Dulles's immediate reaction mirrored that of most persons. How could one make sure that the nuclear fuel would not be stolen and used for offensive purposes?

The president was far ahead of him. Admiral Lewis A. Strauss, Chairman of the United States Atomic Energy Commission, much admired by Eisenhower, had already found a way of preventing theft by holding uranium diluted and in solution. Also, the pool would issue a small amount of fuel only to responsible nations and, by regular inspection, make sure it was being used for peaceful purposes.

An air of expectancy raced through the United Nations General Assembly of December 8, 1953, as President Eisenhower began to outline his program. He mentioned the need to reduce the fear of nuclear energy and then proposed his program for peaceful uses in cooperation with the Soviet Union.

> The more important responsibility of this Atom Energy Agency would be to devise methods whereby this fissionable material would be allocated to serve peaceful pursuits of mankind. Experts would be mobilized to apply atomic energy to the needs of agriculture, medicine and other peaceful activities.
>
> A special purpose would be to provide abundant electrical energy in the power-starved areas of the world. Thus the contributing powers would be dedicating some of their strength to serve the needs rather than the fears of mankind.
>
> The United States pledges before you—and therefore the world—its determination to help solve the fearful atomic dilemma—to devote its entire heart and mind to find the way by which the miraculous inventiveness of man shall not be dedicated to his death, but consecrated to his life.

Eisenhower's program was a resounding diplomatic victory for the United States, showing leadership, idealism and altruism. The world could now begin to see atomic energy's better profile. Perhaps there was some reason for hope, after all.

The press named the program Atoms for Peace. It did not come into being immediately, but in time the president's vision became solid reality.

Although Eisenhower's decisions on Atoms for Peace and other key issues had been made despite the objections of Dulles, it was clear to insiders that the president and secretary of state could work harmoniously, in agreement or disagreement.

Explosive Islands, Open Skies

Before dawn on September 3, 1954, the Chinese Communists shelled the island of Quemoy, just off the coast of the Chinese mainland port of Amoy. A complex of islands farther north, called Matsu, was related to the Quemoy happening. These pieces of real estate in the Formosa Strait would be front-page news for months, because they appeared to be the hissing fuse for World War III.

When General Chiang Kai-shek, Nationalist leader, and his forces were routed from China by the Red Chinese in 1949, they took refuge on the island of Formosa (Taiwan), some 125 miles from the mainland. Chiang's troops had also occupied Quemoy and Matsu. They would be useful as a buffer to discourage the Red Chinese from trying to capture Formosa.

The Red Chinese reacted to Chiang's troops on Quemoy as the United States would have reacted to Russian soldiers occupying Staten Island. As Eisenhower once explained to me, "It was like looking down gun barrels."

Farther east, perhaps 100 miles from the mainland, were the Nationalist-occupied Pescadores, an island chain 25 miles from Formosa itself. Far to the north were the Tachen Islands.

The United States was involved due to its mutual-assistance pact with Chiang. The only question was, did the defense of the Nationalists involve only Formosa and the Pescadores, or also Quemoy and Matsu?

Peace-loving Americans with only a gross appreciation of the situation typically said, "Formosa is the only important thing. Just get Chiang to abandon Quemoy and Matsu!" Simple advice for a complex situation. Chiang had a greater ambition than refuge on Formosa: rebuilding his army to invade the mainland. Without Quemoy and Matsu as logistical stepping-stones and morale boosters, his troops would lose hope and heart.

The United States Seventh Fleet anchored near Matsu, convenient to Quemoy for any emergency. Premier Chou En-lai, of the Peoples Republic of China, announced his intention to "liberate" Formosa. He would tolerate no interference from the United States.

Events heated up. Asked at a White House press conference what would happen if the Chinese Communists were to attack Formosa, President Eisenhower replied, ". . . I would assume . . . any invasion of Formosa would have to run over or through the Seventh Fleet."

Members of the Joint Chiefs of Staff and John Foster Dulles advised holding the offshore islands and helping the Nationalists bomb the mainland. Eisenhower killed the idea. Dulles then recommended that the offshore matter be placed before the United Nations Security Council. This plan pleased Eisenhower.

On the heels of this, the Red Chinese announced that thirteen American airmen captured in Korea had been sentenced from four years to life for espionage. Senator William Knowland insisted the United States Navy blockade China and force the Red Chinese to release them. Eisenhower gave Knowland a resounding no. Such an act would be self-defeating and might possibly provoke Russian intervention. He urged patience.

After New Year's Day of 1955, when 100 Red Chinese aircraft bombed the Tachen Islands and launched an amphibious attack on Ichiang, a small post near the Tachens, Dulles proposed evacuating Chiang's forces from the untenable Tachens with the Seventh Fleet. Eisenhower approved.

In a special message to Congress, the president asked permission to defend Formosa, the Pescadores and, at his discretion, other principal islands.

After his second term, the president explained to me why he did this. "First, I wanted the backing of Congress for any major military action. It seemed to me that the executive function had previously taken unwarranted liberties in unilateral decisions. Second, I wanted to establish in the minds of the Communist Chinese that the executive and legislative branches were in complete harmony.

"It is my strong belief that the Korean War started because the Communist Chinese erroneously thought that the United States would not back the Republic of Korea. With the backing of Congress, I knew that the Communists would not again mistake our intentions and be too quick to attack Formosa. Third, if we left our options open relative to Quemoy and Matsu, this would give the Communists pause and possibly delay or discourage any military action there."

Red Chinese belligerency troubled him. The Communists were intoxicated with their successes: having driven UN troops in Korea from the Yalu River back to the thirty-eighth parallel, having overwhelmed the French at Dien Bien Phu, and having forced the United States to evacuate Nationalists from the Tachens.

Chou En-lai brought the matter to a climax. In a war with the United States, he could lose 150 million men and still have 450 million left, he boasted.

A shudder went through Washington, D.C.

Eisenhower, John Foster Dulles, Allen Dulles, the secretary of defense and the Joint Chiefs of Staff discussed Quemoy and Matsu daily.

The president was due for a press conference.

"We were meeting with him . . . discussing questions that might arise and making suggestions for him to consider for his response," General Andrew J. Goodpaster wrote me in a letter of January 17, 1970.

> On this question, we all recognized that it was tremendously important that he not be "smoked out" . . . that he keep the Chinese Communists uncertain, and face them with the threat of response over the forward positions without pinning himself down and giving up his flexibility.
>
> Unfortunately, we were unable to suggest how to do this. After hearing us out, he finally told us, in the direct and incisive way he had, "All right, boys, I know how I will handle this. I'll confuse them."
>
> You may recall that this is exactly what he did, and the wails that went up over his mixed-up sentences. In fact, as the saying goes, he "kept his options open."

This story throws a revealing ray of light on Eisenhower's much-berated syntax in press conferences. Many a Washington correspondent asked a simple question and got an answer so circumlocutive and incomprehensible that he or she was sorry to have asked.

Eisenhower became known for his tongue tanglers, which often made him appear bumbling and dumb. Yet this quality of expression was contradictory from a man known for lucid writing in the army and the Lincolnesque Guildhall address.

Not only did his Quemoy-Matsu comment confuse the press, it must have given migraines to Chinese translators and pause to Chou En-lai. It was a Chinese puzzle.

I once asked the president whether his suspect syntax was intended as a confusion factor. He laughed heartily.

"Is that your answer?"

All he did was continue laughing.

Obviously, I wasn't going to get an answer. At least he had spared me from having to untangle his syntax.

The Washington suspense continued. Meanwhile, the CIA looked forward to the African Nations' Conference in Bandung, Indonesia, starting April 17. Possibly attitudes or statements there would tip Chou's hand. Overtones of the conference indicated that the Chinese Communists had hoped to win the offshore islands and Formosa by a military-diplomatic bluff. Chou's bluff had not worked against an old poker player named Eisenhower.

At Eisenhower's suggestion, India's Krishna Menon was sent to Peking by Prime Minister Nehru to make peace between the Communists and the United States.

Then the crisis was over. Eleven of the American flyers were released, and the explosive little islands of Quemoy and Matsu, which had almost caused World War III, faded from the front page.

The United States breathed a collective sigh of relief. Eisenhower and Dulles couldn't join the nation, because they knew that only one crisis was out of the way. A major one still festered. Was atomic annihilation of the United States among the Soviet Union's war plans?

Eisenhower could not live in a knowledge vacuum.

In a closed society such as the Soviet Union, it is difficult to gather data on military capabilites and preparations. In an open society such as the United States, intelligence agents can travel and observe freely and assemble critical information from tons of available public sources.

I was jarred by a statement from General Ira Eaker, who commanded the Eighth and Fifteenth air forces during World War II: "We have provided the Russians and all other potential enemies with far better pictures, details and information about our big military installations than we were able to obtain about those of Germany and Japan after four years of warfare."

Then a panel headed by Nelson Rockefeller, presidential assistant for security, disclosed phenomenal breakthroughs in aerial reconnaissance photography that would permit shooting clear pictures of Russian military installations and movements from extremely high altitudes.

Rockefeller recommended that Eisenhower propose all major powers open their skies to permit photo missions that would prevent covert preparation for a surprise attack. The president liked and broadened the plan. Dulles, who did not relish Rockefeller working too closely with Eisenhower, said, "It just won't work."

Open Skies involved exchanging blueprints of all military installations, establishing a specified number of airfields on which to base airplanes and, on all flights, including at least one representative of the nation to be inspected.

With a summit conference scheduled in Geneva for July 18–23, Eisenhower tried not to get bogged down in Dulles's characteristic pessimism about the Russians. He hoped the summit would lead to peace, or at least to useful exchanges, although he feared that the Russians would use the platform strictly for propaganda purposes.

Even in Geneva, the president was not sure that he wanted to present Open Skies. He consulted with Nelson Rockefeller and then General Lauris Norstad, head of NATO. (Norstad was one of Eisenhower's black-book boys. When in North Africa, General Tooey Spaatz needed a chief of staff for the Fifteenth Air Force. General Ike recommended Norstad, an obscure captain. His rise was breathtaking.) Norstad's enthusiasm helped to convince the president that he must make this bold move for peace.

It was cloudy the next morning, when parties from the USSR, Great Britain, France and the United States entered the Palais des Nations' enormous square Council Chamber, with its imposing ceiling of blue-gray and its gold murals.

During the session in the air-conditioned, windowless chamber, no one was aware that an electrical storm had started. Eisenhower surprised and amazed conferees with his unique Open Skies peace plan. Without a warning, the loudest thunder Eisenhower had ever heard rumbled the building. The lights went out. "I didn't know my remarks were *that* strong," he announced. The chamber roared with laughter. The lights came back on.

Khrushchev and Bulganin promised to consider the proposal, but Eisenhower did not deceive himself. Open Skies suffered a lingering death, but the spirit of Geneva persisted, and the United States had again internationally demonstrated its desire for peace.

A Man and His Heart

A giant, juicy hamburger, stacked high with white onion slices—Ike's favorite food at the clubhouse of Cherry Hills golf course in Denver—got the blame for the president's stomach distress. That was shortly after 1:30 P.M. on September 23, 1955.

No matter. The problem would soon disappear. Or would it?

Twelve hours later, at approximately 1:30 A.M., the symptoms had progressed from mild stomach distress to deep fatigue and then to a full-fledged heart attack.

While the president, deathly pale and immobile, remained in a morphine-induced haze at Fitzsimmons General Hospital, a shocked nation waited apprehensively at radio and TV sets for the latest medical bulletin. The stock market plunged.

And, wherever the name of Ike was known, hopes plunged, too. Was the general who had fought for peace in both war and peace waging his last fight? Many lost hope and found it again in faith—in simple prayer. The prayers of millions were heard and answered. He was better.

Yet doctors could not breathe easily. An unpredictable strain could cause his heart to worsen. Medical reports continued to improve. Eisenhower was definitely mending. Smile again, world!

Soon he was sitting up and receiving selected guests in addition to Mamie and John. A get-well gift that pleased him especially was a pair of tomato-red pajamas from the working press. Inscribed above a pocket were the words "Much Better, Thanks."

Doctors had issued strict orders that no stressful subject should be brought up to the president by anyone. Eisenhower was shielded from Washington whispers and editorials that asked pointed questions: Will he heal enough to stand the rigors of the job? Will he be well enough to run for a second term? If so, would he want to run? Can a man with a serious heart condition win an election?

At least these were positive questions, dealing with objective issues, not the subjective editorializing directed at him in the past by some of the liberal press. Certain writers had characterized his low-profile executive techniques and "up-the-organization" methods as *no leadership* and *do-nothing*.

He had been called "the first nonworking president in history," "an absentee president," and "a golf player who never lets the presidency interfere with his game." One book about his administration was called *The Invisible Presidency*. Governor Stevenson supplied the whipped-cream topping when he charged the president with "gazing down the fairway of indifference."

Dulles was said to run the State Department with little interference from the chief executive. Governor Adams supposedly had built an organizational barbed-wire fence around Eisenhower, arbitrarily deciding which cabinet members or advisers should be admitted. Adams, allegedly, was the real president, the man who made the important decisions.

A favorite capital question prior to Eisenhower's illness was, "If Sherman Adams dies, who will become president?"

In talking with Ann Whitman, the president's secretary, and

Sherman Adams, I got a somewhat different picture of Ike as a policy-making executive who utilized his hours in the office with efficiency and little time wasting. I learned that he often would do night reading, to saturate himself on upcoming subjects for discussion.

A letter of September 1, 1970, from Tom Stephens, Ike's appointment secretary, offered me more sidelights on these issues:

> . . . When I would see him in the morning, which was generally at 8:00 A.M., Ann and I had gotten there at 7:30 A.M. . . . . His schedule for the day was in front of him, having been typed late the previous day. . . .
>
> The first appointment would be brought in generally at 9:00 A.M., which gave him time to sign any mail he might have or see General Goodpaster regarding matters which he had gotten from the State Department, the Security Council or other such agencies since the previous afternoon.
>
> No cabinet member, National Security Council member, senator or congressman who had to see the president was turned down—delayed, on occasion, yes, when the president had higher priorities. He was, after all, a man with a hundred different duties and functions.
>
> If somebody ever delayed appointments, it was I, as appointments secretary, who did it. Sherman Adams didn't encroach upon the presidency. . . . We were all encouraged to offer recommendations, but, make no mistake about it, the president made the decisions.

In a letter of November 29, 1971, Henry Cabot Lodge told me:

> The impression that President Eisenhower did not fully discharge the duties of the office and that someone else was actually making the decisions is untrue. I speak as a member of the cabinet who was in and out of the White House all the time over a period of eight years.
>
> The assertion that anyone prevented me from talking to President Eisenhower on the telephone is also untrue. Nobody ever did, and I am sure nobody ever tried to.

I asked similar questions of Neil McElroy, successor to

Charles Wilson as secretary of defense. In a letter of December 20, 1971, when he was chairman of the board of Procter and Gamble, he answered: ". . . President Eisenhower made it clear to me from the very beginning that my access to him at all times could be immediate and would be direct."

I also asked Dr. Arthur Burns, head of the Federal Reserve Board, about these matters.

"Many people believe that Sherman Adams made some of the decisions and handled high-level policy. This is simply not true. Adams did handle a multitude of details, and he took much pressure off the president, but he did not make high-level policy, and the decisions enunciated by Eisenhower were his own."

A member of the president's inner circle, who asked not to be named, revealed:

> Sherman Adams was the principal assistant to the president, but to say that the cabinet members could reach the president only through Adams is the sheerest nonsense. Tom Stephens was appointments secretary. Either he arranged for such appointments or, often as not, the cabinet member would talk to the president directly on the phone, explain what was bothering him, and the president would then see the cabinet member, either in his office or at the residence.

Senator George Aiken once told me he cringed at the innuendos that the president neglected or avoided his responsibilities:

> I did not call at the White House very often, and then only when matters of importance required the president's attention.
>
> At the time he took office, the agricultural attachés of our embassies abroad were used largely as guides for very important persons visiting those countries. Some of them knew very little about agriculture and were not expected to.
>
> Congressman Hope, of Kansas, chairman of the House Committee on Agriculture, and I called on the president one morning to tell him that a change should be made in this system. He listened to us and without hesitation called the State Department and stated that from then on he wanted the agricultural attachés

to have the same standing as the military attachés in foreign countries.

At another time, a serious agricultural problem arose. It was Saturday noon when I learned of it, and action had to be taken before nine o'clock Monday morning. The secretary of agriculture had gone to the mountains to spend a weekend.

Ordinarily, one would not have expected to find top officials at the White House, or even in Washington, on a Saturday afternoon.

I took a chance and called the White House. The president responded almost immediately. I told him the problem. He said, in characteristic fashion, "I will look after it myself."

Secretary Benson was called back from his weekend vacation and the problem was solved by eight o'clock Monday morning.

Now, fully recovered from his heart attack, Eisenhower began thinking ahead.

Some years after the fact, Dr. Paul Dudley White, noted Boston heart specialist, and I talked in his offices. He admitted to having advised the president to give up the thought of a second term.

"Not because your health wouldn't permit, but you should really spend full time as a messenger of peace," he told him. "I am interested in international medicine. I have a connection with a trust which would provide the necessary funds for us to travel and work together."

Dr. White told me that he emphasized that "no one in the world enjoys the universal respect, love and trust that you do. You are in a unique position to further a lasting world peace."

The president listened attentively and promised to consider the proposition. Several months later, he phoned Dr. White. "Doctor, so many colleagues and friends are putting heavy pressure on me that I've decided to run for a second term. As for your proposal, I am convinced that, as a former president, I would not have sufficient prestige to carry on a worldwide crusade for peace. Anyone conducting such a program must have the power of the White House behind him."

Dr. White pleaded with him, but the president had made a firm decision!

Critical Canals–Alimentary and Suez

Traditionally, June is a month of weddings.

In 1956, June was a month of divorcement for Dwight D. Eisenhower. He was divorced from part of his ileum and from a fair-weather friend, President Gamal Abdel Nasser, of Egypt.

Both events were front-page news.

First came the president's ileitis, an acute pain in the midsection that caused him to be hospitalized and merited almost as much media coverage as his coronary occlusion, while provoking far more curiosity.

Eisenhower let the nation in on his current physical problem. He followed the same pattern as he had after his heart attack, when Press Secretary Jim Hagerty had asked him how much he wanted revealed.

"Everything—the whole truth," Eisenhower had replied. He had remembered the hush surrounding the long illness of President Woodrow Wilson.

The nation had a right to know, he felt.

Few persons realize that President Eisenhower brought about a whole new, frank style of hospital reporting. Before his coronary occlusion, medical bulletins were generally a compound of evasion, medical jargon and words that said something without saying anything.

For an individual who believed in strict privacy about personal things, Eisenhower's was an unusual position. He was shocked at the candor of the medical bulletins. His cherished privacy had gone public. Even his inner functions belonged to the nation.

During Eisenhower's healing from ileitis, President Nasser was about to sign an agreement with the United States, the World Bank and Great Britain for financing the gigantic, billion-dollar Aswan Dam project to irrigate more of the barren Sahara and generate electrical power. It was also to be a monument built by Nasser for the glorification of Nasser.

Two factors upset finalization. Nasser refused to accept conditions he had previously agreed upon. Intelligence reports disclosed that he was playing the United States against the Soviet Union for a better deal.

Eisenhower put his foot down, and the United States stepped out of the Aswan Dam deal.

President Nasser became enraged. On July 24, he scalded the United States in a public attack. Two days later, he nationalized the Suez Canal.

As the president once informed me, "He was seizing the world's largest public utility, and the implications were horrendous. Would the Egyptians have the capability to operate it? Would Western Europe be cut off from using it, as Israel had been in 1950? What would be the response of the British? the French?

John Foster Dulles recommended that the canal be internationalized, but took no action in this direction. President Eisenhower feared that the dispossessed British would invade Egypt to regain control of the canal and warned Prime Minister Anthony Eden several times to desist.

Eden could not clearly interpret Dulles's stand and was upset that he refused to cooperate with prime canal users to exert pressure on Egypt. A communications blackout developed between London and Washington.

On October 28, the Israelis smashed into Egypt. With no advance notice to the United States, the British and French staged ineffective bombing raids and half-heartedly invaded Egypt; the weak Egyptian army somehow succeeeded in fighting them off. The Israelis penetrated to within twenty miles of the canal.

Eisenhower set up an emergency meeting that night, in the executive mansion, with the secretaries of state, defense, the head of the Mutual Security Council, the Joint Chiefs of Staff and the CIA director.

General Wilton B. Persons described the scene to me some years later.

After three hours of intense discussions, during which latest reports and Intelligence information were reviewed, the disappointed president said quietly: "We simply cannot go along with the British and French. We cannot approve of their action, and we must oppose it. Our policy will be that the situation must be handled through the United Nations. It is at times such as these that the United Nations can grow in strength or it will sink back into a virtually meaningless operation."

The president was deeply grieved by his decision, because it had to be taken against his oldest and closest allies. Many British officials, starting with Churchill and Prime Minister Sir Anthony Eden, were among his most valued friends. Nevertheless, he was firm.

Arthur Burns confided to me several other generally unknown aspects of the Suez crisis. He had been meeting almost daily with the president, who was puzzled about the ineptitude of the British and French.

"I cannot understand what they are doing. They must have a plan. If so, why don't they move in, hit hard and get it over with quickly? The British and French seem to be operating as if they were confronted by the vast armies of Hitler, rather than by Nasser and the Egyptian armed forces."

Still later, the president told Burns, "Our information is that Prime Minister Eden virtually tied the hands of the military when the operation began. Due to his humanity, he insisted that bombings not involve or endanger civilians. That is no way to wage war if you want victory. Since the British and French were willing to risk world opinion and to carry out an aggressive campaign, they should have been ready to pursue their plans vigorously."

Many years later, the president explained to me why he had requested that the UN handle the dispute. "The United Nations calls for settling disputes peacefully. If we don't use the UN for that purpose, we will destroy it. We could not stand idly by and watch force used against force. If this rule applies to those who are not our friends, it must apply to our friends."

The Anglo-French invasion failed and the UN eventually had the Israelis pull back from their greatest penetration. The UN voted sixty-five to one for the eviction of all invaders from Egypt. The British and French withdrew.

Eisenhower was uneasy upon learning that Russian armament had been captured by the Israelis in Egypt. Now the rumor had become truth. The specter that bothered him most was Russian influence in Egypt and the Communists' strategic position to move toward the rich Arab oil fields.

General Goodpaster told me: "Some members of the administration thought the countries involved may have felt they had President Eisenhower at their mercy, because of the approaching election. If this was their attitude, they were dealing with the wrong man."

After his White House years, Eisenhower explained to me that the Suez crisis had put the United States into a peculiar position. It seemed that the nation was abandoning its traditional allies and siding with the Russians.

"We never sided with the Russians," he informed me. "And the Soviets—Bulganin—had cabled me to join with them in suppressing the aggressors in order to prevent a possible World War III. I am sorry the British got the wrong impression. We took our position for vastly different reasons than the Soviets. It just so happened that our action paralleled, in some instances, the course taken by the Kremlin."

Eisenhower was very much hurt that Anthony Eden had not told him of the British invasion plan. He never expressed to me feelings of anger toward Eden, although several books state that he felt this way.

During one of my last talks with Eden at his country manor near Salisbury, he said: "There has been a great deal of misunderstanding about the relations between Britain and the United States and my own personal relations with President Eisenhower at the time of the Suez Canal crisis. . . . Mr. Dulles could have been more explicit on the United States stand. There has been a great deal written and said about the alleged break between Ike and myself . . . . Articles have stated that he became angry and used violent language to me on the trans-Atlantic telephone. There is not a word of truth in this."

Different in character from Suez was the blood-chilling situation in Lebanon in mid-1958. A desperate call for help had come to the United States from President Camille Chamoun, a virtual prisoner in his palatial mansion. For two months, with assassins in the streets, he dared not stand in front of a window.

Dulles was well aware of the United States commitment to help defend free Middle East nations against an aggressor. He also was aware of CIA reports from the Middle East that the United States was now considered a nation that talks a great game of helping but does nothing.

Military action alone wouldn't do it. "Let's send Bob, too," said the president. Dulles agreed on Eisenhower's longtime friend and handler of delicate diplomatic missions, Robert Murphy.

Eisenhower asked approval of Congress to send United States armed forces to Lebanon. It seemed paradoxical for a former military man to ask Congress's permission, while modern civilian presidents before and after him—Roosevelt, Truman, Kennedy, Johnson and Nixon—had ignored the practice. Approval was voted.

The president called out the marines and the army, sped

overseas by C-119 Flying Boxcars and C-124 Globemasters. Within 24 hours, 10,600 men—6,600 marines and 4,000 army men (outnumbering the Lebanese army) — rolled into the sea-port resort city of Beirut with tanks, armored amphibian vehi-cles and atomic cannons. The 75 Sixth Fleet vessels rode the swells outside the city's harbor—a powerful reserve punch.

The United States took a deep breath and anxiously awaited word from Lebanon. Would this be just a local police action, or a flame that would set the world on fire? Would the Egyptians and the Russians back the rebels with arms and men?

Early reports relieved the suspense. Not a shot was fired as Americans occupied Beirut, but there was still danger.

The rebels operated from the ancient part of the city, the Basta (a Casbah-type area). Intermittently the whine of bullets from the Basta troubled American commanders and Bob Mur-phy. If even one American were killed, it could mean a bloody battle to clean up the Basta.

Already the Soviet Union had charged the United States with a Hitler-type invasion of a sovereign nation.

The United States disclaimed this. The duly constituted pres-ident and his government had requested American help.

A local part of the problem was Chamoun's intention to run for a second term. Murphy urged him to drop this objective and call for a general election. Chamoun agreed.

Meeting with the rebels, Murphy explained, "We are pre-pared to use our weapons and men, but we prefer your friend-ship and peace. We request that you call off firing from the Basta. If an American is killed, this could cause great harm."

Murphy's persuasion convinced the rebels. It was soon over.

I once asked Eisenhower if at any time in his eight White House years there had been serious problems with Dulles.

He grinned. "We had differences, but that was to be ex-pected. We both had strong opinions. Foster had clashes with Anthony Eden. On these occasions, I acted as the honest broker and worked out suitable compromises."

On summit conferences, they were like Siamese twins, believ-ing in careful advance planning, with details worked out in lower echelons. Both feared that Soviets would use summits for propaganda.

Why, if Eisenhower made the major decisions, did Dulles get credit for them?

Eisenhower's long-standing practice of giving full credit to persons in charge of departments made him appear to be a non-doer and achiever. Since earliest days in the military, he made key decisions and let others take the bows.

Did Dulles dominate him?

"I have always believed in selecting intelligent, knowledgeable, and strong men and giving them responsibility and authority. Foster was that kind of person.

"It was my policy to give him firm guidelines for conduct. When he was on a foreign mission, he would phone me daily so that we could consider important issues jointly. When in Washington, we talked in person or by phone as much as a dozen times daily."

The public papers of Dwight D. Eisenhower for 1954 offer this statement: "So far as I know, Secretary Dulles has never made an important pronouncement without not only conferring and clearing with me but sitting down and studying practically word by word what he is to say."

In a final statement, he told me, "I regarded it a great loss to the nation and to myself when Foster lost his battle with cancer. While he helped formulate policy, the final decisions were always mine to make, and I made them."

The U-2 Furor and Credibility

Hundreds of us correspondents within the jammed Palais de Chaillot knew that USSR Premier Nikita Khrushchev would torpedo the 1960 Paris summit conference.

The only mystery was *how*!

As I slipped into my seat near the aisle of the fourth row center and marveled at the gigantic stage for presenting ballets and spectacular pageants, Khrushchev was already speaking.

He had conducted himself like a gentleman during the first session, but now, suddenly, dramatically, he thrust his pudgy hands aloft, as if stabbing the air, and cried out: "This man Eisenhower comes here posing as my friend. All the time I was at Camp David, he pretended to be my friend. At the same time, he was directing overflights of our territory by American U-2 airplanes to gather Intelligence information.

"He calls me his friend. Actually, he stands there with blood dripping from his hands down to his elbows and falling in pools to the floor."

His melodramatic gestures were almost as grisly as his words. "I demand an apology from the president and an official apology from the United States, with pledges of no more over-flights. Otherwise, I shall return to Moscow."

As Eiscnhower—first shocked, then flushed in anger—remained quiet, a roar went up, intermingled with boos.

President Charles de Gaulle, seated on the stage with Eisenhower, Britain's Prime Minister Harold Macmillan and other notables, leaned over to Eisenhower. "You don't have to take that kind of attack. There is no reason in the world for Khrushchev to humiliate you before the whole world."

Amid the confusion, the summit crashed to earth.

After the layers of diplomatic cosmetics have been removed, what is the true complexion of the U-2 incident? Was the shooting down by the Soviet Union of a U-2 observation aircraft piloted by Francis Gary Powers the first information that Khrushchev had that the United States was spying from the air?

Not at all.

Eisenhower had proposed earlier that the USSR and the United States should eliminate the possibility of surprise attacks by permitting on-site inspections of each other's military installations. The Russians flatly turned down the proposal. Why open their closed society? Why give up their advantage, when it was so easy to gather military intelligence in the open-society United States?

Eisenhower turned to the U-2 as an equalizer.

The CIA's Allen Dulles furnished specifications for Lockheed Aircraft Corporation, of Burbank, California, to design a special long-range airplane that could reach altitudes of 100,000 feet, fly over Russia and take photos.

Called the Black Lady of Espionage by the USSR, this strange-looking bird had incredibly wide, thin wings that drooped from the weight of fuel, and a towering tail rudder.

The Black Lady's push-button camera was phenomenal. It could capture clear photos of serial numbers on the sides of guns or aircraft from maximum altitude.

To keep up with Russian technological development, the U-2 photographed the Tyuratam Cosmodrome (the USSR equivalent of Cape Kennedy), intercontinental-ballistic-missile sites, air bases and other key installations.

The CIA had assured the president that a U-2 aircraft would never land on Soviet soil to leave proof of espionage. Its foolproof self-destruct system would blast it to bits. Nor would its pilot ever be taken alive. He possessed a special CIA suicide device—a poison needle within a hollow silver dollar.

To the United States, more than four years of U-2 flights brought revealing information and satisfaction. To the Russians, they brought great frustration. Neither their antiaircraft guns nor their interceptors could reach high enough altitudes to down the U-2s.

President Eisenhower, with whom each flight was cleared, felt that these missions should soon be ended, because Russian antiaircraft technology was catching up.

John Foster Dulles disagreed. He believed that no matter what happened, the Russians wouldn't protest. That would be admitting to the world their engineering inferiority.

Now the United States was working on the Samos satellite, a spy in the sky that eventually would be able to take photographs of Soviet military installations, although from far greater altitudes and with less clarity than the U-2s.

That was the stage setting for Gary Power's late April flight across the Soviet Union, planned to head northward over the huge USSR industrial center of Sverdlovsk to the Arctic Circle and landing at Bodo, in north Norway, a NATO airbase.

Powers started his craft down the runway of the Peshawar, Pakistan, airport. After a clumsy, bumping, oscillating takeoff, the black U-2 flew effortlessly. Below him in the bronze dawn was the Khyber Pass, a narrow, steep-sided passageway linking Pakistan and Kabul, Afghanistan: a trade route and the invasion route of the historic armies of Tamerlane, Babur and Alexander the Great.

Powers put the U-2 into a 45-degree climb so steep that he seemed about to tip over backwards. What a thrill to make that power climb! Above 60,000 feet in no time, he transmitted a single beep to the base that all was well and then switched off his radio.

It was an emotionally moving scene: everywhere around him were dark blue skies—incredibly blue skies—a world without a horizon. A few dabs of white clouds far below reminded him that there was such a thing as weather. He was all alone, but not lonely.

Now a cloud cover hid the ground. Soon it slid away, and sunlight glared off the snowcapped Ural Mountains. So far beneath him in the distance that it seemed small and insignificant, was the cosmodrome.

He switched on his automatic pilot and got a sinking feeling. It wasn't working! Quickly he switched back to manual. He was 1,300 miles into the Soviet Union and about 30 miles from Sverdlovsk, when he started the cameras.

Then, without warning, he heard a dull thud. Something drove the aircraft forward. An orange flash lit up the sky. The U-2 quickly began to spin downward. Powers' first impulse was to activate the ejection seat. Rather than that, he jerked open the canopy, which ripped off and floated into space behind him. Standard procedure would have been to turn on the destruct system and bail out before the aircraft blasted into a million metal shards. Instead, he just bailed out. At 15,000 feet his automatic parachute billowed open, and the earth rushed up to meet him. He landed abruptly in an open field at the edge of a village. A welcoming committee with guns received him.

It was May Day, and celebrating villagers encircled him. They seized his pistol, marked with the incriminating acronym, USA. Even more blatantly incriminating was a colorful poster in his seat pack, which announced in fourteen languages, "I am an American." A bunch of cards—identification, social security and credit—left no doubt about his nation of origin.

His captors lost no time flying him to Moscow, where he revealed full details of his flight. Blocky Nikita Khrushchev learned of the news during the May Day celebration. Was this a provocation to wreck the Paris summit conference? Probably

Eisenhower wanted peace, but not the imperialists and militarists around him.

As soon as the U-2 disappeared from the radar screen, the CIA became concerned. General Andrew Goodpaster phoned the bleak news to the president at Camp David. Troubled, Eisenhower immediately flew to the capital by helicopter.

The National Aeronautics and Space Administration's director, Keith Glennan, issued a cover story: A U-2 research plane on a NASA-USAF weather-report mission was missing near Lake Van, Turkey. The pilot, a Lockheed Aircraft employee making high-altitude weather studies, had radioed about oxygen trouble.

On the heels of this announcement came one from a State Department press officer. This incident was not an attempt to violate Soviet air space. The plane may have continued northward after the pilot blacked out. An announcement by the National Aeronautical and Space Administration stated that the name of the weather pilot was Francis G. Powers.

Khrushchev played his hand perfectly. He was silent. Let Washington weave the rope, form a noose and slip it around its official neck. That is exactly what happened.

Only then (on May 6) did Khrushchev lay bare the sequence of United States lies. He announced that Gary Powers had been captured alive, not just over the Russian border, but some 1,300 miles inside Russia.

Powers had confessed to being on a spy flight that had started in Pakistan (not Turkey) and was to have ended in Norway. The purpose of his flight was to gather classified information on Soviet guided missiles and radar stations. Film taken from the crashed plane bore out Powers's statements. He was going to be tried for espionage.

Even at this point, Khrushchev offered a way out for Eisenhower. He was ready to accept that the flight had been authorized without the president's knowledge. But Khrushchev wasn't going to let him off easily. He recommended that the CIA people involved, Allen Dulles, Richard Bissell, and the men in charge of the flight be fired.

President Eisenhower wanted nothing to destroy the summit conference, an important step toward peace, but he couldn't let Khrushchev run the CIA or influence his ethics. Eisenhower regretted the issued cover stories.

In a press conference of May 11, 1960, he admitted that he had authorized U-2 flights:

> . . . No one wants another Pearl Harbor. This means that we must have knowledge of military forces and preparations around the world, especially those capable of massive surprise attacks. Secrecy in the Soviet Union makes this essential. In most of the world, no large-scale attack would be prepared in secret, but in the Soviet Union there is a fetish for secrecy and concealment. This is a major cause of international tension and uneasiness today. Our deterrent must never be placed in jeopardy. The safety of the whole free world demands this.

Khrushchev burned with embarrassment. He had given Eisenhower an out. Now he had to make an about-face to save his own skin. Why had President Eisenhower broken all rules of diplomatic protocol and taken responsibility for the flight?

Prime Minister Macmillan of Great Britain was horrified. If he had perpetrated some unwise or dastardly action, responsibility would have been taken by the British Secret Service, Scotland Yard, or someone other than the resident of 10 Downing Street.

After Eisenhower left the White House, I asked him about the U-2. He told me, "The greatest asset any occupant of the White House has is the trust of the American people and total credibility. If the president loses this, he has lost his greatest strength. Therefore, I admitted to ordering the flight."

Even today, there are unanswered questions about the U-2. Why was this flight scheduled just before the summit conference? Why was Powers permitted to carry so much incriminating evidence? Posing as a civilian pilot, why was he allowed to carry cards showing the military schools and bases where he had been stationed?

Why didn't he activate the U-2's destruct system, according to the CIA pledge to Eisenhower? Why did he not use the poison needle, rather than incriminate his nation? Before other flights, Powers had been completely inspected. All of his personal clothes and effects had been taken off. Nonidentifiable clothing and equipment had been issued for each flight. Why, on this particular flight, was this procedure not followed?

It has been suggested that agents of the Politburo had made on-the-ground arrangements to undo the U-2 in the air, arranging an incident to explode the summit conference.

I asked Eisenhower why the flight of the U-2 had been timed before the summit. "The weather was favorable. If we had waited several weeks more, the area would have been fogged. It would have been impossible to photograph Sverdlovsk."

Khrushchev and the Politburo knew all about the U-2 flights. And they knew that the United States knew that they knew. After all, American radar had picked up USSR radar homing on U-2 flights for more than four years. Khrushchev was well aware of them while a guest of Eisenhower at Camp David in 1959. He was also aware that Soviet spies had been captured in the United States.

Then why had he been hypocritical? Why did he purposely break up the summit conference? For some very practical reasons.

His policy of conciliation toward the United States, the failure of his agricultural program and his repeated use of force within the Communist party to carry out his policies had made enemies.

Then, too, he had had a falling out with the Red Chinese for refusing to share atomic-bomb secrets with them. Also he feared the consequences of keeping his promise to host President Eisenhower in the Soviet Union.

He remembered too vividly the disturbing reactions of the Politburo to the visit of Vice-President Nixon and Milton Eisenhower. On a nationwide telecast, Nixon had talked about the incredible production records of the United States, about its modern schools and vast transportation systems and (probably most telling) how much the laborer's family could buy on his annual income.

Khrushchev had a sharp mental picture of his own personal appeal, compared with Eisenhower's. The premier had been given a cold reception in India, while Eisenhower had received a hero's welcome there.

It was Eisenhower's considered opinion that, even before the U-2 incident, Khrushchev had decided to blast the summit conference and his visit to the Soviet Union.

To quiet growing opposition, Khrushchev had to take a firm line in Paris. He had to refrigerate the Cold War several more degrees. If he canceled the summit conference, he would probably return to the good graces of the men who run the Soviet Union: the Politburo and the Red Marshals.

Khrushchev's desperate move for political survival had wrecked the president's best efforts to forge a lasting peace with a nation that wanted no peace.

Intolerance for Intolerance

President Eisenhower's only intolerance was for intolerance.

Having been brought up in Kansas, a turbulent mixture of north and south, he saw much hatred and abuse of blacks. The happening which left the deepest cleat marks in his thin white skin was the firing of Jack Briscoe, his Abilene High School teammate, merely for being black. The same spirit that drove him to get Briscoe reinstated made him battle for equality for blacks and other minorities throughout his career.

President Eisenhower's basic reason for his deep belief in equality goes beyond man's law and is best stated in his public papers of 1954: "Man has a soul and for that reason is equal to every other man, and that is the system, that is the principle, that is the cornerstone of what we call the American system."

Throughout his career, he had men of the Jewish faith in key spots. Colonel "Tex" Lee was his close aide and friend during World War II. Four of his top-ranking officials during the presidency were Jews: Admirals Lewis Strauss and Hyman Rickover, Dr. Arthur Burns (head of the Federal Reserve System) and Max Rabb, secretary of the cabinet and Ike's aide in minority matters.

Eisenhower urged Sherman Adams to search for qualified blacks for the executive function. (He asked J. Edgar Hoover, of the FBI, too.) Adams found E. Frederick Morrow, who served as one of the president's administrative officers; Lois Lippman, for the White House secretarial staff (the first black ever to work in this capacity) and J. Ernest Wilkins, assistant secretary of labor.

"You may not realize this, Virgil," Eisenhower told me, "but Wilkins was the first black man in the country's history to attend a cabinet meeting."

On January 23,1970, I had one of a number of interviews with Max Rabb. It was most revealing on the president's civil rights beliefs. Max told me that the president was determined to have citizens of all races and colors enjoy the rights guaranteed them in the constitution.

"He believed with all his being that unless we dispensed justice equally to all citizens, there was little purpose for the existence of the United States of America. His resolve to advance human and civil rights occupied much of his thought and efforts for eight years.

"He worked quietly and effectively through individuals and with a minimum of publicity or fanfare. In fact, he played down publicity and self-glorification. He did not say, as his successors did, 'I have instructed the secretary of defense to take immediate action because I have discovered a situation which needs correcting,' or 'I have determined that our policy pertaining to inflation should be as follows. . . .' Rather, he said, 'The secretary of defense informs me that a situation exists which needs correcting, and we are taking the appropriate steps.' "

Eisenhower felt that there had been enough water treading in civil rights. A great deal that could have been done by the executive branch had not been done.

One afternoon, as the shadows were falling across the rear of the White House, Dwight D. Eisenhower called Max Rabb into his office. He told him that there had been too much talk, too many promises, and too little action advancing civil and human rights. He wanted to do something helpful in this area, as he had promised in his campaign.

The president said, "We do not dare go to the nation with this issue unless we put our own house in order first. This means carrying out integration in the armed forces and then putting conditions right here in the District of Columbia.

"I want you to start with the navy. Go to the secretary of the navy, Bob Anderson, and tell him it is my desire that segregation cease. Tell him I do not want excuses. Action is long overdue, and I hope he can attain this goal."

Eisenhower explained that the Veterans Administration, and especially its hospitals, had to be reoriented for equal rights, too.

"The president asked me to tell Anderson that he wanted integration of the navy accomplished within ninety days," Rabb told me. " 'Max, if there are any roadblocks, let me know immediately, and I will move them out of the way.' "

Anderson, a Texas Democrat, lit up. He was intrigued and inspired by the president's wishes and Max's ideas. It wasn't going to be easy—not with resistance to change and layer upon layer of prejudice solidified by the passing years. He notified commanders of the twelve naval districts that integration was to be carried out at once, but that there was to be no publicity and that the issue was not to be political.

"This is the desire of the president and commander in chief of the armed forces."

Max told me that Anderson used a non-Quaker brand of "friendly persuasion" on heads of the twelve naval districts. "I expect full and enthusiastic cooperation," Anderson explained. "If I don't get it, you will be relieved of your post!"

Anderson personally handled some desegregation. He began in the giant naval construction yards at Charleston, South Carolina, on a Saturday. This change would cause less confusion and be better received if the first big step were taken over a weekend.

All DRINKING WATER FOR WHITES ONLY signs were taken down,

as were those warning blacks away from lavatories for whites. On the following week, navy mess halls were integrated.

"Then we moved to the next big base of operations, until the job was done," Max informed me.

Ninety-one days after Rabb went to Anderson, he received a telephone call from him: "I would like to come to the White House and report personally to the president. Segregation is at an end in the navy."

The transformation was breathtaking.

From that time, Eisenhower kept his eyes on Anderson and, as the months passed, often said that he was presidential material.

White House public-relations people clamored for a major press conference to announce the civil rights gains. The president vetoed the idea. Civil rights could best be advanced through quiet, personalized work, he said. Eisenhower wanted results, not publicity.

Soon the air force, army and the Veterans Administration followed suit. Eisenhower formed two committees to make certain that companies receiving government contracts hired minority groups.

Desegregating the District of Columbia was a sticky problem, because offending institutions were privately owned. Attorney General Herbert Brownell appealed to the Supreme Court for a ruling that restaurants in the district could not refuse service to blacks, and the court gave a unanimous ruling to this effect.

Eisenhower then phoned commissioners of the District of Columbia and suggested that they set an example for the nation through desegregation of their schools. They cooperated, and it was accomplished without incident.

The president used personal persuasion to get motion-picture theaters and hotels to admit blacks.

Max Rabb informed me that a marked change came over the District of Columbia. He recalled that when President Truman had asked Dr. Ralph Bunche to become an under-secretary of state in 1950, Bunche had forcefully declined. "I cannot raise my family in an area where there is rampant segregation. I would not submit my children to the indecencies of growing up in the District of Columbia."

Upon visiting Washington, D.C., in 1956, Dr. Bunche was immediately aware of dramatic changes. "I would have accepted President Truman's appointment if conditions in 1950 had been comparable with those in 1956."

After the president's civil-rights gains, the United States Supreme Court, on May 17, 1954, decreed racial segregation in schools unconstitutional. This was reaffirmed by the court a year later, and local authorities were ordered to comply gradually.

No one needed acute foresight to see the threatening thunderclouds of major tests between pro- and antisegregationists. Soon—who knew how many months or years ahead?—the southern system of all-white and all-black public schools on opposite sides of town would be broken down.

Feelings in the South rose to the highest pitch since pre-Civil War days. Eisenhower called on evangelist Billy Graham to prevail upon southern ministers to soothe heated emotions, rather than to inflame them.

In many areas of the South, blacks were not permitted to vote. Blacks who overtly favored desegregation were fired from jobs, even beaten. They often feared to claim their rights. Those who suffered violence or witnessed it were afraid to talk of it to police.

Eisenhower proposed a revolutionary piece of legislation to guarantee equal rights: the establishing of a civil-rights commission and a civil-rights division in the Department of Justice; a stronger law to guarantee voting rights, and amendments to laws allowing the federal government to use civil courts to gain relief for those denied their rights.

Despite a coalition of southern senators and reactionary Republicans, Eisenhower and his aides pushed through Congress the first new civil-rights legislation in eighty-two years.

Two months later, the outbreak that the nation feared took place in Little Rock, Arkansas. Central High School was the setting. Several blacks arrived to take advantage of their newly found freedom and enroll.

Thousands of noisy, belligerent, stick-brandishing individuals formed a thick, impenetrable cordon around the school, defying them: "Just try to get in!"

The blacks, apprehensive, hung back, and mob rule prevailed over the rule of the land! Governor Orval Faubus refused to lift a protesting finger.

This encouraged the mob even more. Finally, the governor called out Arkansas National Guard units to surround the high school to "preserve peace and order." The Faubus version of peace and order meant preventing blacks from entering.

Mayor Mann, of Little Rock, in panic, sent a telegram to the White House: "The immediate need for federal troops is urgent. The mob is much larger in numbers at 8 A.M. than at any time yesterday. People are converging on the scene from all directions and engaging in fisticuffs and other acts of violence. Situation is out of control and police cannot disperse the mob. . . ."

Eisenhower knew this was no time for indecision. It was his constitutional duty to have the court decrees implemented and strictly obeyed. He signed an executive order to federalize the Arkansas National Guard and dispatched 500 paratroopers of the 101st Airborne Division from Fort Campbell, Kentucky. In the afternoon they arrived and were supported by 500 more that evening.

On the next morning, the violence was over. Eisenhower had brought peace and a major victory for integration.

Max Rabb emphasized to me that when Eisenhower took his civil-rights action, he did it in an indifferent-to-hostile climate. "The nation and Congress were not as concerned about civil rights during the Eisenhower years as today."

Wherever Eisenhower saw intolerance, he opposed it. General Lucius Clay told me a revealing story about him. He and Mrs. Clay, General Ike and Mamie had gone to an island off the coast of Florida near Miami to enjoy a brief holiday. At the reception desk, Eisenhower noticed a card which said, "Negroes and Jews not welcome."

Just then the desk clerk handed him a pen to register. General Eisenhower turned to General Clay and said, "Lucius, there isn't any way I could stay at a place like this. Come on. Let's go back to Miami." They did.

Like the great black scientist Booker T. Washington, Eisenhower believed in gradualism in integration. "You must move slowly, because one thing you cannot legislate is love. This is the sort of thing that must grow, and generally growth takes place slowly.

"The way to assist blacks is not to entertain them at a tea party, but to give them a proper education and to provide them with the learning tools necessary to succeed."

The Bottom Line

President Eisenhower was upset.

A disturbing news item had come to him—an item having nothing to do with cold, lukewarm, or hot war. He had just heard the results of a physical-fitness test given to American school children between the ages of six and sixteen.

Kraus-Weber tests for maximum muscular strength and flexibility had revealed that 57.9 percent of United States children had failed to reach minimum standards. Only 8.7 percent of the children from similar communities in Italy, Austria and Switzerland had failed.

Shock that the United States children's failure rate was more than six times that of the European children spurred him to found the President's Citizens Advisory Committee on Youth Fitness (to upgrade the physical condition of young Americans) and to form the President's Physical Fitness Council.

Eisenhower recommended more athletics, swimming, bike riding, walking and improved diets and started the first national movement for upgrading health as a national resource.

This is one of his little-known accomplishments. I decided to

351

check official records to note the major achievements of Eisenhower's eight White House years. I also talked with Eisenhower and his aides for additional information. Here are my findings, according to subjects.

Ended Korean War: "Six months after this administration took office, a cease-fire order had been achieved that assured the safety of South Korea and ended the fighting," Eisenhower told a Republican rally on November 2, 1960.

Avoided Vietnam War: He resisted strong influences, including that of John Foster Dulles, the French, Vice-President Nixon and Admiral Arthur Radford, and kept the nation out of war in Vietnam.

"After the election of John F. Kennedy, who asked for advice, Eisenhower urged him not to send troops to Vietnam," I was told by Percival Brundage. Kennedy listened, but did not hear.

Lyndon Baines Johnson, Kennedy's successor, often sought Eisenhower's advice, but still expanded national commitments and war efforts in Southeast Asia.

SEATO: Eisenhower and Dulles put mind and muscle behind formation of the South-East Asia Treaty Organization, another strong line of resistance against Communist conquest.

Formosa (Taiwan): He prevented the Communist Chinese from capturing Formosa and the offshore islands of Quemoy and Matsu.

Philippines: The president's aid to the Philippine Islands eliminated Communist guerrilla warfare.

Eisenhower Doctrine: To stabilize the delicately balanced Middle East, the president formulated the Eisenhower Doctrine, an agreement to protect nations there from aggression by the Soviet Union.

Iran: He kept Iran from falling into Communist hands and, with it, one of the world's greatest reserves of oil.

Guatemala: Through Eisenhower's intervention, a Communist bridgehead in Guatemala was destroyed.

Suez: Eisenhower averted international disaster by prevailing upon Israel, Great Britain and France to pull out of Egypt and increased the United Nations' usefulness and prestige by calling in the UN to settle the dispute.

Lebanon saved: Eisenhower responded to Lebanese President Chamoun's call for help and, with congressionally authorized American troops, set down a Communist-inspired effort to take over the government. Not a life was lost. A Communist Lebanon would have brought the Soviet Union a step closer to Arab oil resources.

No Communist territorial gains: During the Eisenhower years, not one inch of territory was gained by the Communists, where American influence or arms were involved.

Not a single American death: After the Korean War's end (started in the Truman administration), not a single American lost his life in combat.

Waging peace: "Into our armed forces, we integrated weapons of tremendous deterrence, many of them unknown eight years ago, through a program more than three times larger, in dollar amount, than only ten years ago," Eisenhower said in Philadelphia on October 28, 1960, in the last innings of his presidency.

"And we have proof of the respect the Soviets have for our power and our resolution: the Communists have been turned from a strategy of military penetration to a strategy of infiltration by political and economic means.

"Now in glib oratory, we have heard this progress called, 'standing still.' Now if the great things you [citizens of the United States] have done are 'standing still,' then I say America needs more of it."

Revolutionary defense weapons: Eisenhower started and developed defense weapons: guided missiles, ballistic missiles, atomic submarines carrying ballistic missiles, sophisticated electronic computers, various satellites (communications, weather, navigational applications, earth resources and spy-in-the-sky types) and the space program.

Defense economy: To create an international buffer against Soviet Union aggression, the United States, under

Eisenhower, gave $17 billion in direct military assistance, stimulating other free-world nations, which put $107 billion into their own and common defense. This was the kind of bargain Eisenhower relished: 200 divisions of friendly military forces, 27,000 aircraft, 2,500 naval combat vessels.

Atoms for Peace: Eisenhower's revolutionary plan for the "have" nations—the United States and the Soviet Union—to share nuclear material and know-how with the "have-not" nations took the accent away from the use of atomic energy for death and destruction and turned it to peaceful uses.

Open Skies: His dramatic proposal at the 1955 Geneva summit conference to open the skies over the United States and the Soviet Union and permit mutual inspection of defense installations to prevent surprise attack did not enlist Russian cooperation, but it demonstrated to the world United States sincerity and dedication in seeking world peace.

Creative diplomacy: "Eisenhower succeeded because in the conduct of the presidency, he sensed that the nuclear deadlock had introduced a literally unprecedented factor in human history," writes Eisenhower aide Arthur Larson in *Eisenhower: The President Nobody Knew.*

> In bluntest terms this new factor is that *major cold war conflicts simply cannot be resolved* in the sense of disposing of them once and for all and making them go away.
> . . . While the nuclear deadlock lasts, we must reconcile ourselves to living in a divided world in which the objective of foreign policy is not to make the big disputes dissolve, but rather to manage them in such a way that they do not break out into a large-scale organized war. It was this limited but realistic task that Eisenhower devoted himself to and performed successfully.[1]

Goodwill missions: Never, before Eisenhower, had a president carried on personal diplomacy with so many countries. He visited nations in Europe, Asia, Africa, South Africa, the Pacific and South America.

Enhanced relations with Latin America: Eisenhower's goodwill tour of Latin America—thirty-seven addresses, two television appearances and private meetings with four presidents—brought greater unity and harmony between the United States and Latin American nations. In *Waging Peace,* the president quoted the summary of Tad Szulc, *New York Times* reporter on the tour: "relations between the United States and South American lands appeared today to stand on the highest plateau since the end of World War II. . . ."

Alliance for Progress: Eisenhower secured an appropriation of $500 million to fund the Alliance for Progress plan for Latin America.

St. Lawrence Seaway: Many words flowed from the mouths of many presidents—for fifty years—about the gigantic Saint Lawrence Seaway project, but no action was taken until 1954, when Eisenhower pushed Congress to authorize the project. Opened in 1959, the Seaway permits ocean vessels to travel to Great Lakes ports, giving the United States and Canada a fourth seacoast.

Closer relations with Canada: Cooperation with Canada on the Saint Lawrence Seaway and Eisenhower's warm relations with Canadians created the closest ties ever experienced between the two countries.

Innovation: Just before flying to Switzerland for the Big Four conference at Geneva (July 15, 1955), Eisenhower addressed the nation about his unprecedented trip to seek peace:

> Other Presidents have left the continental limits of our country for the purpose of discharging their duties as Commander in Chief in time of war, or to participate in conferences at the end of a war to provide for the measures that would bring about peace.
>
> But now, for the first time, a President goes to engage in a conference with the heads of other governments in order to prevent wars, in order to see whether in this time of stress and tension, we cannot devise measures that will keep from us this terrible scourge that afflicts mankind.

Peace: He stopped a wasteful war in Korea and prevented others.

Restored armed forces to strength: After World War II, the armed forces of the nation were cut back to their lowest ebb since before war with the Axis. Eisenhower rebuilt them. After the first two Eisenhower White House years, Admiral Radford, chairman of the Joint Chiefs of Staff, said that United States defenses were better prepared for any emergency than ever before in "my forty years in the armed forces."

Unified armed forces: Eisenhower continued work he had started with the Truman administration to unify the armed services and overcame great resistance to complete the job during his presidency. This move did much to eliminate competition between the armed forces and to secure greater cooperation, effectiveness and a saving of defense billions.

Better coverage for veterans: War veterans with service-connected disabilities received increased compensation. More beds were provided for sick and disabled veterans in a 12-year $900 million construction program. VA services were upgraded.

Broadened Social Security: Through his urging, Congress extended Social Security coverage to 10 million more Americans.

New states—Alaska, Hawaii: The territories of Alaska and Hawaii were admitted as the forty-ninth and fiftieth states of the union.

Civil rights: He championed the first civil-rights legislation in eighty-two years and started integration in government agencies, the armed forces and the District of Columbia.

Superhighway construction: To modernize (or futurize) the nation's horse-and-buggy road system, Eisenhower spearheaded construction of the world's most comprehensive highway network—41,000 miles—enough paving to make a sidewalk that would reach to the moon and back.

Percival Brundage, Eisenhower's director of budget, explained to me: "Eisenhower favored financing this program by user charges—a very sound fiscal policy. He envisaged paying costs out of excise taxes on gasoline and truck tires. This turned out to be one of our most successful federal programs."

Congress wanted to draw more than $20 billion out of the treasury. Eisenhower opposed this as inflationary, because it would encourage the printing of more money. Finally, Congress funded the program with a federal gasoline tax.

Antipollution: In 1955, President Eisenhower was concerned about the elimination of the wastes in water and air. "Pollution and its control are the world's greatest problems for this and future generations," he told Brundage. "Our government should give a shining example of how pollution may be solved. We should tackle it with all-out research for successful solutions."

Brundage recalled his first budget meeting with Eisenhower on the subject. "The president requested $50 million. The next year he increased it to $100 million." The following year, Secretary of the Interior Marion Folsom proposed to Brundage that $500 million be appropriated for antipollution. "This is not possible, in view of our fiscal situation," protested Brundage.

Folsom would not be stopped. He had breakfast with Eisenhower, to lobby for the cause. "Shortly after the meeting, the president phoned me to come to his office," Brundage informed me. "He had the expression of an impish boy on his face. 'You haven't had breakfast with Secretary Folsom, have you?' I asked.

"Eisenhower grinned broadly. 'Yes, I have.'

" 'Did Folsom get your O.K. for the $500 million?'

" 'Yes, he did,' replied the president."

He knew he had to stretch the budget, or pollution would grow out of control.

Balanced budget: No president in modern times was able to balance the federal budget until Eisenhower did it and kept his election promise.

Strong dollars: Running a large federal deficit had become a way of life in America. Spending far more than was collected was cheapening the dollar and making the national debt and interest payment harder to meet. Taxes steadily became a more crushing burden. Eisenhower stopped deficit spending and even created budget surpluses.

Brundage, Eisenhower's director of budgets for some years, explained the president's fiscal philosophy:

> Many times in cabinet and National Security Council meetings, the president insisted on a sound dollar, on reducing expenses

consistent with our security and meeting national commitments and objectives.

He frequently talked about cutting taxes. One of his greatest concerns was defending the value of pensions and income for retired people. He was conscious of costs in government as in his personal life. As a youth, he learned the necessity of hard work, thrift and frugality. He had income taxes cut by eleven billion dollars at a time when the dollar had genuine value. It was by far the largest reduction up to that time.

Defeated inflation: ". . . Since the birth of the United States, costs have risen, on an average, about 3 percent a year," writes George Aiken in *Senate Diary*.

"Only during the eight years of the Eisenhower administration did the country get by without an increase in inflation, and it seems to me we are making up for lost time."

Most of his legislation passed: During one of our post-presidential chats, General Ike told me that 87 percent of his most-important proposed legislation had passed.

This surprised me.

During his first administration, he had a majority in the Senate of one vote, but in that majority was a handful of Republicans who rarely, if ever, backed his legislation (the radical Republicans—Joe McCarthy, Mundt, Jenner, and Knowland). So, in effect, he had a minority.

After the 1956 elections, the Democrats had a clear majority in both houses.

My face must have been a big question mark. General Ike never did answer my question. A phone call interrupted, and we failed to discuss that subject again.

I was never sure I would hear the inside story, until the afternoon I interviewed Robert Anderson in his New York offices and unexpectedly picked up some exclusive information:

> After I had resigned as secretary of the navy to go back into private business, the president phoned me.
>
> "How about coming to Washington for lunch one day next week, Bob?"
>
> "Of course, Mr. President," I replied.

Next week, in his office, after a few minutes, he said, "Bob, I would like to have you as secretary of the treasury." [George Humphrey had resigned to go back into his Cleveland business.]

"Secretary of the Treasury?"

The president nodded. Now my curiosity shot up.

"We're swimming upstream in Congress. We need some help. We simply cannot permit the nation to mark time because we have a heavy Democrat majority on the Hill and a Republican in the White House."

I was bewildered about my role.

"Bob, I happen to know that you went to school with Senator Lyndon Baines Johnson and were the man who raised the first eighty-five thousand dollars for the Sam Rayburn Library."

How did he know that? I asked myself. He obviously had done his homework, as usual.

"Bob, I want you to serve as liaison man between me and the Hill—between me and Johnson and Rayburn. Knowing them intimately, as you do, you can help legislation go through.

"I want you to tell them that anything that comes from you comes from me and is to remain between the four of us. And anything they tell you will be brought to me and remain between the four of us.

"Bob, tell Johnson and Rayburn I don't want them to be surprised or startled by any legislation which I send to the Hill. I want them to see it first. Tell them that any suggestions they have that will help passage will be welcome.

"Get to know them outside office hours and socialize with them.

"If it takes more time on the Hill than as secretary of the treasury, please take it. You can delegate some of your other work and review it to make sure it's up to your standards. Number-one priority is getting needed legislation through promptly. We must work through Lyndon and Sam."

Bob accepted. Now, at last, I was beginning to understand, at least in part, Eisenhower's high batting average in Congress.

Many liberal writers, some of them intellectuals, still offer the stereotype of Eisenhower as the man with the smile, the amiable bumbler whose decisions were made by others and who got all the lucky breaks.

For some, the stereotype is beginning to crumble.

Murray Kempton, the acerbic liberal columnist of the New York *Post,* had a longer, deeper look and wrote an article titled "The Underestimation of Dwight D. Eisenhower" in the September, 1967 *Esquire* magazine.

One paragraph in particular shows a new assessment:

> The Eisenhower who emerges here intermittently free from his habitual veils is the President the most superbly equipped for truly consequential decision we may ever have had, a mind neither rash nor hesitant, free of the slightest concern for how things might look, indifferent to any sentiment, as calm when he was demonstrating the wisdom of leaving a bad situation alone as when he was moving to meet it on those occasions when he absolutely had to.

In an interview on the "Michael Jackson" program (KCET-TV, Los Angeles, April 27, 1979), Theodore White manfully swallowed previous slighting statements about President Eisenhower:

> I was one of those who called Eisenhower a do-nothing president. . . . He was a jovial fellow. I thought he wasn't getting anywhere. When I reflect on the eight years of the Eisenhower administration, the first two years were plagued with his fight with Joe McCarthy. Once he eliminated Joe McCarthy in December 1954, he went on to what were probably the happiest six years in American life.
>
> He believed in doing nothing unless it was absolutely necessary to do something, and then he did it spanking smart and efficiently. Later on [1958] he was threatened with a Communist coup. . . . Eisenhower put the Sixth Fleet on the coast of Lebanon, landed American marines and paratroopers, had them out in three weeks. Not a single American boy was killed. Not a single Lebanese was killed. The Communist coup was squelched.
>
> How I would love a president who could move troops that quickly and efficiently, with that little bloodshed and calm the Middle East. He refused to attack Red China when John Foster

Dulles and Admiral Radford wanted to do that. He refused to use the atom bomb in French Indochina.

He did nothing when it was entirely appropriate to do nothing. And I regard him now as one of the major presidents of our time in the USA.

The Truth About Ike and Kay Summersby

Did General Dwight D. Eisenhower have an affair with Lieutenant Kay Summersby, former model, when she was one of his drivers during World War II?

Two books make this sensational charge: Summersby's *Past Forgetting: My Love Affair With Dwight David Eisenhower* and Merle Miller's *Plain Speaking: An Oral Biography of Harry S Truman.*

It is difficult to trace stories and rumors, because many of the sources are dead. It would be trying to chase down ghosts. General George C. Marshall, President Truman, and Eisenhower himself are gone. So is Kay Summersby, who died of cancer, leaving the completion of her book many months later to ghostwriters.

The nub of the matter is that General Eisenhower purportedly wrote a letter to General Marshall, his military superior, saying that he wanted to divorce his wife, Mamie, marry Kay Summersby and bring her back to the United States. Supposedly, Marshall told President Truman about the letter, and Truman came to the Pentagon personally to burn the letter. That is the account in Miller's book.

Are the charges true or false?

"False," says United States Navy Captain Harry Butcher (author of *My Three Years With Eisenhower*), who spent more time overseas with the general than any one individual.

I recently interviewed my friend Butch in the living room of his mountainside home in Santa Barbara, California's fashionable Montecito suburb. He was totally frank.

"As you know, Virgil, I was with the Boss almost everywhere during World War II. He was commanding the most-critical war in the nation's history. He worked incessantly, was always protected, always watched. There was no time or opportunity for an affair.

"If General Ike had been in love with Kay and wanted to marry her, he would have arranged for a divorce and married her. That's what I did. I divorced my wife and married Molly, because I loved her. Ike would have done the same thing if he had loved Kay."

Butcher's black miniature poodle, Mary, jumped into his lap, and he continued. "There was no love affair between Ike and Kay. Sure, they liked each other, but that was as far as it went. Ike liked and was kind to a lot of people. Kay was really in love with a guy named Colonel Richard Arnold. Ike knew that. Everybody knew it.

"Ike encouraged their getting married. He even let them borrow his villa, Sailor's Delight, outside of Algiers, ride his stallions, and have a quiet place away from military activity to make their wedding plans. He arranged to have her flown to Egypt to marry Arnold. Does a man having an affair with a gal do *that?*"

To unearth further information on the Summersby-

Eisenhower relationship, I flew 3,000 miles—California to Washington, D.C., via Abilene, Kansas—to meet Mickey McKeogh, Eisenhower's orderly before and throughout World War II. After breakfasting with Sergeant Mickey and his wife Pearlie, I came away with the strong impression that Kay Summersby loved to be associated with glamor and had sensationalized an affectionate but platonic relationship with one of the most-prominent men in recent history.

"That stuff about an affair with Kay is sheer nonsense," snapped Mickey. "I put the Boss to bed every night, and there was no one else in the bed. In the mornings when I would wake him up, there was no one else in the bed, except one time when I found Telek, his black Scotty, on his pillow.

"I traveled with him almost everywhere. If I wasn't with him, it was Captain Butcher or General Mark W. Clark. There was no time for him to be alone with Kay or any other woman. The war was his whole life—that and regular correspondence with his wife, Mamie, throughout the war. Never in all of our years together did he speak of his wife in anything but tones of endearment."

The Summersby book mentions love in an air-raid shelter. Mickey laughed openly about this supposed episode. "Near Telegraph Cottage in England, we had a small air-raid shelter into which twelve of us—more if we had guests—would squeeze during a bombing. There was no room for hand holding by the General and Kay, or lovemaking. These quarters were so tight that even sardines would have been uncomfortable."

Summersby's book frequently negates itself. In one place, Kay, whom I knew in Africa, London, and on the continent, mentioned three occasions when she and the general supposedly tried to make love, in hopes of having a son. She says that the general was physically incapable.

If this were so, how could the two, as claimed, possibly have had a love affair for several years after that?

Pearlie McKeogh, also a driver in the pool for military VIPs, including General Ike, says that he was an extremely compassionate man, with genuine concern for others. On one occasion, she had the sniffles.

" 'Pearlie, you go right over to the dispensary and get treatment,' the general commanded. 'I don't want you coming down with a cold.'

"He was always that considerate with me and other members of his staff."

Pearlie, who chatted with Kay for hours during slow times, told me that Kay let her imagination get away from her in interpreting the general's concern as love for her.

Having met Kay on numerous occasions in Africa, England and on the continent, I knew her well. Photographs showed her off better than she actually looked, which is true of many models.

A correspondent of a large eastern daily described her as "straight up and down, like a wall, with none of the feminine curves in the right places." Kay was not particularly fastidious, while Ike was. She had rather large feet, which made the correspondent—in a bitter mood—comment, "What's all this talk about a shortage of landing craft? They can always use Kay's shoes."

I asked Mickey McKeogh if he had ever noticed anything beyond normal friendly relations between Summersby and the general.

"At least a dozen of us made up the Eisenhower household, or family, overseas," replied Mickey. "If there had been even unusually warm exchanges—looks, remarks, touching or caresses—someone would have seen or learned about it. If they had had sexual relations, someone would have told or written that story for money. You can usually count on one Judas among twelve, but no one ever told such a story."

I phoned my friend General Mark W. Clark at his home in Charleston, South Carolina, and asked whether General Ike had had an affair with Kay Summersby.

"No. None whatsoever," he replied tartly. "In all the years I was in Europe and Africa living with or near the general and seeing him almost daily, I never noted anything but friendship between him and Kay. I deeply resent such talk. For people to write or say what they have about this imaginary attachment is deplorable—an offense to Mamie and to Ike's memory," he said.

Relative to the alleged letter to Marshall, it was not unknown that Truman originally idolized Eisenhower. That warm relationship rammed an iceberg when Eisenhower refused Truman's offer to run on the Democratic ticket and, during the subsequent political campaign, Truman turned upon Ike.

Except for a few lulls, that feeling grew in Truman, for in time he was quoted as calling Eisenhower a coward not fit to be president. Then he came up with the story of the alleged Eisenhower letter to Marshall, suggesting a divorce from Mamie, which Truman claimed he destroyed to protect Eisenhower. Detesting Ike as he did, why would he want to do this? The statement has a false ring. If Truman protected Eisenhower for the good of the service in 1952, why did he tell about it later?

What's the truth about the alleged letter?

President Truman burned it, if we accept the Merle Miller account. I phoned the Alexandria, Virginia, home of General Harry H. Vaughn, a close crony of Truman, to get the exact story: "As I recall, the president told me a day or so later that he had returned the letter to Marshall with a covering letter," he said. "But we never could find such a letter. I searched the Pentagon files for two days. You cannot burn a nonexisting letter."

Dr. Forrest C. Pogue, official biographer of General Marshall and the man who controls all Marshall's papers, told me in a telephone interview from his home in Arlington. "There's not the slightest intimation of any such letter in the vast correspondence I have read and handled. The whole yarn sounds fishy."

In the book *Letters to Mamie,* John Eisenhower states that his father handwrote his mother 319 letters between 1942 and 1945, an average of two letters weekly.[1] Many letters in this collection puncture the allegation that General Ike intended to divorce Mamie and marry Summersby.

Several refer to apparent concern by Mamie about attractive women in and around her Ike's headquarters. He asked her never to let such things enter her mind. "I love you all the time," he wrote. "Don't go bothering your pretty head about WACs. . . . You just hold the thought that I'm not so worn out by the time this is all over that you'll have a wreck on your hands; because I'm on the run to you the day the victorious army marches into Berlin!" [2]

A 1943 letter comments on a reference in *Life* Magazine that Kay Summersby had been assigned to North Africa to join the general: "The big reason she wanted to serve in this theater is that she is terribly in love with a young American colonel and is to be married to him come June—assuming both are alive. . . .

". . . I tell you only so that if anyone is banal and foolish enough to lift an eyebrow at an old duffer such as I am in connection with WACs, Red Cross workers, nurses and drivers, you will know I've no emotional involvement and will have none." [3]

Another letter said, "You must realize that in such a confused life as we lead here all sorts of stories, gossip and lies . . . can get started without the slightest foundation in fact. . . . I love you only!" [4] The words *I love you only*, were underlined three times and followed by big exclamation points.

An excerpt from General Ike's earlier letter of June 22, 1942, from England to his son, John, shows his tender consideration for Mamie: ". . . Please don't write me at the expense of your letter to Mamie. After all, she will always forward your letters to me, and she looks forward to your weekly notes. . . ."

If Eisenhower planned to divorce Mamie after victory in Europe and bring home a new bride, there is no evidence of it. As a matter of fact, there is evidence of just the opposite. After VE Day, Eisenhower was so elated with prospects of going back home that he proposed to West Point classmates that they hold a graduation-day reunion at the Point on June 12, 1945, where they could meet their wives. General Marshall killed the whole project, but Eisenhower would not have suggested inviting Mamie and other wives if he had contemplated a Summersby marriage.

Several times during and shortly after World War II, General Ike told me how much he looked forward to picking up his much-interrupted homelife as it was before hostilities. He looked forward to good times with Mamie.

When the Eisenhowers were getting settled on their Gettysburg farm and Kay had come to the United States, General Ike had her driven to Gettysburg to meet and talk with Mamie. They spent the better part of an afternoon conversing warmly. Eisenhower, a man of great sensitivity, would not have arranged such a meeting, if Summersby had been his mistress.

Why did the news of the Eisenhower-Summersby relationship stay submerged until the writing of two books? If there had been an affair, surely it would have been headlined by political opponents of the general during the 1952 primaries or the campaign. Yet it was not written about until after the alleged participants and major witnesses were dead.

It seems inconceivable that from 60 to over 200 of the world's best correspondents, assigned to Eisenhower's headquarters and seeing him and Kay at headquarters or in the field, could have been fooled for the duration of the war in North Africa, Italy and England. If there had been a romantic attachment, many of them would have parted with at least an arm to get such a story. While some correspondents would not have used a story of this type, many would have.

Had such a situation existed, the British news people, especially, would have pounced upon the news. They never gave up championing Montgomery and Lord Alanbrooke and trying to downgrade Eisenhower.

Sir Kenneth Strong, head of Allied Intelligence in World War II, whose job it was to be aware of Axis and Allied activities, wrote me a recent letter on many subjects. In commenting on rough draft chapters of this book, he wrote: "I have avoided the Summersby episode, as I don't think I have anything new to add except that the whole thing is pure fiction."

My long investigation of the Summersby claim has led me to a triple-headed conclusion:

1   Eisenhower is innocent.
2   Kay Summersby and her ghostwriters were most imaginative.
3   Sexual content helps the sale of books.

Telling Stories

"Any fresh, revealing stories or anecdotes about Eisenhower?" That was a question I usually asked at some point in all my interviews with more than 600 individuals who knew Eisenhower.

It didn't matter whether they were serious, funny or unfunny, as long as they showed a little-known aspect of the man's character, working methods, knowledge, abilities or philosophy.

Some responses disclosed trivia, such as Lieutenant General Sir Humphrey Gale's quotation of Eisenhower speaking about a fellow officer: "That fella is trying to pick up nits with boxing gloves."

Others had scope, depth, color and turned the man's thinking and reacting processes inside out. Still others were just stories that hadn't been made public before.

My friend Walter Williams told me an unusual World War II Eisenhower story, which he had heard from General Raymond McClain.

Just before an offensive by United States troops into Germany, General Ike, visiting McClain's command, was asked to offer impromptu words of encouragement. Rain had fallen earlier, and several GI carpenters had hammered together a rude platform on a mound. After some cheering remarks, General Ike stepped off the platform, onto the mound of slick gumbo. His feet slipped out from under him, and he took a spectacular pratfall.

The troops hollered and laughed.

General McClain sucked in his breath. Certain commanders would reprimand the troops for such behavior.

"General Eisenhower merely got back on his feet, brushed himself off, turned to the troops, saluted them and smiled his famous smile," Williams explained. "The result? Those troops let loose with a chorus of cheers that could be heard in Berlin."

In a letter, Williams gave me another of his favorite Eisenhower stories. Shortly before the 1952 Republican National Convention, in Chicago, where General Ike was nominated for the presidency, he spoke at the annual gathering of the Eighty-second Airborne Division. On the eve of D-Day, he had visited the men of the 82nd and 101st Airborne divisions and wished them well in their hazardous drop. This reunion, which he had long anticipated, was like coming back to his boys before D-Day.

As the Citizens for Eisenhower chairman, Williams had accompanied the general to the gathering. "It was, without doubt, the most emotionally filled event I have ever experienced," Walter informed me. "First, with a blare of trumpets, the lights were dimmed, and the color guard marched in.

"Then came the honor guard, some forty to fifty Congressional Medal of Honor winners. They marched the length of the dining hall, then reversed direction to seat themselves at the head table.

"Next followed other head-table guests, making the number at the head table perhaps sixty. After an invocation by the chaplain, Sergeant Funk, presiding, called upon the chaplain for a memorial service.

"As the chaplain read off various units of the Eighty-second Airborne, giving the number of dead and wounded, an aide would light a candle on the head table."

General Ike and Williams, deeply moved by the ceremony, watched as, one by one, some forty candles flickered to full golden glow.

Sergeant Funk made a few somber remarks and, then, in introducing General Ike, said in a lighter vein, "When General Eisenhower came down to visit us the night before our jump-off [Normandy invasion] I was plenty scared, but not nearly as scared as I am right now."

As General Eisenhower took the microphone, there was no doubt in anyone's mind that he was visibly shaken.

"He stood before his audience, stroking his neck and otherwise trying to keep his emotions under control," writes Williams. "After a few moments, he started to speak. He referred to Sergeant Funk's being scared.

"Then the general said, 'I, too, am scared—scared that I shall break down.' Then he did. It took him a few moments to regain his composure, after which he paid a tribute to the men of the Eighty-second Airborne, the like of which no one could excel.

"General Eisenhower concluded his remarks by saying, 'No matter how long I may live, I can never repay the debt I owe you men.'"

Turning a quick left, and facing the sergeant, the five-star general said with deep feeling, "Sergeant Funk, I salute you, Sir." He sat down and buried his head on his hands.

Sensitivity, warmth and humanity were so much Dwight D. Eisenhower's nature that he expressed them even when split-second reactions were required.

At a White House state function early in his presidency, he was shaking hands with an almost endless line of officials. As the line moved toward him, he suddenly was confronted with a minor official, a German war veteran whose right hand, blown off in combat, had been replaced by a glove.

Instantly the president shifted his feet and thrust out his left hand to shake with the German's left. The official and others who observed the lightning action were amazed.

Sometimes Eisenhower's highest affairs of state lost priority to human affairs, as I learned when talking to Maurice Stans.

Shortly after he became director of budget, his red telephone rang. The president! Stans prickled with excitement.

"I hurriedly grabbed the telephone. The president, with a degree of urgency, said, 'Stans, I have a problem right here in my office. I understand that Fred Seaton's private secretary has a sixteen salary grade. My own secretary, Ann Whitman, has only a fifteen. I hope you can straighten this out quick, before all _____ breaks loose.' "

Eisenhower disliked the stuffy protocol thrust upon him by his station and office. It got in the way of his relaxed, natural Kansas style. So, when he was notified that his friend Harold Macmillan had been appointed prime minister of Great Britain, Eisenhower sent two messages of congratulations—one formal and the other informal and personal, which follows:

Dear Harold,

This morning, upon learning of your designation by Her Majesty as the new Prime Minister, I sent you a formal message of congratulations, the kind that is approved even by State Departments.

The purpose of this note is to welcome you to your new headaches. Of course you have had your share in the past, but I assure you that the new ones will be to the old like a broken leg is to a scratched finger. The only real fun you will have is to see just how far you can keep on going with everybody chopping at you with every conceivable weapon.

Knowing you so long and well I predict that your journey will be a great one. But you must remember the old adage, "Now abideth faith, hope and charity—and greater than these is a sense of humor."

With warm regards,
As ever,
D. E.

Many times during the years I knew General Ike, people commented on his excellent memory. It was far above average. The only individual I ever knew who could top him in this regard was General Al Gruenther, *"Supermemory"* and "Super Bridge Player."

Once during World War II, I was discussing General Ike with several leading British parliamentarians.

"His memory is incredible," volunteered one of them. "He can recall instantaneously names, dates, facts and figures about industry, transportation, and communications."

When I repeated this remark to General Ike, he smiled broadly and responded—not about his memory but another subject—the scope of his reading. "Maybe this will indicate to them that I read something other than western stories."

During a luncheon given at the Palm Desert home of Pollard Simon, General Ike was the guest of honor among a host of golfing greats—Arnold Palmer, Jack Nicklaus, Billy Casper and other prominent individuals, including Amon Carter, Jr.

After being introduced to General Ike, Carter mentioned having been taken prisoner of war in North Africa. Eisenhower told him exactly where he had been captured, which prison camp he had been taken to and its precise location. Carter was awed when General Ike recalled the names of a dozen villages and bases in and around the area, because he had forgotten most of them.

On a number of other occasions, I was a witness to his noteworthy memory. One in particular comes to mind. Claude Terraill, owner of the Tour d'Argent in Paris and captain of a visiting polo team, saw General Ike come in for breakfast before a round of golf at Eldorado Country Club.

He hadn't seen Eisenhower for twenty years and impulsively rushed over to him, shook hands and said. "How fit you look, General. But you probably don't remember me, or when we met."

"Yes, Mr. Terraill, I do," replied Ike. "It was in Paris, and we talked about Joe DiMaggio. Furthermore, you and your family entertained many of us generals at a dinner following the liberation of Paris."

They chatted for a few minutes more, and when Terraill started back to his table, General Ike called to him, "By the way, Mr. Terraill, your first name is Claude, isn't it?"

Few of the Ike stories can top this one, which Mamie Eisenhower told me in Palm Desert, where I spent many enjoyable, sun-filled years.

Mamie was present at a huge Washington dinner given to honor General George C. Marshall. Presiding over the dinner, former Ambassador Joseph C. Grew misspoke in a remark to the group: "General Marshall wants nothing more than to retire to his Leesburg, Virginia, home with Mrs. Eisenhower."

Laughter roared through the hall. Grew was humiliated. General Marshall tried to smile away the *faux pas,* and Mamie could not restrain laughter. Grew tried to remedy his remark. "My apologies to the general," he said.

In the sudden quiet, Mamie piped up, "Which general?"

The Ultimate Decision

There had been no clue.

I had no idea General Ike was so near the end.

Our conversations began to tend less toward war, peace, politics, government and the presidency than toward the distant past of Abilene days.

He had always referred to Abilene with deep affection, but he did so especially near the end of his life. He reminisced about camping out on Old Smoky River with Bob Davis, sleeping under the stars, of the breeze that rustled the cottonwoods and the golden grain from horizon to horizon, under the hot Kansas sun.

It was poetry, the way he referred to these things—poetry without rhyme.

A number of times, as soldier and president, he had gone back to Abilene and loved every minute of it. He recalled the Benson sisters' restaurant on the crest of a hill outside the city, and the excellent catfish his brothers and he had eaten there during reunions. He remembered the time Lena Benson, who traditionally paddled kids and adults on their birthdays, had paddled the president, when he had lunched there on his birthday.

Another memory bobbed into his consciousness: a homecoming parade through Abilene while he was president, and the Secret Service men's consternation when he ordered his limousine stopped and jumped out into the crowd to kiss Gladys Harding, his high-school sweetheart.

Then he told me about attending the funeral of the assassinated President John F. Kennedy, one of the most elaborate in Washington, D.C. history.

Harry Truman had turned to him and commented, "I certainly don't go for these Hollywood theatrics."

"I agree," replied General Ike. "When I die, I want the cheapest casket there is—a sixty dollar GI job and no medals on my chest." He said he wanted Icky's remains brought back from Denver to be buried beside his in Abilene. Mamie would sleep on his other side.

During one of our last talks, I asked him who was the greatest man of our times. Without hesitation, he replied, "Winston Churchill. But the greatest person I ever knew was my mother. She taught me the principles of life that guided me. Had she lived while I was in the White House, she would have been invaluable to me and the nation. She was the greatest reader of character I ever knew. She could have advised me on appointees for the cabinet and other important positions. With her, I would never have gone wrong."

Then I made a comment that brought a surprising answer, "General Ike, you're one of the few persons I know who has realized his every dream in life."

That quick, broad Eisenhower grin seemed to split his face horizontally, and amusement brightened his blue eyes. "Wrong on several accounts, Virgil," he replied. "I had longed to give the United States and the world a lasting peace. I was able only to contribute toward a stalemate. About the presidency: that was more a duty than a dream. As far as fulfillment is concerned, I still would like to have played shortstop and hit like Honus Wagner."

After the presidency, General Ike did not idle. He had made a standing offer to presidents and the nation to be on standby whenever a consultant was needed. He had counseled President Kennedy in person and by phone and, on many occasions, Kennedy's successor, Lyndon Baines Johnson.

Many book ideas percolated in his mind, and he started writing projects. Also, he golfed, cooked and did some painting (very little portrait work, because, despite Churchill's instructions, he was still not great at painting eyes and mouths). The scenic southern California desert enchanted him, and he used this vast, colorful panorama and other natural settings for many of his paintings.

I can still remember every detail of the day we golfed at Eldorado and he asked me to write this book, and the appointment for the following Thursday for us to play golf at Seven Lakes—an appointment that was never fulfilled, due to his heart attack.

Then I recall too well how I almost became ill when told that General Ike had died.

True to his wish, the funeral was as simple as Washington protocol would permit: a sixty dollar GI coffin and no ribbons on his chest—just General Ike wearing his self-designed Eisenhower jacket. One of the dreariest days of my life was attending the funeral, seeing the casket on a caisson and, behind the caisson, a soldier on foot, leading a black riderless horse with stirrups reversed.

It was another devastating journey for Mamie—as with Icky to Denver—but she and John proceeded to Abilene with the body. And now the promise was kept. Before Ike had left for West Point, he had promised himself that someday he would return to Abilene.

The story seemed to be over, but it was not.

I learned many things that had happened before the end, one of them from comedian Bob Hope. Ike loved to play golf with Bob and considered him an amateur who played like a professional.

Bob and his wife, Dolores, chatted with Ike in his room at Walter Reed Hospital. Then they went outside with Mamie for a while. She said, "You'd better go back in and say good-bye to Ike, or he'll be mad."

"As I was walking back to the room, I tried to think of something funny to say, so I told Ike about the golfers who walked into the locker room after a bad round. One said, 'I am the worst golfer in the world.'

"The other fellow said, 'No, I am.'

"The first guy said, 'Let's compare scorecards.'

"The second guy said, 'Okay. What did you have on the first hole?'

"The first guy said, 'I had an X,' and the second guy said, 'You are one up!'

"Ike almost fell out of bed with laughter."

Among the many eulogies presented by congressmen as the body lay in state, the one that seemed most memorable to me was that of Representative Larry Winn, Jr., of Kansas. It included a poem by Barbara Hanna Gray, titled "Wheat: In Memory of Dwight David Eisenhower."

Fifty children from Kansas had visited the national capital, bringing with them a beautiful box of long-stemmed wheat—a symbol of their love. The Gray poem, endorsed by the children, read:

> A shock of wheat—Ripened in the sun of a Kansas prairie,
>   tendered gentle there from small green sprout
>   until tall and golden—unbent by the winds
>   that blow hard.
> A shock of wheat—Filled with the grain of a Kansas youth,
>   harvested by God to feed his flocks with the bread
>   of his life—unbent by the winds that blow hard.
> A shock of wheat—Having borne its fruit must die to live anew,
>   returning now to the promised land of everlasting life—unbent
>   by the winds that blow hard.

I shall never forget the tribute to Dwight David Eisenhower by cartoonist Bill Mauldin, whom the general had defended against George Patton's censorship. It was Bill's all-time best, as far as I am concerned. The setting was a hillside cemetery, covered with row upon row of white crosses. From one grave came a voice, "Pass the word along . . . it's Ike."

President Richard Nixon's eulogy was equally moving, especially his quotation of Ike's last words to Mamie: "I have always loved my wife, I have always loved my children, I have always loved my grandchildren, and I have always loved my country."

I had many thoughts about the faith of Ike Eisenhower; how much he had been like Lincoln, with a deep, quiet faith in God. It was a private and precious thing to him.

Wherever he was quartered or headquartered, I never saw Ike Eisenhower without a Bible somewhere in sight—on his desk, in a bookcase nearby, or on a table in his office. It was a Bible for use, as the well-worn pages showed.

He once said, "Like stored wisdom, the lessons of the Bible are useless unless they are lifted out and employed. A faithful reading of the Scripture provides the courage and strength required for the living of our time."

One gift that seemed to please him above others was the 500 millionth copy of the Scripture disseminated by the American Bible Society—a nine-pound King James Version family Bible bound in red morocco.

One night, Norman Vincent Peale and Mrs. Peale spent the night in the White House. Before going to bed around 11:00 P.M., Dr. Peale asked the president if he prayed regularly.

"Yes, I do. I do most of my praying at night, just before I go to sleep, and every morning as soon as I rise. At night I say, 'Dear God, I have done the best I could today, so won't You please take over until tomorrow morning?' "

It was Eisenhower who started the Christian prayer-breakfast session in the White House.

Many times, President Eisenhower invited evangelist Billy Graham to the White House and telephoned him at his retreat in North Carolina to ask advice, guidance, and prayers.

Some years ago, I had an appointment to meet with Billy Graham at the Bel Air Hotel in West Los Angeles for a breakfast interview. Promptly at 9:30, Graham, wearing a sky blue cashmere sweater, a white polo shirt open at the collar, gray flannel slacks and gray suede shoes, came striding down the path toward me. As we entered the coffee shop, I was impressed with his slender physique and catlike grace.

At our table overlooking lush gardens, I learned that he had been invited to Walter Reed Hospital, where the ex-president was under treatment for his heart condition.

"That was on the day before I was leaving for Vietnam to spend Christmas with the troops in the field," he stated. "It was the last time I saw him alive.

"As I got halfway across the room on my departure, the general, who was propped up in bed with pipes and tubes in him, said, 'Billy, may I ask a big favor of you?'

" 'Certainly.' "

" 'When you get out to Vietnam, will you tell the boys that there is an old general in Washington who prays every morning and night for their safety and eventual victory?'

" 'Of course, I will, General,' I replied.

" 'Thank you, thank you, thank you, Billy,' he responded.

"Then when I reached the doorknob and started to open it, the general raised his head slightly. 'Billy, can I ask you one more question?'

" 'Of course,' I said.

"In a firm, strong voice, he asked, 'Can an old sinner like me ever go to heaven?'

" 'Of course, General Ike. You have made the ultimate decision—the greatest single decision that anyone can make. You have accepted Jesus Christ as your Saviour, and you have asked for forgiveness of your sins. Of course, you'll go to heaven. The moment you stop breathing, you will automatically be in heaven.' "

As Billy Graham quietly closed the door, he glanced back once more. Tears were streaming down the face of Dwight D. Eisenhower, who had lived, loved and fought as a true Christian.

Acknowledgments

Any book about a person of stature and achievement requires a tremendous amount of assistance and teamwork. During my ten years of intensive research in all parts of the world and in the preparation of this manuscript, I have benefitted from the efforts of associates who spent many long hours and gave generously of their skills.

In particular, I would like to acknowledge the sacrifices and contributions of my wife, Virginia Beth, who gave up nights, weekends and vacations so that I could concentrate my efforts on the book. She did a great deal of the typing, proofreading, research and correcting of the manuscript. She created the book's title.

My personal secretary, Bunny Durkin, organized the production of chapters and mailings to the Fleming H. Revell Company and did many tasks over and above the call of duty.

I am grateful to Carolyn Scheer, wife of James F. Scheer, who collaborated with me on the book, for her help in research, taking dictation and typing.

Bert E. Stolpe helped immeasurably in the coordinating of the project.

I gathered important information from Forrest C. Pogue, military historian for the American army and biographer of General George C. Marshall.

Dr. John Wickman, director of the Eisenhower Library and Center, built and administered by him from the first day, and his well-trained and selected staff, were of special assistance to me on many occasions.

It would make for tedious reading if I listed everyone interviewed in the course of researching this book. The most prominent are:

Sir Winston Churchill; Anthony Eden (Lord Avon); former South African prime minister Jan Smuts; Admiral of the Fleet Mountbatten, Earl of Burma (formerly, Lord Louis); Field Marshal Bernard Montgomery; Admiral A. B. C. Cunningham; Air Marshal Sir Arthur Tedder; Herbert Brownell; Viscount Alexander of Tunis; General Sir Kenneth Strong; Sir Francis de Guingand; Walter Cronkite; Trygve Lie; American generals George C. Marshall, Omar Bradley, Jimmy Doolittle, Mark W. Clark, Ira Eaker, Al Gruenther, Lauris Norstad, George Patton, Walter Bedell "Beetle" Smith and Carl "Tooey" Spaatz; United States Navy Captain Harry C. Butcher (*My Three Years With Eisenhower*); Israeli Prime Minister David Ben-Gurion; Admiral Arthur Radford (later chief of staff); former Philippine president Ramón Magsaysay; Carlos Romulo; Eisenhower presidential assistants Sherman Adams, Tom Stephens, and Bob Gray; presidential press secretary Jim Hagerty; Eisenhower's personal secretary Ann Whitman; secretary of Eisenhower's cabinet, Max Rabb; UN representative Henry Cabot Lodge; ambassador to the Soviet Union Charles Bohlen; Dr. Ralph Bunche; Secretary of State John Foster Dulles; Ambassador Robert Murphy; senators George Aiken, Barry Goldwater, William Knowland and Mike Mansfield; Mamie, John and Dr. Milton Eisenhower; George Allen; Freeman Gosden; Paul Hoffman; Sigurd Larmon; Bob Hope; and, among many others, ex-presidents Herbert Hoover, John F. Kennedy, Lyndon B. Johnson, Richard Nixon and Gerald Ford.

Source Notes

Chapter 6—Baseball, Prejudice and a Girl

1. Dwight D. Eisenhower, *At Ease: Stories I Tell to Friends* (Garden City, New York: Doubleday and Company, Inc.,) 1967.

Chapter 9—Soldier Takes a Wife

1. Eisenhower, *At Ease,* p. 113.

Chapter 10—Improvisations

1. Eisenhower, *At Ease,* p. 133.
2. Ibid., p. 142.
3. Ibid., pp. 155, 156.

Chapter 11—Learning From the Fox

1. Eisenhower, *At Ease,* p. 173.
2. Ibid.
3. Julie Eisenhower, *Special People* (New York: Simon & Schuster, 1977), p. 205.
4. Eisenhower, *At Ease,* p. 195.

Chapter 12—A Time of Uncertainty

1. Eisenhower, *At Ease,* p. 201.

Chapter 13—MacArthur Plus Eisenhower Equals Trouble

1. Stephen E. Ambrose, *Ike: Abilene to Berlin* (New York; Harper & Row, 1973), p. 75.

Chapter 14—Peace and War

1. Dwight D. Eisenhower, *Crusade in Europe* (Garden City, New York: Doubleday and Company, Inc., 1948), p. 14.
2. Ibid., pp. 21, 22.
3. Ibid., p. 22.

Chapter 16—Intrigue With French Dressing

1. Eisenhower, *Crusade in Europe,* p. 105.

Chapter 18—Roosevelt Behind the Scene

1. Robert Sherwood, *Roosevelt and Hopkins* (New York, New York: Harper & Brothers, 1948), p. 651.

2. Ibid.

3. Ambrose, *Ike,* p. 112.

4. Sherwood, *Roosevelt and Hopkins,* p. 654.

5. Ibid.

Chapter 19—End of a Campaign

1. Robert Murphy, *Diplomat Among Warriors* (Garden City, New York: Doubleday and Company, Inc., 1964), p. 143.

2. Eisenhower, *Crusade in Europe,* p. 112.

Chapter 21—D-Day or Disaster Day?

1. Eisenhower, *Crusade in Europe,* p. 240.

2. Stephen E. Ambrose, *The Supreme Commander: The War Years of General Dwight D. Eisenhower* (Garden City, New York: Doubleday and Company, Inc., 1970), p. 416.

Chapter 24—Monty's Foes—Germany and General Ike

1. Bernard L. Montgomery, *Memoirs of Field Marshal Montgomery* (Cleveland: World Publishing Company, 1958), p. 286.

2. Eisenhower, *Crusade in Europe,* p. 372.

Chapter 27—The Dove Is a Hawk

1. Eisenhower, *Crusade in Europe,* p. 444.

2. Ibid.

3. Ibid, p. 447.

4. Allan Taylor, ed., *What Eisenhower Thinks* (New York: Thomas Y. Crowell Company, 1952), p. 91.

5. Ibid.

6. Ambrose, *Ike,* p. 190.

Chapter 28—Five Stars Over Columbia

1. Eisenhower, *At Ease,* p. 337.

Chapter 30—Amateur Strategists, Professional Results

1. Dwight D. Eisenhower, *Mandate for Change* (Garden City, New York: Doubleday and Company, Inc., 1963), p. 20.

2. Relman Morin, *Dwight D. Eisenhower: A Gauge of Greatness* (New York: Simon & Schuster, 1969), p. 141.

3. Ibid.

4. Eisenhower, *Mandate for Change,* p. 34.

5. Ibid., p. 35.

Chapter 32—An Unconventional Convention

1. Eisenhower, *Mandate for Change,* p. 45.

2. Ibid., p. 66.

Chapter 33—Who Knows Exactly How to Be President?

1. Henry Cabot Lodge, *As It Was: An Inside View of Politics and Power in the Fifties and Sixties* (New York: W. W. Norton & Company, Inc., 1976), pp. 48, 49.

2. Eisenhower, *Mandate for Change,* p. 95.

3. Ibid., p. 97.

Chapter 35—Inside the White House

1. Eisenhower, *Mandate for Change,* p. 265.

2. Robert Keith Gray, *Eighteen Acres Under Glass* (Garden City, New York: Doubleday and Company, Inc., 1962), p. 138.

Chapter 36—Guilty Until Proved Innocent

1. Morin, *Dwight D. Eisenhower: A Gauge of Greatness,* p. 169.

2. Eisenhower, *Mandate for Change,* p. 274.

Chapter 37—Showdown

1. Lately Thomas, *When Even Angels Wept: The Senator Joe McCarthy Affair, a Story Without a Hero* (New York: William Morrow & Company, Inc., 1973), p. 472.

2. Ibid., pp. 585, 586.

3. Ibid., p. 586.

4. Ibid.

5. Eisenhower, *Mandate for Change,* p. 331.

6. Thomas, *When Even Angels Wept,* pp. 605, 606.

Chapter 38—Did Dulles Run Eisenhower?

1. Eisenhower, *Mandate for Change,* pp. 145–147.

Chapter 44—The Bottom Line

1. Arthur Larson, *Eisenhower: The President Nobody Knew* (New York: Charles Scribner's Sons, 1968), pp. 194, 196.

Chapter 45—The Truth About Ike and Kay Summersby

1. John Eisenhower, *Letters to Mamie* (Garden City, New York: Doubleday and Company, Inc., 1978), p. 7.

2. Ibid., pp. 98, 99.

3. Ibid., pp. 104, 105.

4. Ibid., p. 99.

Index